Never a Dull Moment!

c/o

My good friend Gwen

With best wishes

Terry

Never a Dull Moment!

Published by The Conrad Press in the United Kingdom 2020

Tel: +44(0)1227 472 874
www.theconradpress.com
info@theconradpress.com

ISBN 978-1-913567-22-4

Typesetting and Cover Design by:
Charlotte Mouncey, www.bookstyle.co.uk

Illustrations by B. Day

The Conrad Press logo was designed by Maria Priestley.

Printed and bound in Great Britain by Clays Ltd, Elcograf S.p.A.

Never a Dull Moment!

working on Britain's railways 1962-1996

Terry Collins

Contents

Foreword by Peter Hancox

I really enjoyed reading this fascinating book. As a typical commuter I had no idea what went on behind the scenes and the number of dedicated, caring people involved in making the journey safe and on time. Terry Collins spent his whole working life as a railway man, as did his father before him. How he still remembers it all in such detail I don't know. But he does, and now it's here for us to share.

Terry has an engaging narrative style covering detailed and complex technical operations in a way we can understand, as well as a welcome fund of anecdotes – hilarious at times. It is reassuring to read about the meticulous safety procedures put into place when there is an incident and how problems are thought out and resolved, very often against the clock.

This book extends the horizons of railway enthusiasm and should make any train journey more interesting – a voyage of discovery. What happens in signal boxes and control centres? How is the track made safe for those workers down there? There is much more of course.

Forget train spotting and collecting numbers. Find out instead what really made our railways and their history the envy of the world.

PJH - June 2020

Peter Hancox is a professional proof-reader
and an experienced commuter by rail

Introduction

This account is not intended to be a technical treatise. Nor does it purport to be an absolute authority on the procedures concerning accidents or incidents and their investigations and recovery. Where technical matters arise, as they inevitably do, I have tried, drawing from my personal experience, training, and knowledge, to be accurate and correct in my descriptions. Other publications will have far more technical detail contained within them.

In this account, I have tried very hard to avoid any embarrassment to colleagues past and present, and in many of the incidents I am about to relate, I have referred to people only by their first names. In some cases, names have been omitted altogether.

The purpose of this book is to share with readers some of the many incidents I have been involved with in some way or another, to highlight some of the wonderful characters I have been privileged to work with, men and women, who were real railway people, to whom the job was not just a job but a way of life, as it was with me.

They were, and some still are, people with a lifetime of experience, who knew what to do in any crisis, who were immensely professional, and who were always willing to share their experience and knowledge with me. It really was a privilege to work with them and learn from them.

The other reason for this book is to show what life on the

railway was really like from the inside, from the early 1960s to the late 1990s. It includes the Beeching era, the gradual changeover from lever frame signal boxes to panels, super panels and computerised I E CCs. It includes the last days of main line steam locomotives and the coming of diesel and electric traction. It begins with wagon load freight traffic and ends with block load freight trains, It begins with a publicly owned railway and ends with a privatised one.

It was against this background that I experienced a career of over thirty-four years. Most of the time I enjoyed it. Most of the time I found it very challenging and very rewarding. Sometimes it was frustrating and there were some sad times too. But sometimes it was hilariously and almost unbelievably amusing.

Through it all, through all the adventures – and misadventures – runs the thread of the real professionalism and expertise, and the camaraderie of the people I worked with.

I really enjoyed my career. It was much more than a job. Without exaggeration I can say with complete honesty that it was a way of life.

Most of the railwaymen, and women, who appear in these pages will understand and agree with that view. I have enjoyed writing about it and preserving accounts of the many incidents, and those who helped me so professionally in dealing with them. I hope you, the reader, enjoy reading it.

Terry Collins May 7 2020

Chapter One -
How it all began - and nearly ended!

When I left school, reluctantly, in July 1962, there were only two choices open to me. I had wanted to stay on and do the Sixth Form courses, as did my teachers, but we were not a rich family and it simply wasn't possible.

The two jobs open to me were a position as a clerk in a builders' yard or a position as a clerk on British Railways. My father Arthur (1899-1968) was a lifelong railwayman on the Southern. He had joined in 1919 after leaving the Royal Horse Artillery at the end of World War One.

He became at first a South Eastern Railwayman in 1919, then a Southern Railwayman in 1923, and finally a British Railwayman (Southern Region) in 1948. He retired as West Yard Inspector at Tonbridge in 1960. He was considerably older than my mother, this being his second marriage. My mother Esther (1919-1973) also worked on British Railways (Southern Region) and that's how they met.

Given this background, it was almost inevitable that I should choose British Railways. And so it was that three days after my sixteenth birthday, on the 8th August 1962, I was introduced to Mr George Wright, the Goods Agent for Tonbridge.

He was second only in seniority to Mr Stan Burrows, the Station Master for Tonbridge, a fine railwayman, a Christian, and acknowledged by even the toughest railwaymen, to be a real gentleman. He was to play a vital part in my career.

Having completed my Induction Course and passed the Medical Exam at London Bridge, I was assigned to the Chief Clerk, Mr Stevens. At the same time, an old school friend of mine, Alan S also joined and for a short time we worked in the same area, although not the same office.

Tonbridge East Yard and Goods Depot was a fascinating and very busy place. It was where the goods traffic was transhipped to and from the trains. All day long, three-wheeled Schammel tractors towed trailers into the Goods Shed with consignments from outlying districts around Tonbridge. Those same trailers were then loaded with goods from wagons from all around the British Isles and from the Continent too.

To deal with all this traffic there was the main Goods Office, which dealt with the movements of the goods, liaised with customers, dealt with matters of Insurance Claims, Demurrage, where goods were held in wagons waiting customers to collect or accept, and for which a variable charge was raised, costing the movements of goods and issuing waybills and invoices, the movement of livestock and liaising with the various veterinary services, paybills for the clerks, shunters, Schammel drivers, and what is now called 'Human Resources.'

We rarely saw Mr Wright, the Goods Agent, but we were in awe of his deputy, the Chief Clerk, that is until my friend Alan, who was carrying a tray of full teacups, tripped and spilt quite a lot of it down him. Apparently he took it all very calmly.

The Depot also had a British Transport Police Office and also a separate Her Majesty's Customs and Excise Department, for the continental traffic.

In addition to the traffic brought in and out by the lorries, what was known as a 'raft' ran once on the early shift and once on the late shift. This consisted of wagons that had been loaded in the East Yard Goods Shed, being taken to the West Yard to be shunted into trains that would take them to their destination.

Each 'raft' returned with wagons loaded with goods destined for Tonbridge and District, which had come into the West Yard from various starting points, and which were to be unloaded in the Goods Shed and put on the trailers for the Schammel lorries to take to the customers. Each raft would comprise between thirty and fifty wagons, hauled by a diesel shunting locomotive.

Often a little 0 – 4 – 0 class 204hp locomotive was allocated (known as a 'coffee pot' because of its odd shaped funnel) and when this loco was used, the signalmen were instructed to give it a clear run through the station because if it stopped with such a full load on, it might not be able to start again.

Later I was often able, from the signal box, to watch this little locomotive, waggling from side to side as it struggled with its heavy load. Pathways through Tonbridge Station could be difficult to find, but it was important to run the raft as early as possible to give the West Yard Shunters time to insert the wagons in the right order on the appropriate train.

The primary function of the West Yard was to marshal the 'wagon load traffic', so that these wagons were in the right order on the trains, and when they had to detach wagons in yards and sidings on their routes before their final destinations, those wagons were easily accessible and caused the minimum of delay.

Other factors affected the order of wagons. If for example a large crane or other heavy plant was being conveyed, this, regardless of the order of the train, had to be marshalled next to the engine, so that when the train was compelled to brake, the weight would not bear down on the more lightly loaded wagons.

I hope this gives the reader some idea of how the West Marshalling Yard and particularly the East Goods Yard worked, and how complex and fascinating it was.

This then, was the complex in which I found myself. I was assigned to various departments. Some I liked more than others. One of my first encounters was with an elderly gentleman and senior clerk called Colin, who walked with a limp and who was straight out of the Victorian Railway era. I was instructed to do my work in pencil so that mistakes could be erased. It was a crime to have to cross something out and rewrite it.

I was issued with a pencil and a pencil economiser, a long metal tube in which you inserted your pencil and used it until you had sharpened the pencil down to a stub. To get a new pencil, you had to submit the stub, and you would not get a new pencil until the senior clerk was convinced that you could no longer use the stub in the economiser. But I was not issued with a rubber.

One day the inevitable happened. Seeing my error, I approached the senior clerk, Colin, and asked if I might borrow his rubber. He looked at me over the top of his glasses and said in a calm, measured voice, 'Young man. Don't you think it is time you invested some of your considerable wages in purchasing an eraser?' And he would not loan me his rubber. I could not continue my work until another clerk lent me his rubber when Colin was not looking.

I really enjoyed working in the Insurance and Claims Department, and to my surprise and pleasure I found that I was quite good at it. The Department was run by a lively young man and woman, both of whom were friendly and encouraging. One day they went out to lunch, leaving me in charge.

While they were gone I had just one telephone call, but an important one. A company had taken delivery of a carpet, and had found one corner damaged. I apologised profusely and asked what the (Railway) Company could do to rectify the situation. In this I made several mistakes, firstly by admitting responsibility, and secondly by offering compensation when we hadn't even seen the damage to the carpet.

The customer appeared to be so taken aback by this that they said, 'Oh, don't worry about it this time. We will hide the damage under a cabinet. Just be more careful in future.' When the clerks returned, I told them what had happened they were amazed. 'That company always but always claims for everything!' the clerk exclaimed. They said, 'Well done, Terry!'

Sometimes we were mistaken by customers for British Road Services, which was also a flourishing business at the time. I would establish that the initials of the company they were complaining about were B.R.S. and then take great delight in politely informing them that it was British Road Services that were at fault, and not British Railways. Apologies would follow and another satisfied customer would go on their way.

I really enjoyed working in that office and I believe a good report about me went to Mr Wright. It was the last department I worked in before I was sent for my formal training at the Clapham Junction Training School.

Clapham Junction Training School was situated on a bridge over the Waterloo/ Bournemouth main line, and it enjoyed the last days of main line steam traction. I travelled there by diesel train from Tonbridge to Redhill, then electric train to

Clapham Junction. For this I was issued with a pass, which showed me to be a member of staff. Using this influence, I often travelled in the brakevan with the guard's permission, which I found exciting.

Having been a working man, bringing in a wage for six months, I was dismayed to find that at the Training School we were treated very much like inky fingered schoolboys. No respect was accorded, and the rules of the training school were spelt out in words of one syllable, repeatedly and at great length.

We began our training with trying to learn over two hundred different types of ticket, including warrants of all sorts and origins. There was also the dreaded Ticket Issue Book (TIB) (Ledger).

The theory was that each pasteboard ticket had a serial number. This was noted at the beginning of each shift (every ticket in the racks). At the end of the shift, the serial numbers were taken again. By subtracting the first numbers from the second, the number of each ticket sold in a shift would be known and this was entered into the Ticket Issue Book. From that, the amount of money taken on each shift could be ascertained.

This money had to be counted and the amount must match exactly the totals in the TIB. The TIB had to be cross cast, horizontally and vertically, totalling each shift, each day, each week, and each month. For any 'passed' clerk to have inaccurate figures was a dismissible offence, because whether or not the error was genuine, dishonesty was always suspected. Maths was my worst subject and I loathed this job. Naturally there was no money to count but I could never get the totals to match and I got more and more frustrated.

Writing out paper tickets came next. We had a small round-faced instructor, who was probably a very nice person, but who spoke with a very quiet voice. I had an additional problem, in that hearing in my left ear was minimal following an apparently life-saving operation when I was twelve years old, in which most of the eardrum was surgically removed. I had quickly learned to lip read and managed very well in normal circumstances.

However, this was Clapham Junction. At regular intervals, the tobacco tin ashtrays on our wooden desks began to vibrate. Then there would be a loud 'whoosh' and a cloud of steam and smoke would billow up through the floorboards. As I sat at the back of the class, I was reliant on my lip-reading skills, but whenever a train passed through underneath, he disappeared, and I could neither hear, nor see him.

I was frustrated and bored. Apart from an unsuccessful attempt to engage the affections of a girl who served in the Station Refreshment Room on Clapham Junction station, there was not much joy to be had. And there was still the three weeks Parcels Course and the three-week Goods Course to come, before the final exam. However, as I was soon to find out, I would not have to worry about the Parcels Course, the Goods Course, or the final exam.

I had done nothing seriously wrong (in my view) but in my boredom had simply filled out silly destinations on tickets, such as 'From Somewhere to Nowhere via Anywhere.' This however was brought to the attention of Mr S, the Training School Principal. It was an eventful week. I had recently been knocked off my bicycle by a motorist who had not seen me and had opened his door at the wrong moment. This resulted in the police being involved and that week I had to appear in court as a police witness. I was very nervous, and the case was dismissed. I was still in this frame of mind when I was summoned to Mr S's office.

'Collins,' he said, 'We are not going to get on, are we?'

I politely disagreed.

'No, Collins, what I said was – we are not going to get on, are we?' was his reply.

I explained about the accident and the court appearance upsetting me. With no change of voice or expression, he said, 'Collins, we are not going to get on, are we?'

Finally conceding defeat, I said, 'No sir.'

'Very well then,' he said, 'One of us has got to go.'

'Yes sir,' I said.

He instructed me, 'Go back to your Station Master and hand in all your equipment. Tell him you are dismissed from the Railway for gross insubordination.' And that was that!

I was horrified. What was I going to tell Dad? He had got me this job with Mr Wright and was expecting me to make a go of it.

I duly travelled back to Tonbridge, and, to my surprise, found my Station Master, Mr Stan Burrows, expecting me. I was still in shock. Mr Burrows was kindness itself. I later found out he was a Christian. He was also a gentleman, and a very knowledgeable and capable railwayman, and he was to become one of the three top managers in my career.

He said he was deeply sorry this had happened. He could not understand what had gone wrong. Mr Wright had spoken highly of me. Nor could he understand why I was studying the Passenger Course, when, because of a known hearing defect (from my schooldays) I would not be put into a Booking Office. He asked me what I was going to do. I told him I had to go home and tell my Dad what had happened.

Mr Burrows said, 'Well Terry, before you do that, I have an idea. Have you ever thought what it would be like to work in a signal box?' When I said I hadn't, he said, 'Well I am just going up to the signal box now. Would you like to come with me and see what you think?' I enthusiastically agreed. It seemed that I might not be going home to tell Dad I had got the sack after all!

I found Tonbridge Signal Box fascinating. It had only recently been opened. It was one of the then new Panel Boxes, controlling routes by 'Entry' and 'Exit' buttons on a diagram, which had an illuminated track circuit diagram and repeaters for the colour light signals. Trains were mostly described on 'barrel describers,' except for the branch line from Tonbridge to Redhill, which was still worked on the Absolute Block System.

My job was to be a signal lad, recording on the Train Registers all the times and description of signals sent and received by the signalmen, and the times of all the movements of trains in the area controlled by the signal box. In addition, I would make the signalmen's tea when they asked, and keep the central heating coke boiler downstairs working properly. In time I would learn the trade of being a signalman and could be getting promotion to signalman.

For someone who had just faced the prospect of being sacked, to be offered a job like this, was like a dream, and I gladly accepted it.

I thanked Mr Burrows. Dad was delighted when I told him. He didn't mind that I wasn't working for Mr Wright. Having a job on the railway was what was important.

I had to go for another medical at London Bridge. That was a bit of a farce. The room in which I found myself, was more like a corridor with a door at each end. When I was asked to get undressed the doors kept opening and men, and women too, passed through. However, the medical was very thoroughly conducted. I passed with flying colours.

In due course I made my way back to Mr Burrows. I was taken to the Staff Office. A lot of papers were signed, and I was measured up for my uniform. I was to have two pairs of trousers, a waistcoat and jacket and an overcoat, plus my pride and joy, a 'cheesecutter' hat. There was no badge for a signal lad, so I was given a crown badge and another badge in Southern green with the word 'Porter' on it.

I was to be on duty early turn, 0600 – 1400, or late turn 1400 – 2200 hrs, alternate weeks. As I was under eighteen years, I was not allowed to work night shifts. I reported for duty on my first early turn and was given three weeks training on the job of Signal Lad, or 'Box Boys,' as we were more commonly known.

So began my real career in Operations on the Railway. Life was never dull in a signal box, as you will see from the next chapter.

Chapter Two -
A Box Boy's life in Tonbridge Signal Box

Perhaps I should begin with a short description of Tonbridge Signal Box. Tonbridge was a significant junction on the South Eastern main line. It worked Track Circuit Block on the up and down lines between Sevenoaks and Tonbridge, the direct route to London Waterloo East, Charing Cross and Cannon Street, handing over to Sevenoaks the control of the up line after crossing the Medway Bridge, and taking control of the down line from Sevenoaks once trains had left Sevenoaks Tunnel.

It worked Track Circuit Block with Ashford Signal Box on the down line as far as Paddock Wood and on the up line from Pluckley. It worked with Staplehurst Signal Box when that Box was open

It worked Track Circuit Block to Yalding Signal Box on the Maidstone West Branch from Paddock Wood, and this included the two level crossings at Swatlands and Wagon Lane, and the Keylands Goods Yard at Paddock Wood.

It worked Track Circuit Block with Grove Junction Signal Box, between Tonbridge and Tunbridge Wells Central on the Hastings/Tunbridge Wells West Lines. It worked with Tunbridge Wells Central Goods Signal Box when that Signal Box was open.

It worked standard Absolute Block Working with Penshurst on the Tonbridge to Redhill Line. When Penshurst was closed the Block Section was with Edenbridge, and if Edenbridge was closed the Block Section was with Redhill 'B' signal box.

In addition, Tonbridge controlled the West Marshalling Yard entrance and exit, both north and south sides, at the south end of the yard and the entrance and exits to the Redhill Branch at the north end. It controlled the West End Sidings, parallel to the down main line, the Jubilee Sidings, next to the West Yard, and the Redhill Branch Sidings, on the other side of the Redhill Lines.

At the south end of the station it controlled the entrances and exits from Tonbridge East Goods Yard. It controlled the Locomotive Depot exit at the south end of the station, opposite the East Goods Yard, and the Coal Sidings.

The station at Tonbridge comprised, platform 1, up platform loop, platform 2, up passenger loop, the up main line through the station, the down main line through the station, platform 3 the down passenger loop, and the bay platform 4.

The station at Paddock Wood comprised up platform loop, up main line through the station, down main line through the station, the down platform loop, the up and down Maidstone Branch, the Hawkhurst Siding (the old truncated line to Horsmonden and Hawkhurst) and Keylands Goods Yard, and later the Transfesa Continental Goods Depot.

In all the Signal Box controlled over 100 miles of track, and it replaced the two old signal boxes, 'A' box at the north end of the station and 'B' box at the south end, and the signal boxes at Paddock Wood.

The Signal Box control panel was of the entry and exit route calling button system. To set a route, the signalman pressed the entry button at the beginning of the route. He then pressed the exit button at the end of the route. The relays in the floor below then did their job.

Starting with the furthermost end of the route, each pair of points was aligned with the route that had been called. When all the points were aligned and locked and there was no possibility of a conflicting route, a row of white lights illuminated the route on the panel, while outside on the track the appropriate signals changed to a proceed aspect, and this too was indicated on a repeater set into the panel.

Above the panel was a row of independent point switches, with three lights to show which position they were in. If the signalman had difficulty in calling a route, he could move the points by these switches, always providing there was no conflicting move and the locking permitted it. Sometimes he needed to switch points to prevent a conflicting move and free up the interlocking before he could call a route.

The panel was divided into two halves. The Tonbridge end down as far as Postern, was controlled with Westinghouse equipment, while below Postern to Paddock Wood and beyond the panel was controlled with Siemens equipment.

The major difference there was that, should a signalman call a route using the Westinghouse equipment, and then for whatever reason had to cancel it, he pulled up the entry button. The signal would change back to a red, stop, aspect, and there was an automatic timeout of 2 minutes before the signalman could call another route from that point. With the Siemens equipment there was no timeout and the signalman, once having cancelled the route, was free to call another route immediately. There was no obvious reason for this difference.

Some signalmen said if they had to wait for a timeout, it made them concentrate more. Others said it simply delayed trains. As a matter of interest, the signal box at Ashford was all controlled by Siemens equipment.

The signalmen were also divided up. There would be two signalmen on duty early, late and nights seven days a week. The Panel was divided. The Tonbridge end signalman would work Tonbridge station, all the yards and sidings including the Locomotive Depot and the Redhill and Tunbridge Wells Branches.

The Paddock Wood end signalmen worked all the lines from Postern down to below Paddock Wood on the down main and from Headcorn on the up main, together with the up and down Maidstone Branch, Keylands Goods Yard, the level crossings at Swatlands and Wagon Lane and the Hawkhurst Siding.

The signalmen were supposed to swap ends so as to retain familiarity with both ends but in practice they rarely did so. There were two box boys, one on early turn and one on late turn.

There were also two Signal and Telegraph (later Signal and Telecomms) linemen on duty on each of the three shifts.

So far this has all been a bit technical, but I hope not too dry. But now we come to the more interesting bit as we meet the characters who manned these posts.

When 'the Management' set up the staffing of the signal box they deliberately chose people who were opposites in character to work together in pairs. This, I was told, was an attempt to make sure the signalmen at Tonbridge did not band together against 'the Management.'

Thus, on one shift we had Jack, who was so laid back he

really was almost horizontal. He even spoke with a lazy drawl. With him was paired Sidney, who was of a somewhat nervous disposition.

The next pair were equally different. Jack was a country-man who took everything as it came. Albert was a man who strived for perfection in every way and only rarely failed to make it.

The third pair were formidable. Ted was a strict disciplinarian and a Justice of the Peace. More than once we box boys experienced the length of his tongue. He addressed us all as 'boy!' Revenge, when it came was sweet. I was there to see it happen!

His opposite number was Dick, a cockney who had worked as a Relief Signalman in all the south London signal boxes. Dick appeared to my eyes to have no regard for authority whatsoever (but that may just have been his sense of humour) and the only exception to this was our Station Master, Mr Burrows, whom Dick once described as 'Too much of a gentleman to have a go at.'

There were two Relief Signalmen. George was a Special Rest Day Relief. He was a Special because as well being the Rest Day Relief Signalman he was also the Rest Day Relief Station Supervisor. Some people did not like him. He could quickly become impatient, and it showed, and as with others I have known on relief shifts, his opinion changed with his job. When he was relief signalman, the station staff were rubbish. When he was on the station, the signalmen were useless.

He had only one real enemy, Jock the Jubilee Sidings and Passenger Shunter. They hated each other with dedication. I actually enjoyed working with George and we got on really well.

The Other Relief Signalman was Alex Hancock. He eventually served fifty-one years before retirement. I knew him as Relief signalman, and he was the very best. The last time I heard of him he had been promoted to Area Inspector London Bridge. He knew Signalling and Rules inside out and he was always calm and usually cheerful. It was a pleasure to work with him.

I also enjoyed being on duty with Jack and Sidney and with Jack and Albert, and I tried to keep a low profile with Ted and Dick. I have to say in all fairness that all of them did a very professional job.

There was also an Area Inspector, responsible for all signalling matters in his area. Ours was Mr Bill --, who had been a signalman at Sevenoaks before his promotion. He certainly was an expert on signalling, and no-one succeeded in pulling the wool over his eyes. He made a point of being nobody's friend and was scrupulously strict but fair.

Our S & T Technicians were characters too. The ones I particularly remember were Bill and Syd, If anything was going to happen, it would be on their shift.

There was one little incident when, late at night, the window of the downstairs front door of the signal box suddenly shattered. A signalman investigating, found a pair of footprints going right up the wall and across the ceiling, as well as the shattered window. Of Bill and Syd there was no sign. They were found at Paddock Wood doing some essential maintenance, so they had an alibi.

There was an S & T Manager, Mr H, who oversaw all the technicians, and he was a sneaky man. He would park his car at one station but then catch a train to another station and try to sneak up to the relevant signal box and catch out the technicians. His efforts were frustrated at Tonbridge because the signalmen could see anyone walking off the station platform towards the Box, and the technicians were always well warned.

The other box boys were also characters in their own right. Ginger was the senior box boy. He did a good job and was also unofficially sometimes allowed under supervision to work the panel. I thought he was destined to become a signalman. I was as surprised as anyone when he suddenly left to be a milkman.

The other two were opposites. One was a big and very 'with it' lad, always into the latest music and fashions. He never entirely settled in and no-one was surprised when he left. The other was a small lad who smoked continuously. He worked hard, but soon left the Railway.

The replacement was a man called Mike. He lived at Penshurst and was a patient and very steady person, always punctual and a good person to work with. He was still there when I left.

The other person who worked regularly in the Signal Box was the cleaner. His name was Albert and he was, and still is, a friend of mine from outside the Railway and I was very pleased when he came to work in Tonbridge Signal Box. It was always fun time when he came up into the box.

I had only been working in the signal box for six months when I witnessed my first collision. At around 7 am two trains of passenger vans were timetabled to arrive at Tonbridge. The first came from Wolverhampton via Redhill and was a mixed consist train. It was a long train and would not fit into the down bay, so it was always signalled to platform 3.

The other train was an express fish train, which left Holborn at around 5.30 am and after Tonbridge ran fast to Ramsgate. This train was signalled to the down bay. Fish from this train was transferred to the other train.

Then the normal move was for the locomotive, one of the powerful '5000' class electric locomotives, to propel its train out of the bay platform across the down main, onto the up main. Then it would be signalled back onto the down main and would be right away to Ashford and Ramsgate. Because of the loads of fresh fish it was designated a class1 express train.

Unfortunately, on this morning the 0638 Hastings to Cannon Street, which was fast from High Brooms was three minutes late and was signalled up the up main. The signalman, not wishing to delay the fish train, routed it instead into the West End Sidings, a much shorter route. I had learned to book these shunts and I watched for the train to start moving out of the platform. When it did, I noted the time and turned to book it.

As pen touched paper, there was a loud but muffled 'Gronk !' sound. Slowly I turned round on my swivel chair and as I did so, I saw an Insulfish van, the last vehicle on the train, sitting right on top of the buffer stops with one pair of wheels each side of it, and gently rocking up and down. For a moment there was complete silence, then came the sound of running feet.

The signalman had blocked the up and down main lines to and from Sevenoaks in case the van toppled sideways onto them. In due course the guard came up into the signal box. He was bleeding profusely from a cut to his forehead. He was in the passenger brake van on this fully brake fitted train.

When he realised where they were going, he leapt up to pull

the emergency brake, but the impact happened before he could reach it and he was catapulted across the van, hitting the end wall with some force. The signalman gave him first aid and I made a strong sweet cup of tea for him.

The driver was missing, and after a frantic search he was found wandering in a daze in the East Yard, having walked right through the station and under the bridge at the end.

Mr Fred C was a Carriage Mechanical & Electrical Engineer, (CM & EE) man who was based at Hither Green but lived at Tonbridge, and he attended.

He had the van made secure on the top of the stops, then he advised the signalman that it was secure and that down trains could pass the site at extreme caution until after the morning rush hour, and he would then arrange for rerailing.

A lot of discussion ensued. Bringing the Hither Green 45 ton Brakedown Crane to the site would entail blocking both up and down main lines. Fred was of the opinion that if sleepers were carefully stacked up against the remains of the buffer stops, and a very long chain was attached, with the other end fastened to one of the diesel shunter pilot engines, the wagon could be pulled back down onto the track. Both main lines would be blocked while the operation took place.

The signalman asked Fred what would happen if it went wrong and the wagon toppled onto the main line. Fred's reply was that the main lines would still be blocked and the Hither Green Crane would have to attend. He had put it on standby.

At a suitable time both main lines were blocked. One of the West Yard pilot locomotives was driven into the station and back into the sidings. The remainder of the fish train had been detached, and, after examination, had continued on its way with a fresh crew.

The chain was attached. The engine reversed until the chain was tight. Then the wagon began to move. Suddenly the rear wheels topped the framework of the buffer stops and the vehicle ran back down the channel of sleepers and straight onto the track. Everyone heaved a sigh of relief. Fred was congratulated and the signalman reopened the up and down main lines to traffic.

Throughout this incident, one of my jobs was to keep Orpington Control advised at every stage, so that the signalmen could concentrate on the job.

This was the first of a number of incidents I was to witness and gave rise to one of my most well-known sayings, 'It was nothing to do with me. I was just there when it happened.'

The next incident was the first time I experienced a runaway. The train concerned was a goods train from Mountfield Sidings on the Hastings Branch. It consisted of some brake fitted mineral open service wagons and some unbraked wagons of the same type. It was loaded with gypsum and was destined for cement works in south London. Because of the unfitted wagons a brake van was attached to the end. The train was hauled by a comparatively new 'slimline' class 33 diesel.

A number of these diesels were built specially for the narrow loading gauge of some of the tunnels on the Hastings Branch.

On the approach to Tonbridge there is a very steep descent through Somerhill Tunnel and down into Tonbridge Station. In order to help the driver control the train, the guard would wind the handbrake on in the brake van as the train passed through High Brooms Station.

We later learned that on this occasion, when the guard wound the brake on, the brake shoes suddenly shattered and flew off like buckshot. The train then only had the locomotive brakes and those of the few fitted wagons on the front of the train to hold it, and it wasn't enough.

As the train emerged from the tunnel, we could hear the continuous sounding of the locomotive warning horn. The signal to admit the train into Tonbridge was at 'Danger.' In platform 2, the 1252 Tonbridge to Eridge steam hauled, was standing ready to leave. The route had been set from platform 2 onto the up Hastings Branch, where just before the protecting signal, it would cross to the down line and go into the tunnel.

The signalmen immediately realised something was wrong. We watched the track circuits activate one by one. The train ran past the danger signal. Then it ran through the trailing points of the crossover, damaging them. It was obvious that the train was going to run into platform 2 at Tonbridge.

The station staff were told by the signalman to evacuate the 1252 Tonbridge to Eridge, and get them clear, and then try to shunt the train, headed by a 2-6-4 tank engine, back up the platform. The passengers were all cleared, and the doors closed.

Meanwhile the goods train continued its slow progress into the station. The crew on the 2-6-4 tank engine were just getting the train brakes off as the class 33 came under the bridge. The buffers on the class 33 just touched the buffers on the 2-6-4 tank and the goods train stopped. Everyone heaved a sigh of relief.

The Signal & Telecomms and the P. Way staff attended to the damaged pointwork. The passenger train was cancelled, and the goods train was shunted into the West Yard. Had the trains collided heavily at that point, they could have brought the station bridge and its road traffic down on top of them. It was a day we would not forget.

Those were the most dramatic incidents I witnessed at Tonbridge but there were many others. One concerned one of our most important trains, the Golden Arrow. This first-class Pullman Express was always hauled by a class 5000 locomotive. These locomotives were a small class of about 25 in total. They consisted basically of a powerful electric motor, which drove a huge flywheel, which gave a continuous current supply to the very powerful traction motors. They were so powerful that they were the only locomotives capable of single locomotive hauling the (up to 17 coaches) Night Ferry. If one of them failed on that train, two of the other classes of locomotive were required to haul the train.

These locomotives had also been tested to pull 100 goods wagons. They drew their electric current from the third rail via collector shoes. But they also had a pantograph. This was to collect 750 v dc, from overhead cables which had been installed at Hither Green and Ashford Yards. This was experimental but was not a great success as the cables were so thick that when they expanded on hot days, they drooped markedly and could not be used. But the pantographs remained on the locomotives.

On this day, the down Golden Arrow was approaching Tonbridge under clear signals, when, as the train approached the footbridge over the main line from Barden Road, to the north of the station, we were watching it, and all three of us saw the pantograph suddenly rise and hit the bridge. There was no contest between the pantograph and the concrete bridge.

The train glided past us with just one finger of the remains of the pantograph sticking up in the air.

The locomotive was disabled and the driver tried to stop the train before it went under the station bridge but was unable to do so and the train came to a stand on the down main with the locomotive just the other side of the bridge. The decision was taken not to try to haul the train back through the bridge in case the remains of the pantograph snagged the bridge and damaged the roof of the locomotive.

Then came the problem of what to do with the train. Not only was it one of the two most prestigious trains of the day, but it also had to make connection with a ship at Dover! There were no main line locomotives at Tonbridge at that moment in time. The services of one of the West Yard pilot 350 hp locomotives was offered to shunt the dead locomotive off, but this was firmly declined by Control. This was the Golden Arrow after all.

A suitable locomotive was found at Hither Green and another one at Ashford. Both were speedily manned and sent light engine to Tonbridge. The first to arrive would work the train forward. Memory does not recall which arrived first, but in due course the train continued its journey, after the failed class 5000 had been detached .Lest the reader should think that the job was all tension, I can assure them that this was not so.

The people I worked with were very professional and I hope and believe some of their professionalism rubbed off on me. I was able to say then, with complete honesty, that there were fewer safer places anywhere than a seat in a British Railway carriage. Many thousands of journeys were made in complete safety and were incident free. I was just privileged to be there when things didn't go entirely according to plan.

But there were also some very funny moments, as the following incidents reveal.

One of the first concerned our cleaner and my old friend Albert. He arrived one morning to do the cleaning in the box. Ted and Dick were on duty. 'Boy' had made the breakfast for the signalman, had placed it on his table beside the panel, and had returned to his own repeater panel.

Albert brought in the 'Dalek' a very large vacuum cleaner on three wheels that really did look like a Dalek. He plugged the lead into the power socket. Then he plugged the waste pipe into the cleaner and switched on. Nobody, least of all Albert, knows how it happened, but somehow, the pipe connected to the waste outlet instead of the suction inlet.

I gradually became aware of a rising cloud of dust, which slowly appeared over the top of my panel. Then it enveloped the signalman and his breakfast. Some very un-JP like language issued from within the cloud.

Albert managed to find the switch and stop the machine. He apologised profusely as the dust dispersed, and order was finally restored. Albert was always very conscientious and was very upset by the incident. How I managed not to laugh I really don't know. The signalman must have seen the expression on my face.

Some railwaymen are renowned for their (distorted) sense of humour, and the staff in the West Yard were no exception. One shunter used to arrive on a bicycle with his dog in a basket on the front. He was very careless about where he left the bicycle.

One day his colleagues decided to teach him a lesson. They hid the bicycle and the driver of a departing goods train took the dog into his cab. Came 2 pm and the shunter was going off duty. He found his bicycle and was just in time to see his dog departing on the locomotive of the 2 pm goods train from Tonbridge to Ashford. He then had to wait until 6 pm for the engine, and his dog, to return!

The coke boiler in the signal box was also the source of some amusement and a lot of frustration. It was the box boy's job to keep it going. It could only be loaded/unloaded from the top. If it went out, as it sometimes did, all the clinker had to be pulled out through the top. A layer of paper and oil, soaked cotton waste (from the S & T room) had to be placed inside and set alight. Then coke had to be fed into it. If it went out (and it frequently did!) everything had to be removed and you had to start again.

One day in mid-November, I had real trouble with this thing. Three times I had lit it and three times it went out. One of our technicians, Syd, saw me struggling and asked what was wrong. He said, 'Leave it to me. You just go back upstairs.' A little while later, my phone rang. It was Syd and he asked me to come down. We went into the boiler room and he opened the boiler door. A sheet of flame roared out! I jumped back and asked him how he had done it. He wouldn't tell me, but he did warn me to close the damper before I went off duty.

Later that morning we had an awkward point failure at Paddock Wood and Bill and Syd were dispatched to the scene. All of us in the box were kept busy. My relief arrived and I handed over and went home. The late turn continued to be busy. Peter and his partner had taken over from Bill and Syd at Paddock Wood, and eventually the failure was rectified.

The night turn signalmen Ted and Dick came on duty at

10 pm. By about 11 pm, Dick commented that the box was very warm. He went over and touched one of the radiators and leapt back, shouting that the radiator was 'red hot!' He went downstairs to the boiler room. He found the damper on the boiler was still open and the needle on the gauge was right over in the red. As he stood there taking all this in, the safety valve blew, shooting a jet of steam at the ceiling.

The night outside was frosty, and the sleepers were white, but the signal box windows had to be kept open to dispel some of the overpowering heat. It took a long time the next morning to remove more than 6 inches of solid clinker from the bottom of the stove. To their credit, Bill and Syd did it for us.

Another incident involved that boiler. I was downstairs one morning, as usual trying, without much success, to get it going. I also needed the toilet fairly urgently. Finally, I saw the thing was alight, and I left it and rushed up the stairs to the toilet. I flung open the door. Unfortunately, this action coincided with that of the signalman who was just rising from the seat. The rapidly opening door struck him on the top of his head and forced him back onto the seat. He just never locked the door went he went in. Thankfully he was not hurt, and neither was I but I had to run. He might have been an older man, but he was very fit, and he could still run fast as he chased me out!

Meanwhile, outside, the trains continued to run well, and the incidents continued to happen. One stretch of line between Hildenborough and Tonbridge was a comparatively straight section and trains ran quite fast.

Sadly, it made it a place where occasionally people chose to commit suicide. One day we had a report from a driver that had seen a man, apparently spread-eagled on the upside embankment, but clear of the track. Staff set out, fearing the worst, but when they got to the man he sat up. He told them that he had found the embankment a perfect place to sunbathe. He apologised for the trouble he had caused and went away. Relieved staff returned to base.

With all the shunting movements going on continuously in the West Yard and the Jubilee Sidings it speaks volumes for the professionalism of the staff that mishaps were very rare, but two I do recall.

When the Jubilee Bridge was built, before we had moved to Tonbridge, it formed a route that was popular for a variety of reasons. It linked the people living on the Sussex Road Estate with those on the Barden Estate.

It was also a direct route for schoolchildren going from the Barden Estate to Sussex Road Infant and Junior Schools and Hayesbrook Secondary Modern School for Boys. It was a very long footbridge, crossing over the entire West Yard, the Jubilee Sidings, the up and down Redhill lines and the Redhill Branch Sidings.

However, one of the bridge supports resulted in one road, West Yard, north sidings, being truncated. As a result, that particular siding could only take eight wagons. One night, a very new shunter pulled the points for a shunt of ten wagons to go into the siding. Inevitably a collision with the buffer stops resulted. The shunter was afraid that this would cost him his job. Sure enough, when he came on duty the next night, the dreaded brown envelope awaited him. When he opened it, he found the following message from the Area Inspector, 'Ten into eight doesn't go!'

The second mishap was much more spectacular and requires

a little explanation. In order for the signalman to call a route from the main line into the West Yard, north or south, the shunter must press a plunger, unlocking the route and enabling the signalman to set it. But there was no such precaution for trains going from the main line into the Jubilee Sidings.

When I walked through the West Yard, early one Monday morning for the start of early turn, using the authorised route to the signal box, I became aware that there were many more lights than usual. Then I saw the Chart Leacon (Ashford) Tool Vans, parked in the West Yard No'2 Road. The crane was nearby. They were just reforming prior to returning to Ashford.

Going up into the signal box I soon learned what had happened. On the Friday night a train of empty minfits (mineral wagons fitted with brakes) had arrived en route to Mountfield Sidings to be reloaded with gypsum. The West Yard shunter had pressed the plunger for the release to enable the signalman to call the route from the down main line to the West Yard.

The exit buttons for the route to the West Yard and the Jubilee Sidings were right next to each other on the panel, and at that precise moment were covered by the pages of the Special Traffic Notice, which the signalman was reading, trying to sort out the order in which engineering trains would go out of the yard. Inadvertently, he pressed the exit button for the Jubilee Sidings. No release was needed and the route 'came off' straightaway.

Because of the length of the train and the convoluted route off the down main, the driver was not aware that he was going the wrong way. The train set back, ran into the Jubilee Sidings and collided with a six coach Hastings unit that was berthed there. The wagons rose up in a heap and fell over onto the up and down Redhill lines. The Hastings unit sustained damage to the cab and was pushed back fifty feet with its brakes hard on. Thankfully no-one was injured.

The up and down Redhill lines were blocked for the weekend for engineering work so the buses had already been arranged, and the cost to the Company was less than it might have been. The wagons had been cleared and the minimal track damage had been repaired in time for the service to resume as planned on Monday morning.

But as the signalman, who had accepted responsibility for the accident, ruefully admitted afterwards, he had been told that thirty-five wagons had been written off in the collision. The Company were less severe than they might have been, noting in mitigation that the Jubilee Sidings ought to have had a separate release. One was installed shortly afterwards.

Two more characters that I had the privilege of working with were Wally, the man in charge of supplying and maintaining of paraffin hand lamps, and Old Ken, the Storeman, whose son Ken later came to work as a signalman in Tonbridge Box In the signal box we had a paraffin hand lamp for use by the signalman to stop trains in an emergency. I only saw it used once, when on a foggy morning, a driver, thinking he 'had the road' to leave the Yard, was driving his train into the little siding just outside the Box, where wagons of coke were stabled and unloaded for the Box. The driver saw the red lamp waved by the signalman and stopped in time.

One of my many little jobs as a Box Boy was to maintain this lamp. I would dismantle it, clean the glass lens and polish the reflector. I would fill the container with paraffin and trim the wick. Then I would reassemble the lamp and test light it to ensure it was working. Then it would be stored ready for the signalman to use. These lamps were very effective as was seen by my little incident. Later they were replaced by Bardic electric lamps that were even more efficient, and now the new lamps are lit by light emitting diodes.

This job that I and the other Box Boys did on a regular but infrequent basis, was a daily job for Wally. Not only did he have the station supply of train tail lamps to service, but the up and down Redhill lines were still worked with semaphore signals that were illuminated at night by paraffin lamps. These had to be checked every three days. This meant taking a supply of newly serviced lamps and walking up the track to the signals, which were some distance away, climbing up the signal posts, removing the old lamps and replacing them with the new ones, then walking back to the station, where the lamp hut was located, with the old lamps, and servicing them. This had to be done in all weathers, sun, rain, sleet, wind, and snow.

Not un-naturally, ways were devised to make this job easier. It was rumoured that some drivers would allow the lamp man to travel with them and stop at the signal to set him and his lamps down. It was also rumoured that much more rarely a few drivers would take the lamps with them and do the job for him, bringing the old lamps back on their return journey.

Then one day came the dreaded 'Time & Motion' man. His task was to accompany each member of staff on his or her duty, measure the time it took and make recommendations on how that time could be reduced. Most of these men were pleasant and conscientious in carrying out their duties, but, as the result of their work was usually the loss of permanent jobs, they were not popular. When they were around, everybody carried out their duties to and in many cases beyond the book.

For Wally, this meant carrying his replacement lamps, and being accompanied by the Time & Motion man, all the way to Leigh intermediate distant signal, a trek of several miles. The signalmen commented later that it was nearly the end of Wally. It was the end of the Time & Motion man, - he never came back!

Old Ken, the Storeman was a tremendous asset to the Company. He never had anything in his stores, or so he said. Another of my jobs was to go to the stores office, located in an archway under the station bridge, and protected by a locked door, with the key jealously guarded by Old Ken. I would go in search of dusters for the signalmen, teacloths and towels, and matches and paraffin for the lamps, which in those days were all standard issue.

The stores were open only at a certain time on a certain day of the week. No-one else was allowed into the Stores. Old Ken would go inside, closing the door after him, and then come back out, bringing the required equipment and get you to sign for it.

Old Ken's invariable response to these requests, was to suck his breath in sharply through his teeth, then, after a moments deliberation, he would say slowly, 'There's none in stock at the moment, they're quite hard to come by now, you know. But I will order some for you. Come back next week.' Back I would go to the signalmen and tell them. Their response was predictable and sometimes unprintable.

Then one day, disaster struck. For the first time that anyone could remember, Old Ken fell ill and was off work for two weeks. A relief Store Manager was temporarily appointed. She was a lovely, generous person. I was invited into the Stores. It was like Aladdin's Cave in there, shelves bowed down with stores. I was given everything I had asked for.

When the signalmen found out, I was sent back for a lot more stores. Word flew like wildfire around the station and yards and long queues formed outside the door, with people returning loaded high with stores.

Old Ken returned to work after his fortnight off duty. When he opened up the Stores, he nearly had a relapse. The shelves were bare. It took him a long time to restock it, and for a little while people were inclined to be more sympathetic when he said, 'There's none in stock at the moment, they're quite hard to come by now, you know. But I will order some for you.'

Another thing that kept us on the alert in Tonbridge Signal Box was the type of rolling stock used on the Redhill line. Because in those days the trains ran through from Redhill to Tunbridge Wells West via Grove Junction, the trains had to negotiate two restricted tunnels, so the instruction was that narrow-sided stock was to be used. But it was not unusual for Redhill to run standard stock on the train.

Tonbridge always kept a spare narrow sided set for these eventualities. It meant that passengers had to change trains, but, with adequate warning, a suitable train would be on the adjacent platform and the passengers were smoothly transferred.

However, Redhill did not always advise us when they had put a standard set on the train. Then the signal box was the first to be aware of the problem. Then there would be a scramble to advise the station supervisor and arrange for a pilot loco to fetch out the spare set, make a platform available (not always easy with the complex service and connections to be maintained).

After the job had been done, we then had to transfer passengers from the next narrow sided set from Eridge, to the standard set and send it back to Redhill. The narrow-sided set would then be stored in the sidings ready for the next occasion it was needed. This may all sound a bit petty, but the fact was that if we didn't store a narrow sided set at Tonbridge, the next time Redhill sent a standard set on the train, it would have to terminate at Tonbridge, which would seriously delay passengers for stations beyond. So it became a regular practice for the signalman or the box boy to examine each train as it came into view on the branch.

Contrary to popular belief at the time, punctuality was important to us. One example sticks in my mind. The hourly services from Charing Cross to Ramsgate were class one expresses, running fast from Waterloo to Ashford, passing Tonbridge at 37 minutes past the hour. To delay one of them would certainly result in a 'Please explain' from HQ Queen Street.

On this night the 2000hrs freight Tonbridge to Ashford with 65 = 80 wagons on, hauled by a class 5000 locomotive was not ready to leave until 2005 hrs. With that load on, the only place for the 'fast' to pass it was Headcorn. The big question was, could the freight make Headcorn without delaying the 'fast'? Driver Dave T on the locomotive promised the signalman that he could. He was given the road.

As the locomotive passed the Box, the signalman made a peddling motion with his hands to urge the driver on. So fast did that powerful locomotive move that, by the time the brake-van passed the signal box, the signalman calculated it was travelling at 40 mph as it snaked through the crossovers. It went through Paddock Wood at speed. George P, one of our technicians, had his head in a relay box as the locomotive went past. By the time he had got his head out of the relay box and looked up, the brake-van was going by!

After Paddock Wood the train went off of our panel and on to Ashford's panel so we could not see its progress. The 2000hrs Charing Cross to Ramsgate raced past the Signal Box at exactly 20.37 hrs. After a short while the Paddock Wood end signalman rang Ashford to see if the freight had made Headcorn. 'Headcorn!,' exclaimed the Ashford Signalman, ' He's just backing into Ashford Yard. The 'fast' has had clear signals all the way!' It was a record run.

With the reader's sufferance, I will end this chapter on a cautionary note. The dreadful collision at Lewisham on 4th December 1957 was one of the worst disasters for British Railways and the worst disaster for Southern Region. The main cause was established as that in the thick fog that enveloped south London (and those of us, who like me, lived through those 'smogs' will know how bad they were) the driver of the 1652 Cannon Street to Ramsgate missed the warnings of two signals and overran the third at St. Johns, with tragic consequences.

What is less well known, was that at the next signal box beyond St. Johns, Parks Bridge Junction, a very busy six way junction, had no Signal Lad on duty that late turn, to remind the signalmen, working a very dislocated service, of the order in which trains were running. Had the trains not been delayed while their identity was ascertained, the 1652 Cannon Street to Ramsgate would still have overrun the signal, but the preceding train would have moved on and there might not have been a collision.

It is a profound thought that, though a junior member of staff might not see himself/herself as important, the first job you do as a junior might be the most important job you ever do, and so it should always be done well, and conscientiously.

Signalmen Alec and George
Tonbridge Signal Box circa 1963

Chapter Three - Becoming a signalman

Overall, I had enjoyed my time as a Box Boy in Tonbridge Box and had learned quite a lot. But I knew that when I turned eighteen, I would be expected to move on, and to begin serious training to become a signalman. One of the preparations I had made to achieve this was to take up evening classes while I was working at Tonbridge Signal Box. I took First Year Signalling and Rules and First Year Commercial Training. I also joined the First Aid Class.

I passed my exams in First Year Signalling and Rules, and Commercial Training. I decided to drop the Commercial Training and concentrated on Second Year Signalling and Rules.

However, the Second Year Signalling and Rules came to an abrupt end. The Area Inspector, who came from Maidstone, and whom I didn't know, arrived at a hired classroom in the local Adult Education Centre one evening, to find it was already occupied. To my amazement a lecture was being given by a man who had been my former English teacher at the Grammar School. A heated argument ensued as to who had the most right to be there. Possession being nine tenths of the law, it ended in defeat for the Area Inspector, who promptly declared that he would no longer take the class in Second Year Signalling and Rules and that was the end of the course.

The First Aid Class however, was something very different. The instructors had a devious sense of humour. On one occasion we were studying chest injuries. We were each shown how to tie on a broad bandage, tying off on the uninjured side. We all had to practice this on each other until we were quite proficient at it. Then an incident was set up. Each candidate was sent in to find an injured man and deal with the injury as we had been shown and had practised.

I opened the door and went in confidently, - to find a woman, whose chest I had to touch intimately as I applied the bandage! I was flabbergasted, and in some confusion, I hurried out of the room and blurted out, 'It's a woman!' Calmly the Instructor replied, 'I am sure that an injured woman would not object to your administering First Aid. Go back in and do it.' I went back in and found that the woman had been replaced by a man!

But perhaps the cruellest trick was played on a Fireman at an exercise at Hither Green. The Hither Green First Aid Team were led by a man called Ted. They were very good and they won most of the competitions in the Division. Exercises were held in the sidings there to make them realistic. An old unit, which had suffered from vandals and was going to be scrapped, was set up in the siding. It was a well worn joke that the Firemen liked to be as destructive as possible in these 'incidents.' The Firemen were encouraged to be as rough as they liked on this unit.

A Fireman approached one of the coaches in the unit to find a man trapped by his arm in a door, which had apparently slammed shut, leaving the 'victim' hanging by his arm. The Fireman struggled to free the door and suddenly it came open. The 'victim' fell out onto the ground in front of the Fireman, but his arm, which had been trapped, fell back into the carriage. The Fireman fainted. Only when he came round was it revealed to him that Ted had used the services of a one-armed member of staff with an artificial arm, to set up the incident.

Another part of my training was my being allowed to visit other signal boxes, in my own time. I spent some time at Yalding, on the Maidstone West Branch. Here I learned to open and close the hand operated gates on the level crossing. I found that motorists could be very aggressive. On one occasion, the signalman was closing one gate while I closed the other. A motorist deliberately drove his car at the gate I was closing, hooked his bumper under the gate bar and forced the gate, with me hanging onto it, back open again. The signalman was annoyed but had no choice but to reopen the other gate and let the motorist through.

On another occasion I was there when the 1842 Maidstone West – Tonbridge van train arrived. This train pulled up right over the crossing so that some four hundred drums of I.C.I chemicals could be loaded into the rear vans. This took some twenty minutes during which time the crossing remained closed to the road.

The signalman advised me to hide somewhere where I could not be seen, and he did likewise. I soon found out why. Despite the fact that there was an obstacle clearly blocking the crossing the motorists being delayed reacted in all sorts of ways. It started with the sounding of car horns. Then people started climbing up the side of the Signal Box to see if they could catch sight of the signalman. When this failed, they hit the wooden walls of the Box, and threw things at it. All the while the car horns were blaring.

Finally, all the drums were loaded. The train moved off, the signalman gave the 'In Section' to Tonbridge Signal Box, and

'Train out of section' to Wateringbury and then went out and opened the gates, to a hail of abuse. He advised me to stay inside. I did!

Yalding, to me, was a fascinating Box. It was a fringe Box, working with electronic describers to Tonbridge Track Circuit Block Signal Box on one side, and 'Absolute Block' with Wateringbury on the other. Trains to and from Paddock Wood were described on 'Barrel Type' describers, while between Yalding and Wateringbury, the Block Bells and associated instruments were in use. Both sections were about ten minutes in length (the time taken by a passenger train to pass through the section). And, of course there were the hand operated station level crossing gates.

There were also two level crossings between Yalding and Paddock Wood, Swatlands and Wagon Lane, but they were controlled from Tonbridge Signal Box, using electronically operated releases at the request of the crossing keepers. Yalding was a 'Class 3' signal box, and as such was ineligible at that time to me.

I also visited Maidstone West Signal Box. Maidstone West had an unusual station layout with two platform roads and one through line. On the down side there was also a bay platform. There were also a number of carriage sidings. There was also a small goods yard. A short tunnel separated Maidstone West and Maidstone Barracks stations.

Another interesting signal box was Slade Green, near Dartford. This signal box was a culture shock to me. It controlled one end of the biggest and busiest Rolling Stock Depots on the South Eastern, holding a big percentage of the suburban rolling stock, which worked the morning and evening rush hours, and also had a big repair depot within the main depot. Trains were coming to and going from the Depot all day, and some during the night too.

Slade Green also had a level crossing with four gates. This was opened and closed by a large wheel. As the crossing was a slewed one and on a sloping gradient, you started winding the wheel gently and gradually increased in power and speed until the climax when the gates slammed shut and the locking bars dropped. There was also a wicket gate, which was not locked by the main gates, so people could still walk onto the crossing when the main gates were shut.

I witnessed an amusing incident one day, when two mature women, who had evidently not seen each other for many years, met in the middle of the crossing. They cried out with joy and flung their arms around each other, oblivious of the closed level crossing and the approaching train. Calmly the signalman slid the window open, leaned out and shouted, 'Scuse me ladies, but there's a train coming.' The two women hurried off the crossing.

But the main thing that amazed me about Slade Green was the shortness of the Block Sections. I was used to ten- minute sections at Wadhurst, but here the sections were just two minutes! When a train came down off the Bexleyheath line, it could be seen when it was 'offered on,' and was 'in section' just one minute before it arrived. Given the density of the traffic and the short sections, Slade Green was a signal box to be reckoned with and I admired the calm way in which the signalmen worked it. And as if that were not enough, the Slade Green area often suffered dense fogs.

I also visited Hither Green Signal Box. This was a similar box to that at Tonbridge, being Westinghouse equipped entry and exit push button panel signal box with barrel type electronic train describers to Parks Bridge Junction up the line and Chislehurst down the line. It also controlled the branch lines to and from the Dartford Loop Line via Sidcup and the Lee Spur which curved around from the up and down local lines onto the Dartford Loop Line.

It also controlled the entry and exit to Hither Green down yards, 'A', 'B' and 'C' sections, the Up Yard, and the Continental Depot. It also controlled the entry and exit from the very busy locomotive shed and sidings, and the entry and exit to the Pre-assembly Depot. This latter was where the Permanent Way Dept assembled track and point sections and loaded them onto flat wagons to be taken to site for installation. Their special rail laying trains, cranes, and other equipment were also stored there. There were four main line tracks, in order from left to right, the up fast line, the down fast line, the up slow line, and the down slow line.

Hither Green was a very busy signal box, and as at Tonbridge, it was controlled by two signalmen, with one box boy to assist.

The last signal box I had the privilege of visiting was the old London Bridge Signal Box. This was something really special. It had a three hundred and two miniature lever frame, controlling points and colour light signals. Many of the signals were semi-automatic, coming 'off' as the routes were called and also by the passage of trains, on the track circuit block system.

The track circuit indicator diagram was unusual (at least to me) in that unoccupied track circuits were indicated by a red light. When a track circuit became occupied by the presence of a train, the light went out. This was the exact opposite of what I was used to. There were two of these huge diagrams, suspended above the frame.

The signal box controlled the South Eastern approaches to the through station and worked with North Kent East Signal Box below London Bridge and between New Cross and London Bridge stations.

To the north of London Bridge was the famous Borough Market Junction, where the lines to and from London Cannon Street Station diverged from the lines to and from London Charing Cross Station. This was known to be the busiest signal box in the country, and it was not possible to visit it.

Indeed, when I later worked in the Orpington Control, we were forbidden even to telephone the signalman in the Borough Market Junction Signal Box during the 'rush hours,' except in a case of real emergency. When the new London Bridge Panel signal box later replaced all these signal boxes, Borough Market Junction Signal Box was preserved in the National Railway Museum at York, where it can still be seen today.

London Bridge Signal Box also controlled the multiple approaches to London Bridge Central Station, the terminus of South Central Division trains from Brighton, the Sussex Coast, and the South Central Suburban train service.

On the South Eastern side, the lines running from right to left were No'1 down, No'2 reversible, No'3 up, No'4 down, No'5 reversible, No'6 up, and the up passenger loop. The signal box also controlled the Tattenham Crossover, where trains from Tattenham and Caterham on the Central Division, and later Thameslink, (now First Capital Connect), to and from Brighton/Kings Cross gained access to the South Eastern Division.

The signal box was staffed by four signalmen on each shift, two working the South Eastern side, and two working the Central side. There were two box boys, on each shift, one South Eastern and one Central, monitoring and recording the progress of the trains, and assisting the signalmen, and each having their own separate desks.

To stand, looking out of the south windows during the morning rush hour, one saw an incredible sight. On each of the up lines there was a steady and continuous procession of approaching trains, one behind the other, just signal sections apart, all moving but very slowly. It really was an impressive sight. I remember thinking every one of those trains was carrying up to a thousand passengers.

Yes, the old London Bridge Signal Box was unforgettable and, of all the signal boxes I have been privileged to visit, one of the most impressive signal boxes I have ever seen. The operations went on calmly and with just a low hum of noise.

While all these things had been going on I was scanning the Vacancy List. Suddenly one week I saw there were vacancies for a class 4 Signalman, at Wadhurst and at Stonegate. I filled in my vacancy forms and applied. In due course of time I was called for an interview. Prior to the interview, I was instructed to go and visit the signal boxes and to choose which one I would like to be considered for.

I duly went, first to Stonegate, then to Wadhurst. It did not take me long to make up my mind. I was not an abnormally fat person, but I had to go into Stonegate Box sideways, partly because of some instrument that was the size of, and resembled a grandfather clock, which was in the doorway. I was under the instruction of the signalman, but in spite of this I managed to pinch my fingers in the frame. I took an instant dislike to Stonegate. At the time both Stonegate and Wadhurst worked the same three shifts with both Boxes being closed out on Sunday nights. I do not remember much more about Stonegate.

I travelled up to Wadhurst. The signal box was situated on the down platform. The moment I walked in, I knew this was the box for me. It was everything a signal box should be. It had a forty- eight lever frame with thirty-two levers in use. The frame faced the traffic and above the frame was a neat shelf lined with instruments. Everything was gleaming and highly polished.

Even the linoleum floor was highly polished. I was told that the signalmen took a real pride in the appearance of the signal box. Cleaning was done on Sundays. There was no box boy and the signalmen kept the Train Register. There was a lovely fire, a comfortable armchair and along the back wall a row of lockers for their personal effects.

The layout at Wadhurst was interesting. The platforms were staggered and not opposite each other. There were the up and down main lines, an up siding and a down siding and two crossovers. The line was on a rising gradient towards Tunbridge Wells. To the north, Wadhurst worked with Grove Junction, just south of Tunbridge Wells, the junction for the then operating Tunbridge Wells West single line. Trains were described to them on an electronic describer, which was operated by a push button. Grove Junction also described trains in the same way on a barrel type describer.

The line continued to rise and there was a tunnel and the intermediate station at Frant in the section. The section time for a passenger train was ten minutes.

To the south, Wadhurst worked with Stonegate on a falling gradient and also with a tunnel in the section. This section was worked by Standard Three Way Absolute Block. When Stonegate was closed out, as it occasionally was, the section was extended to Etchingham. I cannot remember the section time when this occurred, but I believe it was about twenty minutes. Both Wadhurst and Stonegate were equipped with King Levers to enable them to be closed out.

It was important for the signalmen to know these section times because much of the lines then had no track circuits, and the first thing to alert a signalman to possible problems would be when a train had entered the section but had not arrived at the other end of the section in the allotted time. The signalman then had to assess what the possible problem was. He then had to decide, in consultation with his colleague at the other end of the section, on what course of action he had to take.

If there were any railway staff in the vicinity, he could try to contact them. He might decide to send a train forward in the opposite direction under extreme caution, instructing the driver that a train in the opposite direction was overdue and to be prepared to stop short of any obstruction. When the overdue train was located, one of the train crews should contact whichever signalman they could, to advise them of the problem.

If the overdue train had come to grief and the other line was obstructed, a strict procedures, the issuing of wrong line order forms, and other procedures, for example, observing clearance points, and locking any point-work, would come into force before the train stopped by the obstruction could be given permission to reverse.

So those section times and the Train Register were very important to the signalmen. And, in order to ensure that all clocks registered the same time, what was called 'Railway Time,' had been instituted. At 6 am precisely, Orpington Control sent a special signal on the omnibus telephone to all signal boxes and the signalmen would check, and if necessary, adjust their clocks when they received this signal.

Armed with all this knowledge, I attended the interview at Queen Street, London, at that time the headquarters of the South Eastern Division, British Railways. The senior interviewer was a Mr Louis E, and he was accompanied by a man whose first name was Ken. Sadly I cannot recall his last name.

Ken knew my father, and the first part of the interview was taken up with Ken wanting to know how my father was getting on and what he was doing, now that he had retired. Then Mr E started to ask me about signalling in general and Wadhurst in particular. He was quite impressed with my knowledge.

At the end of my interview he told me that they had decided to appoint me as a Class Four Signalman at Wadhurst, and that I would shortly be released to start my training there. I left the interview feeling very pleased that I had succeeded, very excited at the prospect of the new job, but also with some trepidation at the new responsibility. I returned to Tonbridge Signal Box and shared my good news with my friends there.

In due course I received my release date. I now had to solve the problem of how to get to Wadhurst to start the early turn shift. Most of the week I could travel down on the 0335 Victoria – Hastings Newspaper train for an 0600 hrs start, but, as the Box was closed out on Sunday night, I had to be at Wadhurst, on Monday morning at 0500 hrs to open the signal box and accept the 0335 Victoria – Hastings Newspaper train from Grove Junction. With my father's help I acquired a moped from a relative.

This sadly was a fiasco. It was a Raleigh moped with only one gear, which was a plug at the base of the frame, which you pushed in to engage the gear, then pedalled furiously until the engine fired.

It took me an hour and a half to get to Wadhurst, which meant getting up at 0300hrs in order to be there at 0500 hrs. The machine broke down twice and then caught fire.

Finally, it was abandoned and my father, realising my need, loaned me the money to buy my first real motorbike, a small Honda, with a four-stroke engine. This bike was a gem and served me well over several years. At some point I passed my motorcycle test on it. I could now get up at 0400hrs for early turn Monday at Wadhurst.

Just the week before I left Tonbridge, a letter came for me. I am not sure now, but I believe it came from Mr Burrows, our Station Master. He advised me that there was a vacancy for a Class Four Clerk at Orpington Train Supervision Sub Section, more familiarly known as 'Control.'

I telephoned Mr Burrows about it and reminded him that I had not passed the Clerical Exam.

His reply was, 'Don't worry about that. Just think it over. If you are interested, get back in touch with me. They might be able to take you on a six-month trial.'

I took my letter with me to Wadhurst as I started my training there. I met the signalman who was going to train me. His name was Reg W. I also met my new Station Master, Mr Alan M. Reg told me Mr M was a very conscientious man. He said if the TIB in the Booking Office was a penny out, he would worry about it all weekend. Reg was a very knowledgeable and very steady signalman. I had great confidence in him. But the first time a train came thundering by the window, it made me very nervous, as I suddenly realised my responsibility for it.

At Tonbridge I had seen most of the trains we controlled, but the operating floor was so high up that we looked down on most of them, and the only trains we were really close to were those entering and leaving the West Yard and the Jubilee Sidings. Indeed, many of the trains on the Paddock Wood – Maidstone West Branch we never saw at all. They were just a row of red dots on the panels.

But here it was very different. Every train I controlled as a signalman passed right by the windows.

Walking down the platform one day I chanced upon two other characters. I was never quite sure what their role was. They did not look too prepossessing. Their uniform was shabby, and they slouched along the platform. One was short and stout and the other was tall and thin. They instantly reminded me of the two villains in '101 Dalmations,' a popular film at the time.

'You the new signalman?' was their opening gambit.

I said I was.

'Nah then, you listen to us and do the job the way we say, and we'll look after you.' I certainly did not want them looking after me and as very much a new boy I intended very much to stick to the Rule Book, please or offend. I never saw them again.

Training, under Reg's watchful eyes continued. There was friendly banter between the signalmen at Wadhurst and Stonegate, and much pulling of Reg's legs when I had difficulty with pulling one particular signal, resulting on the 'Train or Description cancelled' signal having to be sent on the block bells and the train then having to be offered on again.

All in all, I enjoyed my time there, gradually learning and taking a real pride in the trade of being a Signalman.

But in my pocket was still that letter from Mr Burrows about Orpington Control. I had to weigh up the pro's and con's. A good signalman was respected by his colleagues, and the job was a secure one. If I continued to enjoy doing it, I could progress to bigger and higher graded signal boxes. In those days I had no idea of the sweeping changes that were to come, and the number of signal boxes that would be closed as a consequence of those changes.

Control, on the other hand was an unknown quantity. I had no real idea of what it did. The signalmen at Tonbridge usually treated it with no very great respect. The title, 'Brains Department,' was not a complimentary one. If something did go wrong and providing it did not impact on safety, the rule of thumb was to cover it up, and if it could not be avoided, to tell Control later.

On the other hand, it could be my passport back into the clerical grades. I could then move on as a clerk if I didn't like Control. These opportunities were very rare indeed and I was unlikely to get another one.

Finally, after much heart searching, and with real regrets at leaving signalling, I decided to take up Mr Burrows' invitation. I telephoned him, thanked him, and said I had decided to take up his kind invitation. Again, with real regrets, I said goodbye to Reg and to Mr M and to my career as a signalman.

An interview was arranged with Mr Pat O'Leary, the Orpington Train Supervision Sub Section's Chief Clerk.

Once again, my career on the Railway was moving in a new direction.

Chapter Four -
Orpington Train Supervision Sub Section

I will begin this chapter by introducing Mr Pat O'Leary. Mr O'Leary was a remarkable man, and he was to become the second of the all-time best bosses in my career. He was a small man in stature. He had red hair, which rose to a spike near the rear of his head. The route from his office took him past the windows of the Control, and, so short was he that the only part of him to be seen was this spike of red hair as he passed by the windows. But he was no comic figure.

As Chief Clerk (Controller) he was responsible for all the staff in the Control, all the clerks in the Staff Relief Office, and the staff who manned the Control Switchboard. He would also, upon hearing of any major incident, gleefully abandon his paperwork and come alongside the Deputy Chief Controller (D.C.C) to assist. He knew every one of the nine Control Panels and could work every one of them. He also knew every member of staff by name.

He spoke very quietly. I never knew him to raise his voice.

Mr O'Leary had a gift I have seldom seen elsewhere. If he were pleased with something that someone had achieved, he would summon that person into his office and tell them so. You would come out of his office feeling really successful and appreciated.

On the other hand, if he found someone not doing the job right or doing something wrong, he would summon that person to his office. There, quietly and without raising his voice he would express his disappointment with them and explain why. On those occasions you would come out of his office feeling just two inches tall. He was in constant communication with his D.C.C.'s, and always told them when he had spoken to a member of their shift.

He also had a wonderful knack of being able to defend his staff against written criticisms from Queen Street, our London HQ. He personally read every 'Please Explain' (so called because every critical letter from Queen Street began with the words ('Please explain your actions –'). Those that he thought were justified complaints he would pass on to the relevant member of staff.

Those he thought were 'rubbish,' he would store up. Eventually, when he had amassed a number of these latter and had received a further complaint of a lack of response to their letters, he would make an appointment for a meeting with the Chief Operating Manager at Queen Street. He would call in on his way and briefly mention the items he was going to deal with, then with a grin on his face, and clutching a small brown cardboard case, he would set off for Queen Street.

At the meeting he would take delight, without raising his voice, in demonstrating the folly of the contents of the letters and the incompetence and lack of knowledge and experience of those who wrote and sent them. For this he had the loyalty and respect of every member of his staff, - but he was hated at Queen Street.

This was the man then who was to interview me for a temporary clerical post as a class four clerk in the Orpington Train Supervision Sub Section.

At the close of the interview, Mr O'Leary advised me that he was appointing me to the post. He would monitor my progress. If by the end of about six months he was satisfied with me, my appointment would become permanent.

I should also explain any confusion of the title of the office. When I arrived there, it was called Orpington Train Supervision Sub Section. The clerks complained that this title allowed them to ask for and receive information on incidents on the Division, but no authority to do anything about the incidents, regulate trains, or make decisions about the consequences. Mr O'Leary supported this claim. The Company resisted this because as well as delegating authority, controllers were paid more than clerks.

Eventually the Company conceded the claim, Orpington Train Supervision Sub Section became Orpington Control, Mr O'Leary became Chief Controller, the Deputy Chief Clerks became Deputy Chief Controllers, the clerks on the panels became Area Controllers, Brake-van Controllers, Locomotive Controllers or Guards Controllers, and we class four clerical assistants became Assistant Controllers. Similar arrangements were applied to Redhill Control on the Central Division of Southern Region and to Woking Control on the South Western Division.

From now on, I will refer to everyone and everything in these terms.

The building itself merits some description. During the Second World War the offices were located in what was affectionally referred to as 'The Dug Out.' It was an underground series of offices, the door to which was located in a pillar that supported overhead cable troughing encased in a concrete bridge. Once through this door, you descended some steps until you reached a second door. This door was constructed of very thick metal with a large wheel on the inside. When this door was closed and the wheel turned it formed an air lock. This completely sealed off the underground rooms from anything the enemy might drop on the site.

On descending further stairs, you came to a corridor from which several doors opened into rooms for different purposes. One room housed the switchboard and when I went down into that room, I found all the telephone equipment still intact. It was a fascinating place and I explored it several times. Then one day a large padlock was found on the outer door, and that was the end of our exploration.

The above ground building which replaced the Dug Out at the end of the war, and which was supposed to be temporary, still stands to this day and can be found behind what was then the Locomotive Shed. It housed Orpington Control for many years until major changes swept through the Railway. HQ moved from Queen Street to Waterloo, and Orpington Control was moved to Beckenham. The building then became the Staff Association building. It still stands today, but I do not know what its function is now.

The building was a long rectangle divided into three parts. The first part contained the Control itself and which included the galley kitchen. The middle section contained quite a complex switchboard, which was manned by a very efficient lady operator during the day and with limitations it functioned automatically 'out of hours.'

The last section was the base for our telecomms staff. Around the building were several grounded passenger mail vans, which were used to store old records and paperwork.

The Control itself was divided down the centre by two rows

of seven desks facing each other with an outward leaning frame above the desks. This frame was divided into sections, each one displaying a map of the area of the division that the Area Controller at that desk was responsible for. At the head of the rows of desks was the desk at which the Deputy Chief Controller (D.C.C) sat. It was equipped with a typewriter on which the daily Control Report of Incidents was compiled. Behind his desk was an alcove in which coats were hung. There was also a desk and chair for the use of the Chief Controller, Mr O'Leary, when required.

To the left of this was another little alcove, separated from the Control by a wooden door with a glass window in it. This was the galley kitchen. It was just large enough to contain a gas cooker and a sink. This was provided because the Control was manned twenty-four hours a day, seven days a week, bank holidays included.

Not long before I arrived at Orpington Control there occurred the famous 'Galley Incident.' An Area Controller covering London Area One panel, arguably the busiest area in the division, went into the galley and filled a saucepan with water and placed in it an unopened tin of peas. This he placed on a cooker ring, having first lit the gas. Almost immediately he was recalled to his panel, as Borough Market Junction advised him that a train had failed, blocking the junction and stopping all trains from and to London Bridge, Charing Cross and Cannon Street. The incident took some time to resolve, with up trains terminating at London Bridge and down trains being restarted from there and train crews having to be matched with trains.

Meanwhile the water in the unattended saucepan was boiling. Inevitably it eventually boiled dry. The tin of peas remained intact for some time, but nothing under such pressure lasts forever. Suddenly, with a tremendous 'BANG !!' the tin exploded. The contents erupted like a volcano and welded themselves to the ceiling, where they remain to this day.

The force of the blast flung the door open and slammed it against the wall so hard that it drove the door handle clean through the door, although incredibly the glass survived. Two bricks were also dislodged from the outside wall. Thankfully no-one was in the vicinity of the galley at the time and no-one was injured. All this I was told by several Controllers and the accounts never varied. There was also the evidence of the peas on the ceiling and the hole in the door where the handle used to be.

Sadly, I have no photographs of Orpington Control but there were two identical Controls at Redhill (Central Division) and Woking (South Western Division) and a photograph of Redhill Control is appended. I do not know any of the staff in the photograph.

The South Eastern Division was divided into five Areas. I hope you do not find the next bit too tedious but I have described the areas in some detail because it shows how the South Eastern Division was controlled and because to me it was a very impressive set up.

Area One was one of the two London areas. It encompassed Charing Cross/Cannon Street/ London Bridge (South Eastern) to Chislehurst (South Eastern main line) and included the spur from Blackfriars. It covered the beginning of all four routes to Dartford, including the Lee Spur to Dartford via Sidcup. It also included both routes to Hayes, Addiscombe and Sanderstead, via Selsdon (Central Division) and the Grove Park to Bromley North

Branch, and the flyover from Nunhead to Lewisham. It also included the old Ewer Street Siding at Metropolitan Junction.

The signal boxes we dealt with were Charing Cross, Metropolitan Junction, Cannon Street, Borough Market Junction, London Bridge (Eastern) North Kent East Junction (North Kent West, (Mercers Crossing, and Rotherhythe New Road, on the Bricklayers Arms Branch – Permissive Block) St. Johns, Parks Bridge Junction, Hither Green, and Chislehurst (eastern), on the main line.

On the branch lines the signal boxes and routes are as follows:

The Mid Kent Line from St. Johns to New Beckenham and Hayes via Lewisham and then curving round and under the main lines at Parks Bridge Junction, and the direct route turning right from the main lines .at Parks Bridge Junction. The two routes joined up at a junction south of the main lines. The Mid Kent Line then continued to New Beckenham and Elmers End, where it divided to go to Hayes, Addiscombe or Sanderstead. Another spur line from the Mid Kent Lines, just after Lewisham Station re-joined the main lines to Hither Green. This spur line was also controlled by Parks Bridge Signal Box.

The Greenwich Line to Dartford diverged from North Kent East Junction from North Kent East Junction via Greenwich to Charlton and Woolwich and then to Slade Green and Dartford.

The North Kent Line to Dartford diverged from St. Johns and Blackheath and Charlton to Woolwich, and then to Slade Green and Dartford.

The Bexleyheath Line to Dartford diverged from St. Johns to Blackheath, then turned right at Blackheath and ran via Bexleyheath to Slade Green and Dartford.

The Dartford Loop Line ran via North Kent East Junction, St. Johns, Parks Bridge Junction and Hither Green, where it diverged left and ran via Sidcup direct to Dartford.

The Hither Green Junction also included spur lines, which ran up from the Grove Park direction, then curved round to join the Dartford Loop Line via Sidcup. This latter was useful for empty coaching stock running to and from Grove Park Shed and Slade Green Depot, and for freight trains and engineer's trains running to and from Hither Green Down Yard and Hoo Junction Yard.

Hither Green Signal Box also controlled the junction at Grove Park Station, where the lines for trains to Bromley North diverges to the right of the main lines.

Area One also had two important goods yards, at Hither Green, including the pre-Channel Tunnel Continental Depot, and Bricklayers Arms Goods Depot and Crane Repair Shop.

Hither Green had 'A,' 'B,' and 'C' Sections on the down Yard, and the Permanent Way Engineers Depot, next door to Hither Green Locomotive Depot, and on the upside was Hither Green Up Yard, and the aforementioned Continental Depot. Hither Green Box also controlled the entry/exit at Grove Park Shed where many main line passenger units were stored outside their requirement for the peak hour services.

Area One had one of the most intensive passenger services I have ever known. Any incident, such as a point failure or signal failure or a train breaking down, would immediately delay at least three other trains and the Controller must act quickly and decisively to avoid further delays.

Area One also had a busy freight service with trains from and to Ferme Park (Kings Cross) Willesden, Brent (Cricklewood) and Old Oak Common, as well as divisional freights from Hither Green and Bricklayers Arms from and to Hoo Junction, Tonbridge, Ashford, and Dover. It was also responsible for controlling Parcels Trains and livestock traffic, normally sheep or cattle but including Billy Chipperfield's Circus Train, which used to load up in Ewer Street Sidings (Southwark).

There is a lovely story that one day, before my time, Chipperfield's Circus had loaded some elephants into specially adapted General Utility Vans (GUV's). The elephants were restless and as they shuffled their feet, the vehicles swayed gently from side to side. The train could not be allowed to leave until the elephants had settled down. This was a problem for the Controller because fresh pathways had to be found through the intensive passenger service. And with all livestock carrying trains, there was a strict schedule for feeding and watering the animals at specified places, and rapid access to vetinary services. This meant that a livestock carrying freight train had, on rare occasions, to be given preference over passenger services.

There were also the liquid petroleum tanks (LPG) from the Anglo Iranian Oil Refinery on the Isle of Grain to Angersteins Wharf. Access to Angersteins Wharf was accessed from a line that ran under the Greenwich Line at Westcombe Park.

One day, a Freight Inspector allowed me to travel with him on a return service taking thirty empty LPG tanks from Angersteins Wharf back to the Isle of Grain. Security at the Gas Terminal was extremely tight. Empty LPG tanks are more dangerous than loaded ones because of the vapour that is left in the discharged tanks. So I was quite surprised when, as we came under the bridge at Westcombe Park, we came past a large scrap metal depot, in the middle of which a huge bonfire was burning with flames I estimated to be about fifty feet high. I wondered what the scrap metal merchant would have done, had he realised what was in the train going by him.

Area One also took control of Area Two at night, because the latter was only manned on early and late turns. Justifiably the Area One Controller was given Grade 'E,' the highest grade of Controller, and was also given an Assistant Controller to help him. That in fact was my first job in Orpington Control.

Area Two was a 'B' graded panel. Its Controllers had control of all the passenger trains on all four routes from and to London – Dartford. It continued through to Gravesend. It also controlled Slade Green Depot, which berthed a large part of the suburban passenger fleet, including units 4001 and 4002, the well known double decker units, which ran between Dartford and Cannon Street. The Depot also included a big repair shop.

Although the area was geographically much smaller than Area One, it also had a very intensive passenger service with four routes funnelling into one and stock running into and out of Slade Green all the time. It was a good training area for those intending to make a career on the bigger areas. In those days the Area was worked by a lot of small signal boxes, and a lot of regulating had to be done very quickly by the Controller.

On the Dartford Loop the signal Boxes were Sidcup, Bexley, Crayford Spur 'A', and Dartford Junction, through to Dartford Station Box.

On the Bexleyheath there were Signal Boxes at Bexleyheath, Barnehurst, Perry Street Fork Junction to Slade Green, and Crayford Spur 'B' to Crayford Spur 'A' and Dartford Junction.

On the North Kent/Greenwich route there were Signal Boxes at Woolwich Arsenal, Plumstead, Erith, North End and

Slade Green. The sections were short and this facilitated the intensive service.

In the event of a blockage on one route, the Controller must quickly decide which of the other routes to divert the affected trains and advise the signalmen accordingly.

Below Dartford the Signal Boxes were Swanscombe, Northfleet and Gravesend. Swanscombe and Northfleet both had sidings where cement was loaded. Later on the sidings at Swanscombe were closed and Northfleet was developed as a major cement producer and distributor with a 'merry go round' system for inwards trains of coal and gypsum and outwards trains of cement. In addition there were the freight trains to and from Hoo Junction and the Isle of Grain passing through the area on their way to and from Hither Green.

Plumstead also had a small Goods Depot and Yard, for wagon load traffic to and from Hither Green and Hoo Junction.

My father was in charge of that yard at one time.

There were two passenger rolling stock depots in Area Two, one at Slade Green and the other at Gillingham. They dealt mainly with suburban stock.

Next came Area Three. This area took over the line of route from Area Four after Swanley, via Sole Street to Rochester, and the line of route from Area Two, from Higham, through the junction with the Maidstone West branch at Strood. It continued through Rochester to Faversham, where the route divided, the main line going to Margate and then to Ramsgate, while the branch line went through Canterbury East to Dover Priory, (Area 5).

The signal boxes on the main line were Sole Street, Rochester, Gillingham, Rainham, Sittingbourne (with the branch to

Kemsley and Sheerness) Faversham, Herne Bay, Margate and Ramsgate. The branch from Faversham was controlled by signal boxes at Canterbury East, Snowdown (including the colliery) Shepherdswell, (including the colliery at Tilmanston) Kearsney, Buckland Junction, and Dover Priory.

From the Maidstone West branch line the signal boxes were Aylesford, New Hythe, Cuxton and Strood, where it joined the main line at Rochester Bridge Junction.

From the Dartford direction the signal boxes after Gravesend were Higham, Hoo Junction (with branch to the Isle of Grain, with it's level crossings at Middle Stoke and Lower Stoke) Strood and Rochester,

There was one rolling stock depot in Area Three, at Ramsgate. It dealt mainly with main line passenger rolling stock.

Hoo Junction was the major freight yard in Area Three. Traffic came from Cliffe Cement Works, Queenborough sand and glass producers, and a very specialised traffic from the local abattoirs, the bones from the carcasses being transported to a big factory at Angersteins Wharf in London. When this traffic ran (usually via Tonbridge) it was in tightly sheeted wagons but despite this it was always accompanied by a big cloud of flies hovering over each wagon.

The other important traffic was the oil products and liquid petroleum gas (LPG) tanks. The LPG tanks also ran to Angersteins Wharf (Area One) from where the LPG was pipelined across London.

Area Four was the second London Area, controlling trains from Victoria (Eastern) Holborn Viaduct and Blackfriars. Originally it was a Grade 'D' area, but later, after a long campaign, it was upgraded to 'E' grade. Like Area One, it was a very complex area. The main line ran from Victoria to Ramsgate and Dover Priory via Beckenham Junction and Bromley South, then under the South Eastern main line at Chislehurst and on through Swanley, where it handed over control to Area Two.

There was a suburban service via Beckenham Junction and Bromley South to Orpington, and from Holborn Viaduct to Sevenoaks via Nunhead, Bromley South, Swanley and Otford Junction.

There was also a suburban service from the Central Division to Beckenham Junction via Crystal Palace.

Area Four also took control of the Charing Cross main line from Chislehurst, through Orpington and Sevenoaks to Tonbridge, where Area Five took control.

Area Four was also the source of the two important express passenger trains of the day. The Golden Arrow from Victoria to Dover Marine, with seven Pullman Cars and two passenger brakes, and hauled by one of the 5000 class locomotives, and the Night Ferry from Victoria to France, Italy and Switzerland.

The latter could comprise up to seventeen vehicles, especially during the skiing season in Switzerland. The Southern portion would be detached at Dover Marine (Later Dover Western Docks) and the rest of the train would be shunted into the Ferry Dock and onto the ship for forwarding from Dunkirk. This train, because of its length and weight was also always diagrammed a class 5000 locomotive.

Area Four also had a very interesting freight service. Trains from the Eastern Region, the Midland Region and the Western Region travelled via Latchmere Junction, Longhedge Junction and onto Southern territory at Factory Junction, just above Brixton. These trains had to be regulated to fit into the passenger services.

In addition there was the Widened Lines route. Freight trains, mainly to Ferme Park (Kings Cross) but also to Brent (Cricklewood) travelled up towards Holborn Viaduct but were then signalled onto the steep bank down to Holborn Low Level, where they passed over Underground metals to Farringdon Junction. Travelling in the opposite direction, the ascent from Holborn Low Level was so steep that trains required a banking engine.

This was housed in a siding, known as the Farringdon Siding, just above Holborn Low Level signal box. The train would come to a stand at a marker board. From this marker board a wire ran down the tunnel to the exit from the siding. When the banking loco was in position, its driver would tug hard on the wire and a bell would ring at the marker board. This was the signal for the train driver to start moving forward.

The signalman at Holborn Low Level signal box had to know all the Southern Region bell codes and also all the bell codes of the other regions, which were different, as well. The signal box was situated very close to the Old Bailey. Access was gained by going to a little street which had three identical gates set in a high wall. Two of the gates led to private property. But the third opened up to a spiral staircase, which led down to track level. You then walked alongside the track to the signal box.

One odd little feature I noticed when I visited that signal box was the Control Telephone. This was housed in a wooden box set on the back wall. Above the signal box, at ground level, was a fish market. Water from this had dripped onto the signal box roof. Being of a corrosive content, it had burned a hole in the roof. So now it dripped onto the box housing the Control phone and burned a hole in that. The phone became corroded. So, when we at Control rang the signalman at Holborn Low Level, the bell no longer worked. The mechanism gave an asthmatic cough and a puff of blue smoke was emitted from the box.

Area Four had two stock depots, one at Orpington, which dealt mainly with suburban stock, and the other, Stewarts Lane Depot, near Battersea. This latter was, and still is, a huge spiders web complex with sidings radiating in all directions. It was home to a very elderly breakdown crane and train. It also housed much of the South Eastern main line stock.

The Locomotive Depot at Stewarts Lane was home to the locomotives for the Golden Arrow and the Night Ferry. Stewarts Lane was also a major repair depot, and a storage depot for stock withdrawn temporarily from service. It also had a snow clearing depot. All these facilities for the South Eastern were mirrored by identical facilities for the Central Division. It was a very large depot.

The line of route of signal boxes, which the Controller would need to deal with were as follows:

Victoria (Eastern) Factory Junction, Loughborough Junction (where the line from Holborn Viaduct joined the main line) Shepherds Lane Junction, Herne Hill, Beckenham Junction, Shortlands, Chislehurst, and Swanley. Then from Chislehurst (including the Bickley Junction spur to the South Eastern main line) to Orpington, Sevenoaks and outside Tonbridge.

From Swanley via Otford Junction, to Sevenoaks/Maidstone East. From Shepherds Lane to Nunhead for the Catford Loop line, Bellingham (which stored one set of suburban stock for the morning and evening rush hours) and down to Shortlands Junction, and from Nunhead, to the Lewisham Flyover for passenger trains to Dartford and freight trains to Hither Green.

And finally we come to Area Five. This took control of the main line from Hildenborough to Dover and Ramsgate via Tonbridge, Ashford and Folkestone, and from Ashford via Canterbury West to Minster, for Ramsgate. The area also included the lines to and from Redhill and the lines to Hastings and Tunbridge Wells West, via Grove Junction, for Eridge, and the lines from Hastings to Ashford via Rye. It also covered the lines from Paddock Wood to Maidstone West.

At one time it also included the line from Paddock Wood to Hawkhurst but this line had closed long before I went to Tonbridge Signal Box in 1962.

The signal boxes in the lines of route were as follows:

Tonbridge, Staplehurst (opened only when required) Ashford, Folkestone East, Archcliffe Junction (for Dover Marine and Dover Town Yard) Hawkesbury Street Junction (for Dover Marine, Chatham route, and Bulwark Sidings) Dover Priory, Buckland Junction, Martin Mill (which had the local Post Office as well) Deal, Betteshanger Colliery ground-frame, Sandwich, Richboro Power Station ground-frame and Minster.

The Area also included from Ashford via Wye, Chartham, Canterbury West, Chislet Colliery, Sturry and Minster, to Ramsgate.

Area Five dealt with a wide variety of traffic. It covered the main line services from London to the coast, Hastings, Dover, Ramsgate and Margate, and the services to the Medway area, plus the services to and from Redhill. It included the famous expresses, the Golden Arrow and the Night Ferry.

It was also at the centre of the Royal Mail traffic, with the Travelling Post Offices between Dover and London Bridge, and the ordinary parcel van services from as far afield as Wolverhampton, Holborn (fish) and the connecting subsidiary services from Maidstone, London Bridge and Canterbury.

It also managed a wide network of freight services including gyp-rock from Mountfield for the various cement works in the London Area, Continental freight for Hither Green, mixed goods traffic from Ashford and Maidstone to Tonbridge and Hither Green, and vice versa, coal traffic from the collieries (industrial coal) and from Tyneside (domestic coal) plus livestock trains, and Green Arrow express freight trains.

Area Five was served by Goods Yards at Dover, Ashford (including the Up Yard and the Down Yard and the Livestock Market) Tonbridge (East and West Yards) Paddock Wood (Keylands) Maidstone (Tovil) Tunbridge Wells Central Goods, and Hastings.

Area Five also included the major Carriage Workshop at Ashford Chart Leacon, which also housed the breakdown crane and tool vans, and where a lot of main line stock was berthed and repaired and maintained. Equipment included the wheel lathe, much in demand in the leaf fall season when units required newly maintained wheel sets.

There too was the big Permanent Way Depot, which had cranes and all sorts of other equipment, static and mobile.

And of course, there were the Locomotive Depots at Ashford and Tonbridge.

Area Five was a fascinating area to work because it embraced so many aspects of railway work.

So that was the five Area Panels at Orpington Control. But there were the other essential Control Panels too.

The Guards Controller was responsible for ensuring that there was a guard for every service in the Division. All trains were covered by the Guards Diagram Section at Queen Street but once those rosters had been issued all sorts of things could disrupt them. The first job of the Guards Controller was to cover any shortages left by the Diagram Section. There were never enough Guards for all the services and a list was issued for trains that had not been covered.

Then, whenever an incident occurred and trains were disrupted, Guards duties had to be recovered and matched up. It was the pride of a good Guards Controller that no train in his shift were cancelled due to lack of a guard, and that the first two hours of the next man's shift were also fully covered, to give the relieving Guards Controller time to work on the remaining vacancies before anything happened.

The Locomotive Controller was responsible for seeing that all the diagrams for his shift were covered by a suitable locomotive. Under his control he had class 5000 straight electric locomotives, class 6500 Crompton Diesel Locomotives (three types – standard, narrow sided and push pull) and 6000 class, electro-diesel locomotives with a 1550 hp electric engine and a 600 hp diesel engine.

He had to make sure that the right type of locomotive was diagrammed to the right train, for obvious reasons. But he also had to bear in mind maintenance requirements. Each locomotive diagram included time for maintenance. Should a locomotive fail or be delayed or swapped over for any reason, arrangements had to be made that during its subsequent diagram, it could run to a depot, either Ashford, Tonbridge or Hither Green for appropriate maintenance.

The Locomotive Controller was also responsible for the maintenance and refuelling of the various 350 hp shunting locomotives (and the 204hp locomotive at Tonbridge). This meant finding pathways from the various yards and sidings for locomotives that travelled between 20 and 28 mph. For these, he liaised with the relevant Area Controller.

And lastly the Locomotive Controller was responsible for supplying locomotives for the Central Division and changing over locomotives over there that were due for maintenance and repair. He kept a continuous Locomotive Log, detailing all his arrangements and whom he had advised, and a large Locomotive Chart matching each locomotive with each diagram.

Then came the Brake-van Controller. His job was much simpler, but in those days when trains ran partially brake fitted, brake vans were an essential component of the trains. His job was to ensure that there was a brake-van for each train that required one. Very, very rarely was a train cancelled due to no brake-van being available. He also looked after Green Arrow traffic.

But he also had another task. Because of the steep gradients, particularly between Knockholt and Paddock Wood on the Tonbridge main line, the Hastings Line gradients, and Sole Street Bank on the Chatham main line, but also in other places as well, the brakes on these vans were often applied for quite a few miles.

This resulted in the wheels becoming red hot.

From the window of the signal box at Tonbridge I had often observed these freight trains from Hither Green coming round the corner with four 'Catherine Wheels' under the brake-van, smoke from floorboards set alight by the sparks, and with the guard out on the veranda, trying to get breathable air. In time the Company, recognising this, had the Southern Region brake vans fitted with metal spark guards under the floor. This not only prevented floorboard fires, but the extra weight also made the vans more stable and comfortable to ride.

As a result, they were very popular with guards from the other regions. They were supposed to be returned on workings to the Southern Region. But on numerous occasions, other region's guards 'borrowed' these brake-vans from trains from Hither Green, by the simple expedient of leaving them on the trains as they travelled north.

The Brakevan Controller held a daily conference each morning with his opposite number in the other region's Controls and arrangements were made at that conference to return Southern Region brake-vans to their own region. The conference also established that there was a balance of brake vans to meet all requirements. The aforementioned Green Arrow traffic related to consignments where the consignee paid for the service of being able to ring up at any time to ask where his consignments were.

This was in the days before the Total Operations Processing System, T.O.P.S. All in all, it was an important job.

In addition to these panels, there were also two Area Assistants panels, known as Area One A and Area Three A.

Area 1A assisted Areas One and Four. Area 3A assisted Areas Three and Five. More of their duties will feature in the next chapter.

Area One and Area Four were graded 'E' Controller. Areas Three and Five and the Locomotive and Guards Controllers were graded 'D' Controller. Area 2 was a 'B' grade Controller and the Brakevan Controller was a Grade 'A'. All these ten panels were presided over by the Deputy Chief Controller (D.C.C).

The D.C.C sat at a desk facing the two lines of Controllers. On the left hand side of the huge Area Diagrams, were first, Area Two, then Area Three, then Area Three A, then area Five, then the Brake-van Controller, then the Locomotive Controller, and finally at the end of the room sat the Guards Controller.

To the right of the Area Diagrams sat first the Area One Controller, then Area One A, then the Area Four Controller. The panel beyond that was used for Statistics and Train Running Sheets compiled and amended by the Area Assistant Controllers. Beyond that the panels were spare, not in use.

The D.C.C. was responsible for the safe and efficient working of each panel during his shift. He would advise as required on the handling of incidents and on rare occasions he might even take overall control of an incident, if it was a major or controversial one. He also liaised with the Chief Controller, Mr O'Leary, and with senior officers at HQ Queen Street.

On an old fashioned typewriter he compiled the Daily Report of all the incidents and actions of the Controllers on his shift, which at the end of each day was sent to Queen Street for their leisured perusal and comments. He also received and passed on the 'Please Explains,' passed on by Mr O'Leary, to the relevant staff.

He was also responsible for discipline. If a dispute occurred between Controllers, as sometimes happened during times of high tension, when decisions had to be made and seconds counted, it was his job to sort it out before it affected the job or got out of hand. In this respect he also had to decide what would reach the ears of Mr O'Leary and what might not.

One of his main qualifications for this position was to have a working knowledge of every panel, and in an emergency take over and run it. I have to say with complete honesty that every D.C.C that I worked with ably fulfilled that qualification. It was an example that I did my best to emulate many years later when I became a Duty Line Manager in charge of my own shift in the Control.

So that was Orpington Control in the 1960's. In my next chapter I record what it was like to work in the Control, some of the many incidents we dealt with and some of the wonderful, diverse and memorable characters I had the pleasure of working with.

Chapter Five - Life in Orpington Control

I entered Orpington Control as a temporary London Area Assistant Controller. To my left the London Area One Controller was a man called Fred. To my right was the London Area Four Controller named Ron. Our D.C.Cs worked slightly different shifts to us, so in turn those in charge were Ron C, Ron B, and Bob H.

About the people on the panels on the other side I knew very little. Area Two was covered by Jerry, and Area Three by George. Claude was the Area Three Assistant Controller, a very knowledgeable and helpful man with a great sense of humour. Area Five was covered by Jim. Our locomotive Controller was Bill, a big man with a gruff voice, and our Guards Controller was a small man called Arthur, who spoke very quietly.

As the London Area Assistant Controller, I worked mainly with Fred on Area One. The term 'laid back' was just becoming fashionable in those days and this adequately described Fred. He would never instigate enquiries, even when he knew there was trouble. He always told me to 'wait until they come to us, which they will do when they are ready.'

One morning at about 6.30 am London Bridge tipped us off that Borough Market Junction was in trouble.

Now Borough Market Junction, because of its incredibly busy workload, had a restriction. We were not allowed to ring the signalman there during the rush hours unless it was an extreme emergency. London Bridge warned us again that the train service had virtually come to a halt. Still the signalman at Borough Market Junction had not rung us. Still Fred would not ring him, nor would he let me do so.

Then I was amazed. Fred had an unvarying routine. At 6.45 am he would pick up his towel and his newspaper and take himself off to the toilet block in the Locomotive Shed next door. This morning, with Borough Market Junction at a stand affecting all trains to Charing Cross and Cannon Street, he did exactly the same. He returned, as he always did, a few minutes before his relief walked in. I was going home so I didn't see the outcome of this incident.

A few days later Mr O' Leary summoned me to his office. He asked me how I got on with Fred. Did I have any problems about working with him?

I truthfully said I had no problems. He was always polite and never criticised me.

Shortly after that, Fred himself asked me, in his quiet voice, if I thought he bullied me.

Again I answered truthfully that I was not aware of him bullying me.

He said, 'Only some people seem to think that I do.'

Very shortly after that, Fred suddenly left the Control. I heard he took retirement.

Fred's replacement was Geoff, whom I believed had worked London Area Four. A bigger contrast you could not imagine. He had a fantastic knowledge of the area and was very proactive indeed.

As I remember the fantastic technology available to us in later years, with no less than five computer screens on my desk, I think back to the limited tools available then. The Area

Controllers had a set of timetables to enable them to know the service, a set of pens and pencils, a set of train running sheets, compiled and filled in by the Assistant and a small switchboard to make and receive their calls. Above them was the static chart of the Area. And that was that.

Geoff was such a quick thinker, and he reacted very quickly indeed to every incident. As I would be taking down details of an incident, I could see out of the corner of my eye, Geoff reaching for the appropriate timetable. He had listened to me taking down the details. Before I had finished writing down the incident, he had decided what action to take and was already making phone calls to give people instructions. And he was always right. I never once saw him at a loss as to how to deal with any incident.

Having such a quick mind, Geoff also had a devastatingly quick wit. On one occasion I recall that a train in the rush hour at Charing Cross was delayed while a member of staff retrieved a shoe, which had come off of a lady's foot as she boarded the train, and which had fallen between the train and platform. As I filled in the appropriate place on the running sheet, I asked him what I should show as the cause of the late start. 'Cinderella' he replied immediately.

Geoff's quick wit was also capable of being cuttingly sarcastic, as I found out when this lesser mortal couldn't keep up with him.

Once Geoff had made his decisions, it was my job to advise them out to all the signal boxes. This is one reason why I have taken such pains to list them all in the previous chapter. There were a lot of them, and the job had to be done quickly and efficiently.

I learned from Geoff the valuable lesson that if people were not told the planned response straightaway, they would go off and do what they thought was best, the grip of the situation would be lost and chaos would ensue. This lesson stood me in good stead in later years. Another reason for knowing all the signal boxes was the Staff Relief of signalmen, but more of that later.

Geoff, being so proactive, would never wait for people to come to him as his predecessor had. At the first whiff of trouble, he would be on the phone, getting straight to the heart of the problem. He didn't waste words and he understood exactly what people were saying.

When things were quiet Geoff relaxed and we chatted and had many laughs. I got to know him quite well, and I enjoyed working with him. I certainly learned a lot from him, and he was always willing to answer my questions, although sometimes he got impatient if I didn't grasp the explanation.

Shift work was an education for me. Hitherto I was used to working early and late turns. Now I had night duty and a peculiar early turn. We worked four shifts. On the first early turn week I was early turn Mondays, Tuesdays, Thursdays and Fridays. On Wednesdays I worked from 0950 – 1730.

From 0950 until 1400 hrs I prepared the Running Sheets for Area One. At 1400 I took over as late turn Assistant until 1730 when I was relieved and went home.

On Saturdays I worked late turn. So on this week I would only spend part of my time with Geoff. This shift would be followed by a full week of early turn, then late turn with Saturday off and then a full week of night turn, starting on Sunday night and ending on Saturday morning. I never understood this shift system. The Controllers said it was to save money.

Night duty was always hard for me as an Assistant. No matter how well I had slept the previous day, tiredness would hit me about 1 am, when things had quietened down. At first, I kept going with gritted teeth. Then one night, working with Geoff, I made a bad mistake. It was another of the quirks of this shift system that the Area One Controller was allowed a twenty minute break during the shift. This again was apparently a means of saving money on shift hours.

Only the Area One Controllers were allowed this privilege. I think it had something to do with the fact that on some shifts at weekends they covered the D.C.C. position.

Geoff used to lean forward on his arms on the desk, in what looked to me to be an extremely uncomfortable position and allow himself to nod off. Exactly twenty minutes later he would awake feeling refreshed.

This night I asked Geoff if I could have twenty minutes rest. 'You're not entitled to' he said, 'but OK.'

I went down to the far end of the room where the spare panels were. I lined up three chairs and with the aid of an old cardboard signalling diagram, made myself as comfortable as possible.

I had overlooked one thing, the Control Clock. It was on the wall above me. At intervals of one and three quarter minutes it would give a loud, 'click bonk.' I relaxed and was just nodding off when 'click bonk' and I was awake again. I lay there for some time, anticipating the next 'click bonk.'

Eventually I slept. Now when I say slept, I meant slept. I really went off into a deep sleep. When 5 am came and I hadn't surfaced, somebody came to wake me up. They couldn't do so. There were apparently fears that I might have died. Concentrated attempts were made to wake me, and eventually they succeeded. A lovely hot cup of tea was placed in my hand.

When I felt up to it, I stood up. I was dizzy and I felt sick. I couldn't think straight. I felt awful! I made my way to the Locomotive Shed to freshen myself up. Somebody came with me to make sure I was safe.

I wandered back into the Control, still feeling unsteady. I was no help at all to Geoff. Great was my relief when I saw my relief come through the door. I was even escorted to my train home, by which time I had more or less come to. Needless to say, I made it safely home. Also, needless to say, I vowed that never again would I go to sleep on duty – and I never did!

The weather played a significant part in our work. Controllers were very resourceful people. One snowy winter the roads around Chislet Colliery, near Canterbury, became completely impassable. A large number of miners were stranded in the colliery. Kent Police asked for our help.

The Area Five Controller, together with the Locomotive and Guards Controllers, arranged for an 8 EPB, (2 x four cars), at Chart Leacon Depot, to have their shoes tied up. A class 33 diesel locomotive, fitted with mini ploughs, was attached to each end of the 8 car train. In co-operation with the Electrical Control, the traction current was discharged in the area to avoid short circuits, and the train, carrying Carriage Mechanical and Electrical fitters, (CM & EE), and Permanent Way staff in case of problems, entered Chislet Colliery Sidings.

It got as close to the colliery as possible and the stranded miners were taken on board. They were taken back to

Tuesday and Wednesday, another feature of our strange shift system.

It was still raining hard on Sunday. My mother had gone out for the day on a coach outing with our neighbour. At 5.30 on Sunday evening, the old weir on the River Medway, out towards Leigh, collapsed suddenly under the weight of water, and was swept away. Within an hour Tonbridge High Street was flooded to a depth of two to three feet. Local roads leading to the High Street were flooded and in one road, which had a dip in the middle, the houses were flooded to ceiling level.

Tonbridge Station was flooded to a depth of two feet above the running rails. Both the West and particularly the East Yard and the Locomotive Shed, were flooded, and the main line was under water. The only lines above water were at the Seven Arches on the lines from Tonbridge to Leigh and Redhill. The whole railway system on the South Eastern Main Line came to a standstill. No trains were able to run on Sunday, Monday or Tuesday.

The water had begun to subside on Tuesday and by Wednesday evening preparations were being made to resume the service. Not many people would have wanted the trains anyway because a lot of homes had been flooded and damaged and some people actually had to be rescued from their homes. My mother and our neighbour arrived back very late on Sunday evening, her coach having never got further than Hildenborough and having to be diverted five times before access was regained to Tonbridge.

I returned to work on the Thursday, the first day that any trains ran, for a late turn and found chaos. So much damage had been done by the rain and the floods and it took weeks to get back to normal. Lots of telephone cables had been swept away and signalling and traction current cables had been swept away as well. The service on Thursday was sketchy but by the following Monday almost a normal service was resumed.

Needless to say this disruption on such a scale imposed heavy burdens on railway staff everywhere, and the Control had its share of the pressure, manning services and trying to keep them going, whist trying to arrange engineer's specials to get materials to sites, so that they could restore equipment.

Changing the subject completely, many people will have heard of the expression 'Railway Time,' but perhaps knew no more than that. It originated in the very early days of railway operations. In the early and middle 1800s, village policemen had a responsibility to see and signal railway trains away.

There was no Absolute Block System of signalling and so trains were dispatched on a 'Time Interval' basis. This allowed so many minutes after the departure of one train, before the next train could be signalled away. Passenger trains were allowed so many minutes to reach their next stopping point before the next train was despatched. Goods trains were allowed a longer time. But different villages and towns had variations of one to several minutes in time. Add to that, the constable's watch might be fast or slow, and chaos reigns.

The Railways realised this and eventually introduced Standard Railway Time. With the system of signal boxes being put in place, some means had to be found of ensuring that everyone was working to the correct time. So a system was arranged that at a given time a signal telegraph would be sent to all signalmen. Eventually as time passed and technology improved this message was passed by telephone. It then became the responsibility of the Traffic Control. And finally, that responsibility devolved down to the London Area Assistant (me among others) and the Country Area Assistant.

At 5.57 am, we would put down all the switches on the omnibus circuit that linked us to all the signal boxes, and at precisely 6 am Control Time we pressed the 'Ring' button. The signalmen knew the relevance of that ring and would check and if necessary, adjust their clocks. This job was considered to be very important indeed, and on the rare occasion that the signal might be sent as much as a minute late, the person responsible was severely disciplined. The London Area One Controller kept a very sharp eye on his Assistant to ensure it was done correctly, as I am sure the Area Five Controller did.

So, while some of these things were happening, what was my status? Well I was still a 'temporary member of staff.' Then, one day, some six months after I had joined, I was summoned to Mr O'Leary's office. This was it, I thought. I entered his office confidently and was invited to sit down. Mr O'Leary asked me how I was getting on. Did I like the job? How was I getting on with everybody?

My replies were all positive. I really did enjoy the job and liked the people that I worked with.

He said that was good and I was doing quite well. Then he said, 'But Terry, I have to mention one thing. The other day I saw you reading a newspaper during the rush hour. I know the older staff do it. They think that because I am so short, I can't see what's going on. But I do see them, and I remember. The rush hour is very critical time. Anything can happen and if it does it will happen very suddenly. The consequences to our intensive service will be severe and we need to be constantly on the alert. You can't do that if you are reading a newspaper.'

I agreed.

'So I don't want to see you doing it again,' he continued in his quiet voice.

I readily agreed.

'Good,' he said smiling. 'Off you go.'

I left his office feeling about two inches tall. But he was right.

A week later I was summoned to his office again. I wasn't too confident this time. Again I was invited to sit down. 'Well Terry,' he said, I have been hearing good reports of you from the Controllers and from the D.C.C.s, and I am pleased with your progress. I have asked you here to tell you that I am confirming your appointment as a permanent member of my clerical grade staff. You will get the letter of confirmation very shortly.'

He stood up and as I stood up, he shook hands with me and said, 'Well done.' I came out of his office feeling ten feet high.

And so I settled in on my new job and thoroughly enjoyed it. I began to get to know the characters of the Controllers and to enjoy Control humour, more of that later.

Three characters that I have not yet introduced you to, were the Control Cats. As I walked down the path to the Control one lovely sunny Sunday afternoon for late turn, I counted thirty cats sprawled along and around the path, enjoying the afternoon sunshine. Many of these cats, if not all of them, were feral. They hung around the Locomotive Shed and were fed by the drivers.

The Controllers decided to adopt one. This was a pregnant female and in due course she gave birth to one black male kitten and two tabby females. The mother was then neutered and looked after, but she disappeared.

The three kittens were adopted by the Controllers, and they too were neutered. They soon grew into large healthy cats. They would walk all along the desks over forms that were being filled in and sit on any newspaper that a Controller happened to be reading. At night they would vary this by walking along the keys of the panel switchboards, setting various phones ringing.

From day one, it was obvious that the black male cat was dominant, and he was named 'King.' At feeding times, the D.C.C. would put down a plate of cat food. If either of the tabbies attempted to eat before King had had his share, he would swipe them with his claws out!

Now it so happened that our desks were made of very solid wood, as were the desk drawers. It was very easy to swing round on the swivel chair and catch your knee a nasty knock. So it was standard practice as soon as you sat down, to take what you needed from the drawers and firmly close them. One night I came on duty and found the drawer open. I firmly closed it. The night proceeded as normal.

At 1 am the D.C.C. got the cat's metal food plate out and rattled it several times. This was the signal for food. The door was open. The two tabbies came in, but there was no sign of King. Patiently they sat by the full plate of food but did not touch it. The Controllers remarked that it was unusual for King to miss his supper. 2 am came and went and still there was no sign of King. Eventually and with wary looks around, the two tabbies ventured to start eating the food. They ate it all and went their way.

Glancing up at the clock I saw it was 3 am, time to get my Special Traffic Notice out. As I opened the drawer this black rocket streaked out past my right ear. It looked like a comet because it had a trail of confetti streaming from behind it. I don't know where he landed. King it seems had seen the open drawer and climbed in and gone to sleep. Unaware of this I had shut him in when I closed the drawer. He obviously heard the tin plate being rattled but was unable to get out. I couldn't hear him swearing because of the thickness of the drawer and desk wood. The frustrated cat spent the remaining time he was trapped by dedicatedly shredding my Special Traffic Notice and all my other papers!

Order was restored. Another plate of food was produced for King - and I spent some time trying to find a replacement Special Traffic Notice and all my other documents. When the Control finally closed and was transferred to Beckenham, three Controllers each adopted one of the cats and they all went to good homes.

The next incident also concerned an animal. When you read the account, it may sound incredible but let me assure you it happened. I was there but it was nothing to do with me! The incident had begun on the night shift on Area Four. I was early turn Assistant to Areas One and Four. A train came to a stand outside West Dulwich Station at around 5 am. The driver reported to the signalman that the down line was obstructed, but strangely he was not prepared to say what the obstruction was. This was the story recounted by the signalman to the Controller.

Shortly afterwards an up train approached, and the driver of this train confirmed that the down line was indeed obstructed, but like his colleague this driver also refused to say what the obstruction was, in case they thought he was inebriated. By now it had become necessary to divert trains via the Catford

Loop. A nearby P.Way, (Permanent Way Track Engineer), Supervisor was called and attended.

At first, he too was reluctant to say what he had found, but eventually he was persuaded. 'Well, you asked for it,' he said, 'The down line is obstructed by an approximately eighteen feet long alligator!' 'Is it alive?' asked the signalman.

'Well I'm certainly not going to find out!' said the P.Way Supervisor emphatically.

What does one do with an eighteen feet long alligator on the track. Various of the Vetenery Surgeons we had on call for 'livestock in transit' incidents were contacted but to a man they had neither the knowledge nor the experience, to deal with an alligator. Finally, the R.S.P.C.A. was contacted. A specialist was found, and he agreed to attend with a gun that fired stun darts, in the hope of being able to render the creature unconscious so that it could be removed from the track.

He arrived on site at around 0815. After examining the alligator he explained that a tranquilising dart needed to be fired into the creature but great care must be taken to see that the dart entered between the spines because if it bounced off of the spines the creature would get angry and it would not be possible to move him for about five hours!" Very carefully he took aim and fired and the dart went straight between the spines. There was the sound of a very loud "raspberry" and the remains of a very convincing but inflatable rubber alligator flew up into the air. The trains had been delayed for three and a half hours by an inflatable alligator!

The culprits were never apprehended but it was noted that it was Kings College "Rag Week".

So much for the animal characters around us, now for the human characters. Controllers can move fast when they have to. Take George for instance. He lived in Battle in Sussex. He drove a 2.4 Jaguar. One early turn at Orpington found him having overslept. It was the only time I ever knew him to do that. He jumped into his car.

As he drove across Battle Road Level Crossing, he paused and called up to the signalman, 'Hey Taffy. Give Control a ring will you and tell them I'm on my way.'

Taffy had a quick wash and shave prior to going home. Then he rang Orpington Control as requested – and George answered the phone!

Harry graduated to Control because he had suffered the disapproval of his seniors in Queen Street. Working in the Special Traffic Department at the time, he was responsible for compiling the weekly Special Traffic Notice.

It was Christmas week. Harry produced an item showing a special train from North Pole Junction (a real location) to Dover, Driver S. Claus, Guard R U Dolph. Full timings were given for the pathway and it was classified as Class 1, head code 'ZZ'

His masters at Queen Street, in true Christmas spirit, gave him a final warning and had him transferred to a shift job at Orpington Control. He covered the Assistants panels and occasionally worked Area Two panel.

If you wanted a good-natured argument, Derek was your man. His working knowledge of the railway system and his experience was truly extensive. He had actually been on duty on the afternoon of the Lewisham disaster. His views on the other Controllers varied, depending upon which panel he was working. If he were on an Area panel, he was critical of the Locomotive and Guards Controllers. But if he was on a Locomotive or Guards Control panel, he was critical of the Area Controllers.

In any difficult situation he always remained calm. On one early turn he was covering London Area One. He advised the D.C.C. of a train failure south of London Bridge. When asked where exactly the train was, he calmly replied, 'It's a bit difficult to say. Half of it is in platform six at London Bridge and the other half is standing right by Peak Freans (the famous biscuit factory) at Spa Road Junction).

Because of his argumentative nature, he was sometimes the victim of a set up. When he was down the other end of the room on Locomotive or Guards panels a provocative remark would be made by an Area Controller on the other side of the panels. Derek always rose to the bait and would come round the panels to have a discussion.

Now Derek took sugar in his tea and he had a large old coffee jar full of sugar, which stood on his desk. While he was around the other side of the panels, someone with evil intentions would make a screw out of an A4 sheet of paper, insert it in the sugar and then set it alight.

As the makeshift fuse burned, someone would call, 'Hey Derek, Do you know your sugar's on fire !'

Derek would run back to his panel just in time to pull out the burning paper. Just once he did not quite make it. He extinguished the blaze and then had to deal with three to four inches of carbon on top of his sugar, to the accompaniment of roars of laughter.

He had a wonderful system for dealing with 'Please Explains'.

He would date them on the day he received them, then file them in his locker. Five years to the day later he would take the letter out, answer it and send it off. He reasoned that by that time the people who had sent it would either have moved on or retired. Even Mr O'Leary had given up on chasing Derek for replies.

There were many more equally deserving characters, but it would fill a book to tell of them all.

One final story must suffice for now. George was a keen sailor in his spare time. He obtained permission to use an old grounded Passenger Mail Van (PMV) to build a small boat that he intended to sail on Bewl Reservoir. After early turn he and a small group of helpers set to work. A load of ancient paper files were cleared out of the van and building then commenced.

In due course the boat was built but the builders faced another problem. The boat was far too long to get through the door of the van. George then had to get further permission to knock the end out of the van to extricate the boat. We heard afterwards that the boat performed very well.

Christmas in the Control was something else. I learned that with our peculiar shift system, we would fall for night duty every Christmas for seven years. I never had to work Christmas Day, but I worked several Christmas Eve's. They all had one thing in common. You had to stay on duty until 0600 hrs Christmas Morning. Then you had to find your own way home.

The Controllers were as helpful as they could be. I was advised to bring my bicycle up with me. Then I would be released to go home about 3 am. It took me an hour and a half to cycle from Orpington to Tonbridge. There was no Sevenoaks bypass in those days, so I followed the old A21 down Polhill, through Dunton Green and Sevenoaks, then Hildenborough, and finally Tonbridge. But it was a fine night and not too cold and I enjoyed it.

The following year I did the same - except that this time it was snowing hard from about 8 pm on Christmas Eve. I was alright until I reached Riverhill, south of Sevenoaks. There my front wheel struck a curb hidden by the snow and I came off. I was unhurt and there was just a slight dent in my front wheel, so I was still able to cycle home. On arrival I had to wait on the front lawn until someone was up so I could ring the doorbell.

On the third time, I was allowed to leave my cycle at Sevenoaks, and I got a lift as far as there with Arthur, the Guards Controller. The rest of the journey was uneventful.

All the time the trains were running an intensive service of which we were justly proud. Incidents were occurring and were being dealt with satisfactorily. But times were changing.

Orpington Control Room

Chapter Six - Waterloo Regional Control

A new Control had been prepared in the new South Eastern Headquarters at Beckenham Junction, the staff appointed there would have new grades, and the old Control at Orpington was to be closed. Mr O'Leary took retirement.

Our old building would become the Staff Association Meeting Room, still with the peas welded to the galley ceiling (see chapter four) and painted over many times.

Everyone had to apply for the new posts. There were no Assistant Controllers in the new set up. Effectively the job was regraded to Controller Grade 'A' status. I was disappointed that I did not get an interview for the job.

At the same time, I had applied for a Grade 'A' Controller position in the Regional Control at Waterloo. I had an interview and was delighted to be accepted for the post. I joined the Regional Control on 28th January 1970.

The purpose of the Southern Regional Control at Waterloo was to oversee and manage the three Divisional Controls. We also formed a buffer between the operating controls and the Board and Senior Management. We received the edicts from Senior Management and passed them on to the Divisions.

The set up at Waterloo was vastly simpler than at the Divisional Controls. We were on the third floor in Waterloo Main Line Station, in an oblong room, one side of which had windows looking out over the Waterloo Main Line station concourse.

We sat at the far end of this room. On the side opposite the windows was the only door. Opposite the door was a luggage rack, and behind that a small partition with an equally small Belling stove and tea/coffee making facilities. For water, we had to go to the toilet block down the corridor.

There were just five desks. At the back of the room, facing the door, sat the Regional Deputy Chief Controller (D.C.C.). Just as the Divisional D.C.C.s represented the Divisional Manager out of hours, so the Regional D.C.C.'s represented the Regional Manager, Southern Region.

To the left of the D.C.C.s desk was my desk. As Controller Grade 'A' I was responsible for assisting the D.C.C. maintaining the Control Incident Log, liaising with the News Paper Authority (NPA) and making the tea.

In front of the D.C.C.s desk was the desk occupied by the Regional Locomotive Controller. In front of my desk was another desk occupied by a Controller Grade 'C.'

The other desk in front of the Locomotive Controller was initially empty, but much later on it was occupied by a member of staff from the Regional Carriage, Mechanical & Electrical Department.

Access to the building was gained by an entrance opposite platforms 1 to 3 on Waterloo Main Line Terminus. This was guarded at all times by a Security Guard. A lift and stairs were provided. Most people used the lift, but sometimes it could be unreliable. The corridor leading from the lift to the Control passed over the Cab Road and that part of the floor resounded loudly when people walked along it.

Further along the corridor were the Senior Officers rooms. On the opposite side of the corridor were the Freight, Special

Traffic and Rolling Stock offices. Staff there liaised with their opposite numbers in the South Eastern Division at Beckenham, for Queen Street had also closed, its staff being transferred to Beckenham. They also liaised with the Central and South Western Divisions.

On the day I arrived I was greeted and welcomed by Peter, the Regional Chief Controller, R.C.C. He said, 'Welcome Terry. Can you do early turn tomorrow and Wednesday, 12 hours on Thursday, and then on Friday we will give you a day's training and tell you what you do in your job.' He chuckled as he said this, but he was serious!

I would describe Peter as a gentleman. He was quiet and conscientious and very meticulous. His only 'bête noir' was with the ladies of the Travel Facilities Section, with whom he waged a quiet war. Other R.C.C.s included John, who had a plummy voice and was a magistrate, but was very good humoured, John PJ, who came from Yorkshire, George, who came from the Midlands, Jack F, who also came from Yorkshire, and Colin, who was every inch a Southern man.

On the Locomotive Panel I was delighted to find my old friend from school days and those early days in Tonbridge Goods Office, Alan S. He had developed a very 'Clement Freud' sense of humour, which was to play its part in one notorious incident. Other Locomotive Controllers were Stan, Robert, Davy, and Clifford.

There was also a 'D' grade Relief Controller who covered both the Locomotive Controller and the D.C.C. His name was Alan B, and he came from Cheshire. He was a giant of a man who did everything at great speed. His way of entering the Control was unvaried. He would fling the door back on its hinges, throw his briefcase through the air, where it landed with unerring accuracy in the luggage rack, stride into the room and say, 'Ello Wack! Anythin appening?' Despite his size and speed, Alan was the gentlest of men. He was very conscientious, and he had a great sense of humour. I always enjoyed working with him.

Occupying the desk in front of me between the hours of 9am – 5pm was a man called Colin S. He was another of the Control characters. Aged I think in his late twenties, he was quite a noisy man with a loud but refined laugh. He dealt with Rolling Stock problems and occasionally covered my desk. He was always trying to outwit the D.C.C's. Sometimes he was successful, but revenge was sweet.

This then was the new environment I found myself in. I really enjoyed Waterloo because there was always a lot going on.

The station was always busy. We arrived for Early Turn before the rush hour got under way, but twice a day the station was absolutely swarming with people. The British Railways Board published some astounding figures. According to their statistics, over 600,000 people travelled into London every morning, and returned home at night, using the fourteen London Termini.

A large number of these passed through Waterloo on many of the overall statistic of 1750 trains. Then there were the London Underground and the Waterloo and City Lines which ran between Waterloo and Bank.

But even off peak there was always something to see. Police escorting prisoners, Royal Mail Trains, and an intensive suburban service interspersed with main line services to Southampton, Portsmouth and the West Country to name but a few.

But it was at night that I found it most interesting. First the nightly mail trains departed. Then the stock for the Newspaper trains was shunted into the platforms. No less than five Newspaper Trains departed every weeknight, beginning with the 0145 to Yeovil, then others at 0215, 0245, 0310, and finally the 0340 to Guildford.

Newspaper road vans began arriving from 0030 hrs. Each train had a cut off time of 10 minutes before departure. From the moment of ten minutes before departure, no further vans would be accepted for that train, and the contents of those road vans would have to be transported to their destinations by road. This was to ensure a punctual departure of each train.

There was a contractual arrangement between the News Paper Association (N.P.A.) and the British Railways Board. For every minute the train was delayed by the railway, either through a late start or problems en route, a severe penalty was imposed. That was why the cut off time was so strictly adhered to by station staff. I don't know quite how many road vans came each night but it was around one hundred or more and on arrival each van would be met by staff, frantic to unload the bundles of papers onto trolleys which were then wheeled away to the right van on the right train, and at the same time clear the road van to make room for the next one.

There was so much to do in such a short time that anyone waiting on the station for an early morning train, civilian or military personnel and even vagrants, were roped in to help clear the bundles to the trolleys and railway staff would take them to the right vehicles on the trains and load them on. People who were not railway staff were paid cash in hand each night. This had become well known and there was no shortage of volunteers.

The N.P.A. had a system if the papers were late off the presses. Sometimes news would break late in the evening and the front page might have to have a re-run. This would delay despatch to the station. When this happened, the newspaper concerned would contact the N.P.A. Control and ask for extra time, usually five minutes or ten minutes hold on specific trains. The N.P.A. would contact us, and it was my job to telephone the Station Supervisor and pass on this request. The cut off time for the specified trains would then be extended for the required amount, but only for the newspapers that had asked for it. I would log the request and the time the station was advised.

One night, when I had not been there long, there was a serious incident going on and I was logging the messages relating to it and ensuring the R.C.C. was kept up to date. In the middle of this the N.P.A. rang with a request for time on one of the trains. In the melee I forgot to pass the message on. The train departed on time and a large number of road vans were turned away.

The D.C.C. received a terse phone call from the N.P.A. He apologised and explained that I was new to the job. He assured them it would not happen again.

At around 4 o'clock in the morning, when all the Newspaper Trains had gone, I would be despatched to the Station Supervisors Office to collect a bundle of newspapers for ourselves.

Even then there would still be one or two characters roaming the station. One man I saw frequently, used to walk up to people, stare at them, and then roar like a lion. Then, as the startled people leapt back, he would calmly walk away.

I met one young man who approached me for the money for a cup of coffee. I bought him one from a stall outside the station, and he told me how easy it is to become homeless. He told me his story, and it really made sense. He ended by saying he was determined to make a fresh start. I never saw him again. I hope he made it.

When the Isle of Wight held its famous pop festival, at its end, many of the fans travelled back to Waterloo but could get no further until the morning. When I went for the papers that morning there were bodies everywhere. I stepped over quite a few. There were even youths and girls sleeping on the roof of W.H. Smith's Bookstall.

During the day a number of filmmakers would come to Waterloo Station. Usually they were making advertisements, and sometimes the subjects of their adverts would erect a stall and give away free samples. I was sent down to 'investigate', and, posing as a passenger, I collected samples, always making sure I went to a different attendant each time. We got everything from sweets to shampoos!

But one day I missed, by just five minutes, the shooting of that well know episode of Only Fools and Horses, that marvellous scene where Delboy meets Raquel underneath that famous station clock.

Security at the night entrance to the offices gave rise to one hilarious incident. Coming on night duty one evening I was accompanied by Davy, who was about five feet six inches in height and didn't suffer fools gladly, especially on night duty. We arrived to find the lift had stopped slightly short. The door was slightly open and trapped inside we could see the Security Guard, who was eighty-three years old and asthmatic! The following fantastic conversation took place.

Security, 'I'm stuck. The lift door won't open.'

Davy, 'Where's the emergency door key?'

Security, 'In my jacket pocket.'

Davy, 'Where is your jacket?'

Security, 'In the office.'

Davy went to the office and found the door locked. He returned.

Davy, 'The office door's locked.'

Security, 'I know.'

Davy, 'Well where's the key?'

Security, 'In my pocket.'

A frustrated Davy went back to the Security Office, forced an entry through the window, retrieved the emergency key and returned.

He reached up on tiptoe and inserted the key in the special opening. Immediately the three-section door slid back, taking the key and Davy with it, trapped by his fingers round the key. Davy's language was unprintable and unrecordable.

He was still hanging by his fingers when the Security Guard, trying to be helpful, asked, 'Shall I shut the door again?'

Davy yelled, 'Just get out of there you silly old ****!'

With the Security Guard safely out, the door was closed, and Davy's fingers were, at last, released.

All night long he kept looking at his fingers, and muttering, 'They're going black! They are! Look at them! Silly old fool!'

I too had my adventure with that lift. I was just going off late turn duty, and the lift stuck between floors. I had been sent off at 10 pm, a little early because I was early turn the next day. I managed to summon help, but no amount of winding with the emergency jack would move the lift. All that happened was that Clifford got covered in filthy black grease.

The lift engineer had to come from Chatham, and it was 1.30 am before I was released. I was going to find an empty office to sleep in. I had no wash bag or anything. Then the lift engineer offered me a lift back to Tonbridge on his way back to Chatham. I gratefully accepted. I got back to Tonbridge at about 2.30 am, had about 2 hours fitful sleep and was back in the office at 7 am.

The next incident that I am about to relate, strange though it might seem, is absolutely true! I had only been at Waterloo for a few weeks and was still relatively unknown to my colleagues. I was on night duty, and John (the magistrate) was the R.C.C. I walked down the corridor to get water to make our first cup of tea. At night, apart from the Control, the offices were entirely deserted.

Suddenly I heard soft footfalls behind me. They were getting closer. I ducked into a recess and waited. The figure came into view and then passed me without apparently seeing me. I was speechless. It was a fully dressed Red Indian that had passed me. He had a headband, with long dark hair trailing from it, a buckskin jacket with fringes, buckskin trousers, and moccasins! True I didn't see a tomahawk or bow and arrow, but in every other aspect he was complete.

I collected the water for the tea and returned with the full kettle. I wanted to tell John what I had seen, but I was afraid he would think I was barmy! I sat quietly for some time. Eventually curiosity got the better of me. 'John,' I said, 'I know that you don't know me very well, and I don't want you to think I'm mad or something. But I have just seen something really strange.' I told him what I had seen.

He laughed and said, 'Don't worry. That's the P.R.O. (Public Relations Officer). He often looks like that when he's working late in the evening!'

One incident, which occurred while I was 'long weekend off,' was tragic but also had significant consequences. I found out all about it from the television reports and then when I got into the Control the next day I found the details. It was of particular interest to me for several reasons. Firstly, some of my former colleagues in the South Eastern Control had been involved in dealing with it, and secondly because it had lasting safety implications for signalling.

On the evening of the 4th January 1969, in thick fog, the 2000 hrs Charing Cross to Ramsgate had passed a signal at danger and had collided with the rear of the 1918 London Bridge to Dover Mail and Parcels Train. Sadly, a little girl in a toilet in the front of the train died instantly and the Guard of the mail train also died.

There are more detailed accounts of the accident available, so I won't go into details here, but one aspect is worth mentioning. Because the accident happened at a location deep in the Kent countryside, the D.C.C. who had taken charge of the incident, had great difficulty in identifying the exact site of the accident and therefore had equally great difficulty in directing the Emergency Services to the site.

A lasting result of this accident was that all signals and bridges and some other lineside structures on the whole railway network throughout the country were allocated a grid reference and this can be found on a metal plate affixed to the structure. Now it should always be possible to pinpoint, with some precision, the exact site of any incident. Tragic though that accident was, it led to one vital lasting improvement to the management of future incidents.

I had mentioned once before one of my colleagues, Colin S. He often tried to 'put one over' on the D.C.C.s. Another of his traits was that he always believed absolutely that he was right. When he took Peter's briefcase home by mistake, he rang the Control and asked to speak to Peter. When Peter came on the phone, Colin said, 'You've got my briefcase!'

On another occasion, Colin was covering early turn on my panel and I was rostered to be his relief. I walked into the Control in very good time. Colin roared with laughter. 'You've come in on an 'On Region Day.' What a waste of a good day out!' 'On Region Days were days when we were not rostered a specific duty, and we were encouraged to go out on the region to improve our knowledge in areas we were not so familiar with.

As it happened, I was 'On Region' the following day. On my way in I had called at the Travel Facilities Office to obtain my All Region Duty Pass, to save me coming up to Waterloo on the day. Colin was adamant that I was wrong. I sidled across so that I could see the Roster out of the corner of my eye. I was right, I was late turn.

So I responded, 'Yes, it was a silly thing to do. I'd better go out and make the best of what's left of the day.'

With that I said cheerio to Peter who was R.C.C. and Clifford who was the Locomotive Controller and left. As soon as I was out of the door, I ran down the corridor and dived into the first recess. I was only just in time.

The door was flung open and Colin rushed out. 'Terry, come back!' he called out. Then he went running past me. As soon as I heard him running down the stairs, I returned to the Control. I found Peter and Clifford in fits of laughter.

Colin had realised his mistake as soon as I had left the Control and had gone to find me. They told me to hide in the recess where the tea was made. After some time, a breathless Colin returned to the Control. 'It's too late,' he said. 'I went to the Travel Facilities, but they said he'd been in already and got his ticket. I ran over to the Exeter train but that was just pulling out. He's gone! What are we going to do now!'

'Well it's your fault,' said Clifford. 'You sent him away. Now you will have to cover his shift!'

'What, as well as early turn!' moaned Colin. Then he saw their faces. They could contain their laughter no longer and Colin realised he'd been had. I came out of hiding and for once there was nothing he could say.

Meanwhile the incidents kept happening. One night we all heard a tremendous rumble outside. We quickly learned that as one of the trains to be formed into a Newspaper Train had been shunted, it had gone into the wrong platform and had collided with another Newspaper Train. No-one was hurt and there was no derailment, but both trains were out of action and it was a major problem both for us and for the N.P.A.

On another occasion I was on late turn with Alan B as

R.C.C. when two class 73 locomotives coupled together, ran away at Margate, demolished the buffer stops and continued for some distance 'in the dirt!' Alan looked at me woefully and said, 'Terry why is it that these things happen when you are on duty. If anyone else had taken the incident, the buffer stops would have been demolished and that would have been the end of it. But not you! You have locomotives flying through the air like gliders - and two at a time at that!'

As I have said before, Alan was one of the kindest and most gentle of men it was my pleasure to work with.

The incident that had us all helpless with laughter but mortified him occurred on one changeover time between early and late turns. I was early turn. My friend Alan S was on the Locomotive Panel. Peter was the R.C.C. For some time, we had been given the dubious privilege of advice from a senior manager, who was known as Chairman Freddie, after Chairman Mao. Where Chairman Mao read advice from his little red book, Chairman Freddie, from the Freight Office across the corridor, read criticisms of us from his little green book.

This man spent an hour or more on most days, criticising us and telling us how we should do our job. I was an Assistant, so he didn't talk to me. Most of his wisdom was directed at the R.C.C.

On this day he had been giving us a lot of advice. Peter was sitting there with a glazed expression on his face. Fred was walking backwards, still talking, and had almost reached the door. Suddenly we all heard the rapid beat of Alan B's footsteps approaching the Control. Alan S looked at me. He was at his most 'Clement Freud,' His face was totally without expression. It was all I could do to keep a straight face. Peter was totally oblivious to the situation.

As Fred reached the door, the footsteps outside reached a crescendo, the door was flung back on its hinges, the briefcase flew through the air to land unerringly on the luggage rack, and Alan B ran into the room, calling out, 'Ello Wack! Anythin Appening?'

As the door swung slowly to, Fred came into view. He had been squashed against the wall like a fly and was gently sliding towards the floor, his spectacles at forty-five degrees to his face, his legs buckling, but still clutching his little green book!

Alan was really horrified. He picked Fred up and stood him up, replaced his spectacles on his nose, and dusted him down, all the while saying, 'Ever so sorry Fred. Wouldn't have had that happen for all the world. Are you alright Fred?'

Fred tottered out of the door and down the corridor to his room. He couldn't have gone more than five steps, when we all burst into roars of laughter. We could not hold back any longer. He must have heard us. At any rate we did not see him for quite some time after that.

One final 'internal' incident is worth recording. When the Carriage mechanical and Electrical Engineers, C.M.&.E.E. HQ installed members of their staff in the Regional Control, one of them was rather nervous of possible fire risks in such an old building. So concerned was he that I reassured him that there were many official exits and some unofficial ones as well.

In fact, not that many weeks previously, a colleague on night duty had gone to another office to get some paperwork and on opening the door, he had seen a young man sitting at his desk, head in hands, asleep. Roger would not have taken any notice if the man hadn't woken up suddenly, seen Roger, jumped up, fled to a window and jumped out onto the outside balcony. It had been an intruder looking for shelter for the night!

At all events I promised to take John round the building if it was quiet on the next late turn Saturday. It was quiet and we duly set off. We covered all the floors, ending with the ground floor.

Now this floor contained among other things the Press Office. These were the people we advised of any serious or major incident and they dealt with the Press. We were forbidden to speak to the Press and I for one had no problem with this rule. Only once did the Press actually get through to the Control. The call was taken by Alan S, who answered it in his best 'Clement Freud' style and deflected the caller to the On-Call Press Officer.

Also in the Press Office I was showing John, was the direct link with the B.B.C. Shepherds Bush Studio. When we heard the TV announcer say, 'We are speaking from Waterloo Station,' this was the office from which the broadcast was made. I was in full flow explaining all this to John, who was now much more relaxed, and I flung open the door of the empty office. We stopped in our tracks. There in front of us on the carpet was a body!

It was a man. He was lying face down, with his head and shoulders covered by a blanket, and he was dressed in an old shirt and jeans, with plimsolls on his feet. I shall never know why nervous John did not drop to the floor himself on the spot.

'What are we going to do? He whispered, shocked.

My first thought was that this was the night duty Press Officer, having arrived early and taking the chance of a nap before taking duty. I shared this thought with John and suggested that we withdraw silently and leave him to rest.

'But supposing he's dead,' whispered John.

'Well in that case,' I replied, 'It's too late anyway!'

We quietly withdrew and shut the door. We returned to the Control and nothing further was said.

That was on the Saturday and I was on night duty the next night, Sunday. As it happened, I had cause to speak to the Press Officer over an incident, and I told him he had given us a start, sleeping on the floor.

'I wasn't there!' he exclaimed in surprise.

'Well if it wasn't you sleeping on the floor,' I said, 'who was it?'

'What did he look like?' he asked.

I described the man to him.

He gave a chuckle and explained. 'I brought some old clothes in to change into on night turn and somebody with a distorted sense of humour made a dummy out of them and left it on the floor.'

I said, 'Well there were nearly two bodies on the floor!' and I explained what had happened.

I really enjoyed Waterloo, with all its characters, and with the wide diversity of activities day and night. But there was one thing I missed. I was always recording other people's incidents and reacting to them, advising people as required. But I was not getting any hands-on experience. It was time to move.

I applied for a position as a Controller Grade 'B' at Central Division's Croydon Control. In due course I was given an interview. It was without doubt the most acrimonious interview I have ever had. My replies to their questions, which I knew to be right, were contradicted, I was shouted at and insulted, and I did not get the job. I sat there and took it, but as I left the room, I was fuming and I vowed that no one would ever treat me like that again, no matter what their seniority. I realised later that I had been seen as a 'Regional Man' coming for a Divisional Post.

In the Vacancy List I saw there was a vacancy for a Controller Grade 'B' on Area Three in the new South Eastern Control at Beckenham. It was at that time that the Railway issued the first new Rule Book to replace the old 1950 Rule Book I had been brought up with. I applied and in due course I was advised that I would attend an interview.

The Interview was held at Beckenham. The senior interviewer was Ron C, who had been a D.C.C. and there was a Staff Officer with him. Apparently the choice came down to someone already covering the panel or me.

When I was asked a question on Rules, I asked which Rule Book they were referring to as I had had the opportunity to study the new one.

They specified the new one and I was able to give the correct answer. I think that gave me a slight advantage.

I received my letter dated 23rd October 1972, to confirm my appointment as 'Controller Grade 'B' on Area Three in the South Eastern Control at Beckenham.

John JP, the R.C.C. on duty at Waterloo congratulated me, and then said, 'Terry now you have to prove to them that they made the right choice.'

They were words I have never forgotten.

Chapter Seven -
Area Three - hands-on at last.

The South Eastern Division Control at Beckenham was more complex than the Regional Control had been but not as complex as the original Orpington Control. The five Area Panels had been merged into four. Two were grade 'E' and two were grade 'B.' The Guards, Locomotive and Rolling Stock (new position), were grade 'C.' The Deputy Chief Controllers, D.C.C.s were Managerial Status Two (MS2).

Area One remained basically the same, see pages 18/19.

Area Two took over all routes from London to Dartford and Strood via Gravesend. It also took in the Chatham Main Line from Swanley via Sole Street and on through Rochester, Chatham and Gillingham, after which it handed over to Area Three. It also had the Maidstone West Branch from Aylesford to Strood.

Area Three was the largest Area geographically and I believe also the most diverse. It took in the South Eastern Main Line from below Paddock Wood through to Ashford and Dover, then via Deal to Minster and Ramsgate, and the Chatham Main Line from Rainham to Faversham, then via Herne Bay to Margate and Ramsgate.

It also had charge of the branch line from Ashford to Minster and Ramsgate via Canterbury West, and the branch from Faversham to Dover via Canterbury East, and the line from Ashford to Hastings as far as Appledore and the branch to Lydd and Dungeness Nuclear Power Station. Trains of spent nuclear fuel travelled from there to Tonbridge, where they would be stabled in the West Yard to await onward travel to Willesden and finally to the Sellafield Reprocessing Plant in Cumbria.

There were special regulations governing the movement and stabling of these trains. I still have my copies of both the British Rail and the United Kingdom Atomic Energy Authority (UKAEA) Special Instructions. I was twice to have to invoke these instructions.

Area Four took the Chatham Main Line from Victoria through to Swanley via Shortlands Junction, then the Maidstone East Main Line from Swanley to below Maidstone East, and the branch line from Otford Junction to Sevenoaks. Area Four also controlled the South Eastern Main Line from Chislehurst through to Paddock Wood via Tonbridge, the Hastings Branch from Tonbridge to Hastings and the Ashford to Hastings line from Hastings as far as Rye, after which it handed over control to Area Three. Finally Area Four had control of the Redhill line, from Tonbridge as far as Leigh, the Central Division Control taking over from there. All the Signal Boxes mentioned in pages 28 – 32 were still in existence although this was later to change quite dramatically.

The setup in the Control was as follows.

On the back row, facing outwards from the wall, were three panels. The first, to the left of the D.C.C was the Chief Controllers Panel. In the middle was the D.C.C.'s Panel, and to the right was the Senior Officers Panel. In front of the D.C.C were three more panels. To the left was the Guards Controllers Panel. In the middle was the Locomotive Controllers Panel, while to the right was the Rolling Stock Controllers Panel.

In front of them in each of the four corners and facing outwards, were the four Area Controller's Panels. The reason they faced outwards was to encourage staff to use the internal intercom rather than shouting at each other across the room. Areas One and Two were on the left-hand side with a Grade 'A' Assistant Controller between them, and Areas Four and Three were on the right hand side facing the windows, and with a Grade 'A' Assistant Controller between them.

Area Three Panel had an advantage??? being not only diagonally the furthest away from the D.C.C, but also adjacent to the door of the Chief Controllers Office, which was the other exit from the Control.

Finally, and most importantly, behind the Chief Controllers Panel, next to the D.C.C, was the door to a very well equipped galley kitchen.

Many of the people I had worked with at Orpington had come to the new Beckenham Control. My former Area One Controller, Geoff, was now a Deputy Chief Controller, D.C.C. and I was on his shift, a part of his team. He had replaced Ron C, who had been promoted to Chief Controller. To my right, Area Four was in the charge of Randy, and we had a succession of Assistants. On Area Two opposite me was George H, and on Area One, after a series of changes was Ivan.

Like us they had a succession of Assistants. The other two D.C.C's were the originals Ron B and Bob. Relief Controllers were divided into two groups, Rest Day Reliefs, who did not do nights and General Purpose Reliefs, who covered all shifts. Among their number were George S from the old Control and Maurie D (who had been a driver) and Maurie J, who came from one of the planning departments.

The shifts were much simpler. Three shifts, one of early turn with Rest Days, one of late turn and one of nights. The weekends were interesting. You started nights on Sunday night and finished on Sunday morning. Then you doubled back for late turn Sunday and doubled back again for early turn Monday. You did late turn from Monday to Thursday, then had a long weekend off. On early turn you worked from Monday to Sunday, then doubled back for night turn Sunday.

I was given a period of learning on all three shifts and when Ron C and Geoff were both satisfied, I was passed competent, and from then I was responsible for the whole of Area Three on my shift. It was a wonderful panel to begin on, and though I later was passed competent and covered all the other panels, Area Three remained my favourite. For one thing I was dealing with real dyed in the wool railwaymen. They had taken pride in doing the job well, keeping the trains running in all circumstances and really striving to keep punctuality. They had many skills, and above all they had a real 'feel' for the jobs.

For example, I had Len as Supervisor at Dover Marine, later Dover Western Docks. He had charge of six platforms. He had a regular service via Ashford and via Chatham. He looked after the Night Ferry and its relief train, organising which platform the train of up to seventeen coaches would leave from, depending whether it was going via Ashford or via Chatham.

He was also responsible for dealing with the Golden Arrow in its early days. He also organised the shunting of the Dover to Knowle and Dorridge car transporter train. This train of twenty double deck carflats normally ran via Tonbridge, but if, due to engineering works it was diverted via Chatham, it had to run in and out of Dover Marine to set it into the right direction.

He liaised with the Ferry Supervisor, Archcliffe and Hawkesbury Street signalmen, his opposite number at Dover Priory, the Train Crew Supervisor (TCS), the British Transport Police (BTP), and of course us, Len did all this calmly and competently every day with very few supporting staff.

Then there was 'Sergeant' Fred T, the Station Supervisor at Ashford who dealt with everything relating to electric and diesel passenger trains, parcels trains, stock working, punctuality and a host of other things as well. Ashford was and still is a very busy station. Many times Fred had to find alternative transport for passengers who arrived in England on late running cross channel ferries, who had got to Ashford and could get no further, having missed the last services. He did it all in his calm unhurried way.

One of his remarkable gifts was seen in the way he dealt with frustrated passengers, and just by talking to them, he turned their frustration into good humoured laughter. People had confidence in Fred. They knew he would find a way to help them, and he always did.

I actually witnessed this one night. A friend and I had been across the channel and the return ferry had been late. We caught the last train from Dover to Ashford and there, together with a large number of other passengers, we were stranded. We were standing on the footbridge, looking at the indicators on the platforms and listening for announcements, when I saw Fred moving about between groups of passengers. He had a notebook and was taking note of all their destinations.

Now I had worked with Fred for some time, but we had never actually met. He came to us and asked where we were going.

When I said Tonbridge, he said, 'Well the lines are blocked for engineering work – but I'll see what I can do. Don't go away.' This last was said with a chuckle. Fred knew we weren't going anywhere! Over the years I heard him use that phrase a number of times, 'I'll see what I can do.' And he never failed me once.

Somebody, I believe it was Doug, the night turn Train Crew Supervisor, T.C.S, tipped Fred off that I was on the station. I had rung him to see if any light engines were going to Tonbridge, but there weren't.

In due course Fred returned. Walking up to me, in his slow drawl he said, 'Oive just found out who you are.'

I shook hands with him and said, 'Hello Fred.'

He had fixed up for us to travel on the 0030 Chart Leacon to Stewarts Lane Empty Coaching Stock (ECS). The crew had agreed to stop at Maidstone East to set us down, where a friend was waiting with his car to take us home.

One thing I soon learned with Fred was not to tell him how to do a job. I started to tell him about a complicated passenger stock changeover one day early in my time on Area Three.

He politely interrupted me, then said, 'You just tell us what you want and leave us to do it.'

I did so, and again he never let me down, no matter how short the notice or complicated the move.

His response was always, 'I'll see what I can do.'

And as I say, he always did.

The signalmen on my patch were equally as good. I soon got to know Syd at Folkestone East, 'little' Ray at Minster, and Gordon at Ramsgate, to mention just three. On my Rest Days

I got permission and travelled round meeting these people and getting to know them. Although I was a newcomer, they appreciated that I had come to see them. They showed me their jobs and we became good friends.

I particularly enjoyed my visits to Dover. Len introduced me to the Ferry Inspector, who was responsible for loading and unloading trains from the ferries via the link span. There was a special dock in which the train ferries berthed. This had a pump mechanism, which raised or lowered the water level in the dock.

If the tide was low, it might take some time to raise the ship to the level required for the link span. When the ship was level, the link span with two tracks on it, would be lowered., Very great care had to be taken in moving vehicles on or off the ship. The four tracks on the ship became two just before the point at which the link span connected. On the other end (dock side) of the link span the two roads again became four.

The Ferry Inspector would arrange for two trains of equal length AND weight, to be shunted onto the two outer roads in the Ferry Sidings. The pilot engines would then go down the two middle roads of the Ferry Siding onto the ship. These movements would be exactly synchronised. They would attach to two 'rafts' of wagons on the ship and then, again with absolute synchronisation, they would pull them off the ship. The two pilots would then attach to the two 'rafts' of wagons waiting on the outer roads of the Ferry Siding and propel them onto the ship.

Synchronisation was vital because if either train moved without the other, the weight would cause the ship to tilt and the link span would be damaged. No further transfer of traffic to and from the ships would be possible (including the Night Ferry!) until the link span was repaired again. It really was poetry in motion. It all had to be done in time for the ship to sail away on time.

I once stood on the ship and watched the loading from a little cabin in the middle of the tracks. I was strictly instructed not to move until the shunting had been completed. In the cabin was an instrument called the "Tiltometer." It had a vertical needle that recorded any tilt from level on the ship's decks. If the "Tiltometer" registered more than five degrees of tilt either way, all movements must cease immediately. I have to say that when I was in that little cabin that needle never moved, such was the precision of the shunting.

The Ferry Inspector and the Town Yard Inspector shared another special responsibility. About a year before I came to Area Three, there was, following a period of very heavy rain, a massive fall of chalk from the cliffs which tower above the line between Folkestone East and Archcliffe. A down train had run into this chalk and a 4 CEP unit had been derailed.

The train remained upright, and no one was injured. Passengers had to be evacuated from the unit, to the rear portion of the train, which then conveyed them back to Folkestone, and they were conveyed onwards by road. I later actually saw the unit, still with chalk on the underframe, as it was being worked through Tonbridge to Stewarts Lane for repairs. As a result of this accident a system of three Chalk Alarm Fences were erected, number one fence being closest to Folkestone and number three being between the southern portal of the single bore Shakespeare Tunnel and Archcliffe Junction.

When subsequently any chalk fell, it would strike the fence, set off an alarm, turn the signals to danger and shut off the traction current. The procedure when this happened was for one of the two Inspectors to travel up the line on the Town Yard Pilot to the entrance to the tunnel, checking that the tracks were clear. Then the attending person would reset the alarm, traction current would be restored, and normal working would be resumed.

I also enjoyed my visits to Hawkesbury Street Junction signal box, which took trains from Dover Priory round on the main line to Archcliffe Junction signal box, and also from the Chatham Main Line into Dover Marine. Hawkesbury Street also controlled the entranced to Lyons Siding, and at one time the entrance to the Bulwark Sidings. The latter was closed after the sharp curves caused a number of derailments. The track was taken up and the land became a car park.

Archcliffe Junction signal box controlled the South Eastern Main Line round to Hawkesbury Street Junction and Dover Priory and the entrance from the South Eastern Main Line to Dover Marine. It also controlled the entrance and exit from Dover Town Yard, and movements to and from Dover Locomotive Sidings.

One day I was allowed into the Dover Ferry Signal Box. This controlled all the movements on and off the Ferry Sidings. Some days the area was shrouded in a thick sea fog. Visibility was almost nil, but the work went on regardless. When this happened, shunting movements were controlled by blasts of varying lengths on the shunting horn kept in the cabin.

Yes, Dover was a fascinating part of the area, but by no means the only one. I enjoyed meeting and getting to know 'Little' Ray, the signalman at Minster. Ray had a high-pitched voice. Gordon at Ramsgate told me that Ray was a very little man. He had been told that I was a giant of a man and he was nervous when he heard I was coming to visit. It was a perfect set up, but thankfully I suspected I was being set up.

When I arrived at Minster, I walked up the down platform to the signal box at the end of the platform, and up the steps into the signal box. Ray was a very large and very powerful man. We shook hands and laughed at the joke. Then I watched him walk along the frame, pulling the levers effortlessly with one hand. We became very good friends. So these were some of the people I was privileged to work with and I really learned a lot from them.

I wasn't on the panel very long before I saw them in action on my first incident. In fact, it occurred during my first week on my own on late turn on the panel.

As I settled in on the late turn, Ron C came out of his office and briefed me. 'Terry,' he said, 'The General Manager (Southern Region) is travelling on the 1429 off Dover Priory to London. Under no circumstances must he be delayed. 'I don't care what else you do. You can even destroy the rush hour! But the General Manager must be on time. Do you understand me?'

I assured him that I did.

At 1420 hrs, Number One Chalk Alarm went off. The Ferry Inspector immediately jumped on the Town Yard Pilot and set off for Shakespeare Tunnel. We reckoned that as normally it only took five minutes to check that the line was clear, we would be clear before the 1429 train was ready to leave Dover Priory.

But he didn't come back. There was no word from site.

Then little dribbles of information began to come back, via the signalman at Archcliffe Junction The first said that the Ferry Inspector was still on site. The next was that 'civilians'(non-railway staff people) were on the tracks. Then came a report that Police were on the tracks.

We couldn't send another engine to the site because it would infringe regulations regarding having two trains in a section. When half an hour had passed with no further word, the other Inspector agreed to walk up the track. This would take another half an hour.

At this point, the door of Ron C's office flew open. 'Whatever's going on?' he demanded.

I told him briefly and succinctly.

His next question was 'What are you doing with the General Manager?'

When I told him we were hoping to be clear at any moment, he decided we should not wait any longer. The 1429 off Dover Priory, with the General Manager on board, was diverted via Deal, Minster and Canterbury West and was only half an hour late despite everything.

But a number of traincrews were booked to travel to London on this train for the evening peak services from London. They were very delayed and the evening rush hour was badly affected.

Finally the Ferry Inspector reported back that the lines were clear, and the whole incredible story came out.

A burglar, intent on burgling some tents on the cliff top, had come up from the beach, crossed over the two running lines and their conductor rails. He had then climbed over Number One Chalk Alarm Fence, without setting it off. He had climbed up the cliff and was helping himself to the contents of the tents, when he was surprised by some of the returning campers. Grabbing what he could, the burglar scrambled down the cliff, climbed over the Fence, this time thankfully for him, setting it off, then ran into one of the single bores of Shakespeare Tunnel.

The campers followed him down the cliff, onto the track and into the tunnel. Had the burglar not set the Alarm off, traction current would still be live, trains would have been running at line speed, and there would certainly have been serious casualties. One of the campers saw a passing Kent Police area car and flagged them down. The Police followed the campers down the cliff. At no time did the Police advise us, as they should have done, that they wanted to go onto the track.

So, rather like a knockabout comedy, the burglar ran into the tunnel, followed by the campers and the Police, followed by the Ferry Inspector. On reaching the Folkestone end of the tunnel, the campers emerged, followed by the Police and then the Ferry Inspector. But of the burglar there was no sign. So they all turned round and ran back through the other bore of the tunnel in search of him. They finally reached the Archcliffe Junction end of the tunnel, but of the burglar there was no trace.

Two theories were put forward. There was known to be a large natural drainage hole in the chalk base of the tunnel. It led to the beach. One theory was that the burglar knew of this and made his escape via it. The other theory was that he didn't know about it and fell down it. At any rate, he was never seen again, and so far as I know, the stolen property was never recovered. We told the disgruntled commuters on their delayed trains from London that the delay was due to 'operating difficulties.'

They would never have believed the truth. This then was my first 'hands on' incident. Many others were to follow.

One of the things I enjoyed was going around the patch and meeting the people that I was working with. As well as meeting the signalmen and station and yard supervisors, I enjoyed seeing how the job was done.

On one occasion I was given a cab pass and travelled with a crew on a class 5000 locomotive running 'light' to Shepherdswell. We were to pick up a train of loaded coal wagons in the sidings. Now the 5000 class locomotive was a basically very simple but very powerful machine. It had a very powerful electric motor, the power for which came from a huge flywheel. This in turn was driven by an electric current collected from the third rail (the conductor rail). The fact that the flywheel was used meant that when the locomotive ran over gaps in the conductor rail the momentary loss of power from the third rail did not cause an interruption and the locomotive continued to run at full power.

This also made the following 'event' possible. When we arrived at Shepherdswell, as well as the loaded wagons in the sidings, there was also another loaded wagon, which had been stopped for repairs. The repairs had been completed, and the plan was for us to pick it up. The problem was that the wagon was inside the 'Hole in the Wall,' which was not electrified. With a diesel or electro-diesel there would have been no problem. But we had a straight electric locomotive. I could not see how the crew would get round this one.

The crew however wore confident grins. They asked me what I knew about 'G' force.

I told them I understood the theory.

'Well now you're going to get some practice. Hold tight to your seat' they said. The flywheel was wound up until it was howling madly. The points to the 'Hole in the Wall' were operated. The brakes were released. The locomotive shot back into the siding.

As it buffered up to the wagon the secondman leapt off, ran to the wagon and coupled up. He jumped back onto the locomotive, which then surged forward, and back onto the main line and the conductor rail before the flywheel had slowed down. The driver said laconically, 'Of course it is embarrassing if the flywheel stops before we get back on the main line.' The rest of the trip went according to plan and there was no delay to passenger traffic.

On another occasion, Ron A, a helpful Freight Inspector offered me the chance of a brake-van ride on a trip from Angersteins Wharf to the Anglo Iranian Oil Refinery on the Isle of Grain. This was all out of my patch, but I could never turn down such an opportunity.

Our train comprised thirty empty Liquid Petroleum Gas (LPG) tanks, plus a huge chimney for Kingsnorth Power Station, conveyed on a special long wheel-based bogie wagon, to be detached at Miskins Sidings.

In Angersteins Wharf, security and fire protection was absolute. People could be stopped and searched, and any cigarette lighters or matches would be confiscated. A Gasworks electric locomotive brought the tank cars out of the discharge sidings. Empty LPG rail tanks were even more dangerous than loaded ones, it was explained to me, because of the fumes, which remained in the tanks after the fuel had been discharged.

Our locomotive was not allowed beyond a certain point. The Gasworks locomotive came off and ours went on. From then on I travelled in the brake-van with the guard and the Freight Inspector. The train moved off. Access to and from Angersteins Wharf was via a line, which ran under the Greenwich Line at Westcombe Park.

As our train emerged from under the bridge, I was amazed to see we were running alongside a large scrapyard, in the middle of which was a huge bonfire, with flames rising to more than fifty feet in height. I wondered how the scrap metal merchant would have felt had he known what the train that was passing him contained!

The journey was uneventful and in due course we stopped at Miskins Sidings where the wagon conveying the massive chimney was detached and shunted, then continued on to the refinery.

On the way, Ron told us of another trip when another famous character, who rejoiced in the nickname of 'Mad Jack,' was the Freight Inspector on one of these trips. Getting into the brake-van, he found it freezing with ice on the inside of the windows, and the guard wrapped up like a cocoon. As the train got onto the main line, Jack asked what was wrong with the fire. On being told the chimney was blocked, he told the guard to leave his bag and go out and stand on the veranda.

Shortly afterwards there was a loud bang and the top of the chimney was blown off. No questions were asked. Soon there was a blazing fire, the van was warm as toast and Jack and the guard relaxed in the warmth. The journey was a pleasant one.

Then Jack looked out of the window as the train stopped. He found they were just about to propel the tanks into the Yantlett Siding. Looking up he noticed a plume of smoke and as he looked closer, he saw flames shooting out of the remains of the chimney. Racing back inside he grabbed a bucket full of sand and hurled it on the fire, extinguishing it. No official report was ever made.

Jack was a real and very committed railwayman. My father worked with him, when my father was the West Yard Inspector at Tonbridge, before he retired, and I actually met him once. Two incidents illustrate Jack's commitment. He became the Assistant Yard Manager at Hither Green, where he was responsible for the down yard with three sections, the up yard and the Continental Depot. He also had a supervisory responsibility for Grove Park Carriage Sheds.

Normally Jack worked from 9 am to 5 pm. He was doing that one day, when, at about 4.30 pm, a derailment occurred in the down yard. Rerailing was completed by 2200 hours (10 pm), but then Jack found out that the night turn shunter had not come in, so he stayed all night assisting the shunting of all three busy sections of the down yard.

He was about to go home at 0600 when the early turn shunter for Hither Green had arrived, but then he found that the early turn shunter for Grove Park Shed had failed to arrive, so he immediately walked down to the shed and saw all the suburban trains out for the shed for the morning rush hour.

After that he thought it was too late to go home as he normally started at 0900 (9am) at his office at Hither Green.

This reached the ears of the Divisional Manager. He authorised another Yard Manager to relieve Jack, escort him off the premises, put him in a taxi, and send him home for the rest of the day. Protesting, Jack did as he was told.

The other incident occurred in the up yard, while Jack was making an inspection. It was a principle at Hither Green, as at Tonbridge and Ashford and the other yards, that no train should ever be refused, even when the yards were full. Hither Green up yard was very full, and the continental vans had been stacked back tight against the buffer stops on each siding. Jack was looking for any gap that he could use.

As he reached the south end of the yard, a strange thing happened. There was a 'whoosh' sound, which he felt as much as heard. His hat was lifted from his head and blown away, as a shadow passed briefly by him. Then there was a deep 'thud!' What had happened, he discovered, was that so much pressure had been put on the tension braced buffer stop of the siding he was walking by, that the buffer stop had been forced off the track, flown through the air, and buried itself in the embankment at the end of the yard, missing Jack by inches as it did so.

Jack slowly recovered his composure, and his hat, and then, undeterred by his very narrow escape, set about protecting the siding, which had to be shortened, and then checking all the other buffer stops to make sure the incident showed no signs of being repeated. Only after visiting every siding with buffer stops did Jack then go for a much -needed cup of tea.

It was while I was one Area Three, that we had a number of movements of 'out of gauge' wagons. Ashford had won a contract to build wagons for the then Yugoslav Railways. The loading gauge for these wagons was much wider than that for the British Railways. The only way to convey them to Dover for onward shipping, was to have them offset on the offside (right hand side) in the direction of travel, and because of structural restrictions, for example Shakespeare single bore tunnel, the train could not run the direct route and had to run via Canterbury West and Minster, to Dover.

That meant they had to follow the 0233 Ashford to Margate, a portion off of the 2350 London Bridge to Dover, Royal Mail Train. It was realised quickly that because of the tight pathway, if anything went wrong the early rush hour service was in jeopardy. The train had to be ready to follow right behind the 0233 Ashford. The trip ran once a week.

On one particular night, when I was on duty, the train set off. It had reached Minster, when the signalman at Deal rang me. He told me that there was a raft of wagons in the middle road at Deal, which had been left there in error after some shunting. Did I think the out of gauge load would get by them? If not, an engine would have to come from Dover to shunt them, before the train could proceed. The 0505 Ramsgate to Charing Cross would be heavily delayed.

In the Control we were strictly warned not to give any such advice and, as we were not trained in Rules and Signalling

Regulations, we were not allowed to give any interpretation of them. In addition, I had a bad feeling about this one. The train was a 2-6-3 restriction (not to pass or be passed by vehicles on either side). My training and experience in signal boxes had taught me always to abide by the rules, and never deviate from them. I could only tell him that, if it were me, I would not accept the train until the wagons had been cleared.

We agreed that I would ask Dover to send a locomotive post haste. I asked Ray at Minster to hold onto the train until the line at Deal was clear. In due course the locomotive arrived, the wagons were cleared, and the out of gauge load proceeded. The 0505 Ramsgate to Charing Cross was heavily delayed. The service was restarted from Ashford, while the original train terminated there, and passengers were transferred to another service. The pathways were too tight to allow the original train to go through to London.

The next night I was again on the panel and got a call from Deal. It was the Area Inspector. He asked if I had advised the signalman not to accept the train.

I said I had.

He said, 'It's a very good job you did. If that train had run while the wagons were in the middle road, the out of gauge wagons would have struck the other wagons, and probably been derailed. The signalman would have been taken out of the Box and you would have been taken out of your job.'

It was the line between Deal and Minster that provided the setting for another alarming incident. Again, I was on night duty. Engineering work was to take place on the following weekend, and in preparation for this a train had run from Ashford Pre-assembly Depot to Deal with a number of bogie bolster wagons loaded with rails.

In due course it arrived at Deal and the crew were preparing to run round it at shunt it into the sidings. The first I knew of something wrong came with a phone call from Ray, the signalman at Minster. He asked me if I had been told what was going on at Deal.

I said I hadn't.

He told me that when they ran round the train, the wagon left on the end had been found to have defective brakes.

The locomotive went onto the wagon with the intention of shunting it into the middle of the train, which would have been perfectly acceptable practise. But the wagon hadn't been secured before the shunt was made, and as the locomotive buffers touched it, the wagon, fully loaded with rails, set off on its own. Ray told me the locomotive had been set off in pursuit.

I had visions that if that the wagon stopped and rolled back there would be a fatal collision. I told Ray to stop the locomotive and send it back out of the way.

The wagon was still travelling fast. It had passed Betteshanger, and Sandwich signalman reported he thought it was travelling at around 50 mph when it passed him.

I asked Ray what he was going to do with the wagon. I knew from my knowledge of the layout at Minster, that the speeding wagon would be unlikely to negotiate the sharp curve round to Ramsgate. It was more likely to leave the tracks, cross the triangle and possibly strike the signal box. The only real option was to signal it up the Canterbury Branch.

But Ray said that could not be done as there were engineers working on the tracks and they would not get clear in time. The only other alternative was to signal it into the bay platform. Ray pointed out that it would wreck the station. But we agreed it would be better to do that rather than possibly kill somebody.

I suggested that Ray do that, get traction current discharged, then leave the signal box and find a place of safety. I asked him to ring me when the wagon had come to rest. I spoke to Canterbury Electrical Control and told them what was happening.

Then there was silence for what seemed like forever. The whole Control was quiet as the controllers were all listening intently to what was going on. Geoff, the D.C.C. was standing beside me making notes for the Report.

I rang Minster Box. Ray answered the phone. I asked him what was happening. He told me that the wagon had come to a stop 'right on top of Richborough Bank' The locomotive had once again set off to retrieve it. I suggested they sprag the wagon (put a steel rod through the spokes of the wheels) before they let the locomotive approach. This they did. The locomotive attached the wagon, and hauled it back wrong line to Sandwich and so right line to Deal, where it was put safely away. The line was cleared just in time for the 0505 Ramsgate to Charing Cross to run right time.

Many, but not all the incidents I experienced, occurred at night. One morning at around 5.30 am, Sid, the Signalman at Folkestone East telephoned. He often telephoned me and set my teeth on edge. 'Terry! Terry! Terry!'

'Yes Sid', I would reply with bated breath.

'0508 Dover Priory to Charing Cross right time.'

'Thank you Sid.' I said, heaving a sigh of relief.

But on this morning Sid was different. 'Terry,' he said in

a low quiet voice, 'I think I'm in trouble. I've got the 0435 Ashford to Dover freight in section on the down fast and I've lost all my track circuit indications on the up and down slow lines. I'll let you know in a minute.'

He rang back. 'Yes, I am in trouble. The 0435 Ashford to Dover is 'off the road' (derailed) on the down fast, and there are wagons on the up slow and down slow between Folkestone West and Folkestone Central.' He certainly was in trouble! Only the up fast line remained open – and that with extreme caution. Thankfully there were no injuries.

Under Geoff, the D.C.C,'s guidance we arranged for up traffic only, to run from Dover Priory. The up Night Ferry was diverted via Chatham. Up services from Ramsgate were diverted via Canterbury West. A shuttle service was instituted between Ramsgate and Dover Priory, and buses replaced trains between Ashford and Dover Priory. It was contemplated opening up an old ground frame at Westenhanger, but this was considered to be more trouble than it was worth.

A Circular Twenty (the divisional advice to all stations) was issued, stating that due to a freight train derailment at Folkestone, passenger services would be subject to delay and cancellation.

In the midst of all this, my relief arrived, and thankfully I went home.

By the time I came back the next night, the wagons had been cleared and the up and down slows had been reopened. The down fast was out of use for several weeks. It was reported that one thirty- foot length of rail had been snapped off and driven vertically into the ground until only six feet remained above ground! Such are the ergonomic forces that come into play during a derailment.

With all these incidents, one might think the Railway was a dangerous place, but that would not be true. Thousands upon thousands of journeys were safely made each day, and many of them were on time. The staff, with very few exceptions, were both conscientious and efficient. I could still safely say, with hand on heart, that a railway carriage was one of the safest places to be.

The next incident was, even for me, unusual, to say the least. Again I was on night duty. As daylight came, the driver of the first up train, 0508 Dover Priory to Charing Cross, reported a possible sighting of a body on the upside of the line near a high arch near Folkestone West. The line was blocked, and staff were sent to site.

They quickly reported back that there was indeed the body of a man, but he was lying clear of the track. They thought he might have been in contact with the conductor rail, but this was later discounted. We began the procedures of establishing which were the last trains on the previous evening, so that they could be examined for traces of 'human remains.'

The Police, initially County, and then B.T. Police were called and attended. An ambulance came to the nearest road access. The Police reported back that the man did not show any signs of being struck by a train. They allowed us to call off the search of trains that could have been involved.

Finally, the story came back. The Police believed that the man was murdered on the bridge, and then thrown off the bridge, hoping that the body would land on the track, and be run over by trains in the darkness. But in the dark they had miscalculated, and the body had fallen well clear of the tracks.

Because the scene of crime was actually on the bridge itself, the Police were persuaded to remove the body and the lines were reopened in time for the next up train. We never heard anything more about the incident.

Just occasionally, even with such experts to work with, misunderstandings occurred, with some amusing results. An incident which comes to mind involved the Night Ferry, and I have to admit my responsibility for part of the problem.

I should firstly set the scene. As illustrated earlier, the Night Ferry used the facilities of the Link Span at Dover Ferry Dock. Because of the variations of weather and tides, the international part of the train was often delayed. Because of this the train was allocated three separate pathways, depending on when it was likely to leave. This was essential, because pathways for commuter trains, particularly from Tonbridge and upwards were down to two minutes. Any delay to these trains tended to snowball into real delays, which also affected the suburban services nearer London as well.

So the train was strictly governed. There were pathways at 0620 via Chatham, 0720 hrs via Maidstone East, and 0805 hrs via Tonbridge. Sometimes, as on this occasion, the train ran in two portions. Len at Dover Marine and I had had an argument about something, I forget what now. Unjustifiably I had told him he was useless.

Sid telephoned me from Folkestone East Signal Box and asked me what I was doing with the Night Ferry.

When I asked why, he told me that Len had dispatched both portions of the train, one behind the other, at 0720 hrs.

I knew we could not cope with that. I asked Sid to send the Locomotive hauled portion forward in the 0720 hrs pathway and hold the second portion back, to go forward in the 0805 hrs pathway.

Then I had a slight problem. I do not like swearing and yet I needed to be assertive about this. I rang Len and asked him why he had done it.

He replied, 'You said I was useless, so I thought I would show you that you were right.'

I called him a "Silly Muffin."

He asked me why I called him that. I told him he was daft as a mule and twice as stubborn. Laughter ensued.

We talked it over and apologies followed. The incident was hushed up. Both portions of the Night Ferry arrived in Victoria on time, and no other trains were delayed.

There was only one lasting effect. I was nicknamed 'Muffin' for my sins. This nickname stuck, and much, much later, when I became a manager, when so addressed by colleagues, I insisted on being called 'Mr Muffin – I'm management!'

Whilst on the subject of the Night Ferry, there were other special instructions regarding this train. Passengers joined the train in Paris, the last boarding point, and the train was then sealed by Customs and Excise staff. From that time onward the train was 'considered to be in England.'

When the train arrived on the ship at Dover, Kent Police would be in attendance. What was not generally known was that Kent Police had a vehicle shadowing the train until it reached the Metropolitan Police Area. Metropolitan Police then shadowed the train to its destination.

So one morning, when I was on early turn, and the train was running in the 0805 hrs pathway, and it came to a stand between Staplehurst and Marden, I had to advise the Kent

Police, so that their car could get as near as possible to site. The brakes had suddenly come on, for no known reason.

The train crew investigated but found no cause. They released the brakes and the train continued on its way. Only when the train arrived in Victoria was the cause discovered. An elderly foreign lady made a strong complaint that she had been using the toilet facilities on a Wagon Lit coach, and as she pulled the chain, the train stopped so suddenly that she fell over!

Toilets on trains, strangely, were quite often the cause for delays and disruption. One evening when I was on late turn, Fred at Ashford reported the following incident. The stock for the 2000hrs Charing Cross to Ramsgate was an 8 CEP.

Unknown to anyone, an airlock developed in the discharge pipe in one of the toilets. Pressure built up every time this toilet was used. Finally, an unfortunate passenger was using this toilet on the 2000 hrs Charing Cross. The pressure finally became too much, and the toilet erupted, its contents gushing with some force all over the passenger.

Fred was as sympathetic and helpful as he could be under the circumstances, as this golem type figure tottered down the platform. He apologised and assured the passenger that he would be compensated. Arrangements were made to convey him home. The unit was taken out of service for cleaning and repair.

Toilets were also the subject of occasional practical jokes. Perhaps the most amusing, was the covering of the ring below the seat with 'Clingfilm', which had 'artistic' results.

Far beyond a joke though, was the person who found himself stuck to a seat covered in superglue. The unit had to be taken out of service at Tonbridge and taken down to a siding with road access. An ambulance and the Fire Brigade were called, the latter to dismantle the toilet, and the passenger was taken to hospital for the seat to be removed. Thankfully that was the only incident of its kind that I knew of.

It was while I was on Area Three that we began to experience a series of derailments involving 16 ton mineral wagons, on the Maidstone East Line. The wagons had covered many hundreds of miles. Sometimes they had been badly loaded or overloaded. Sometimes axle boxes ran dry of grease, overheated and disintegrated. The track, I must stress was not unsafe, but it did undulate a bit. A combination of all these and other factors caused three derailments when I was on duty on Area Three.

The first two questions when a derailment was reported were, 'How many wheels off?' and, 'How far has it run?' The answer to the first would tell me something of the extent of the derailment, and the answer to the second would tell me how much track had been damaged or destroyed, usually one to three miles. No casualties were involved in any of the incidents I dealt with, and no other trains were involved.

We got into the routine of arranging to terminate trains at Maidstone East and Ashford with a bus shuttle service for intermediate stations.

These derailments were not restricted to Area Three. One occurred on Area Four, at Weald Substation, near the country end of Sevenoaks Tunnel, between Sevenoaks and Tonbridge. After early turn I motored up to Weald to see for myself the effects of a derailment. I saw a wagon, minus its wheels, and shaped like a weary parallelogram, sprawled across the tracks, with its load of coal spilled over both tracks.

Speed restrictions were imposed on the wagons, which meant

freight trains had to be retimed. Gradually the wagons were withdrawn from service as suitable alternatives became available.

Another incident that occurred on Area Three, well demonstrated the sheer diversity and variety of things that could and did happen.

It was a late turn Saturday on a lovely sunny Saturday afternoon. There were no engineering works and no incidents had occurred. The trains were running normally and on time. We were all sitting back and relaxing.

Out in a lineside field on a farm between Sandwich and Minster, a farmer was spraying his crops. All was well with the world. Then the wind changed. The spray was blown across the railway tracks and fell on the conductor rails. A violent short circuit resulted. The force of the short circuit on the 750 volts supply dislodged the conductor rails that went up in the air, and came down, in the words of a Permanent Way Ganger who attended, 'Like pretzels!'

The lines were blocked between Dover Priory and Minster. A bus service was instituted. Trains were diverted from Minster via Canterbury West. The Permanent Way staff attended, and repairs were eventually completed late in the evening, just in time to run the last trains of the day.

We also had problems with security alerts. The IRA were making and sometimes carrying out their threats. Every threat had to be taken seriously. One night, Len at Dover Marine found a suspicious suitcase on one the platforms. The security forces were stretched to the limit at the time, and we were advised that there could be some delay before they could attend. The two platforms were closed. The 2328 hrs Dover to Knowle and Dorridge car train was in a platform for the

South Eastern route and had to be shunted to another platform for the Chatham route.

Arrangements were made for the Night Ferry to be diverted via Chatham. Various other stock moves had to be made. Around 6 am the security services arrived. A controlled explosion revealed the contents of the suitcase to be a load of dirty washing!

Other Areas also suffered in this way. One morning, just after the morning rush hour, on Area One, Borough Market signalman reported an explosion had occurred outside his signal box, on a train of empty coaching stock from Cannon Street. Investigations revealed that an explosive device had been left on a luggage rack in a coach of a 4 EPB unit, and had exploded, blowing a hole in the roof. It takes no effort to realise the disruption that followed that incident, right outside London Bridge. Thankfully there were no injuries.

We also were affected by criminal activity from time to time. Consignments of shoes were conveyed on the 1945 hrs express freight train from Stratford to Dover. Criminals climbed on top of the signalling gantries, waiting to drop onto the train as it passed underneath. Between Stratford and Hither Green, they unfastened the wagon doors, and as the train passed through Hither Green they threw out boxes of shoes, which were collected by a gang waiting with a lorry.

The firm soon discovered this was happening. From then on, they made their own arrangements. When the thieves opened the boxes, they found they all contained either right shoes or left shoes, but never pairs of shoes. There was no market for single shoes!

Another incident concerned a high-speed freight train from

Hither Green to Dover. The train, conveying washing machines and fridges in long wheelbase four wheeled ferry vans, became derailed on an embankment between Sole Street and Rochester. There were no injuries and no other train was involved. As well as the Permanent Way and Carriage Mechanical & Electrical staff, lorries were sent to clear the loads. But when they arrived, they found the wagons, or what was left of them, empty. 'Travellers' had got there first and cleared the lot.

One gang of criminals, I felt, almost deserved to 'get away with it,' because of their sheer audacity. A Permanent Way gang were working on the trackside, cutting up and preparing redundant rails to be removed. A lorry was expected to take the metal away. In due course a railway lorry arrived.

The Ganger who brought it, apologised but his gang had been called out to an emergency. He asked if the gang on site could help him load the lorry. Of course, the gang obliged. The lorry was soon loaded and went on its way. Not long afterwards, another lorry arrived, with a gang on board.

They reported to the supervisor and asked where the rails they had come to collect were. It transpired that thieves had stolen the first lorry and the uniform found inside, and then had had the audacity to get the railway staff to load the lorry for them and made off with the scrap metal!

So the (mis-) adventures continued on Area Three, as the next chapter shows.

Chapter Eight - More mishaps and misadventures on Area Three

Every incident I dealt with brought its own lessons for me to learn and equipped me for the time when I would eventually become a Duty Line Manager and have my own shift team. But that is some way in the future yet.

It's probably time now to introduce one or two of the senior officers who came and went our way. Some of them were happy with what we did and simply came in to find out what was currently going on and to discuss implications of changes being brought about by the British Railways Board and the Government. They spent most of their time chatting with our D.C.C, Geoff.

One of those was different. I got on with very well with Bob, the manager in charge of the Divisional Freight Office next door. Because Area Three had such a diverse freight service, he often chatted to me. He was very helpful, and on all but one occasion, we got on well.

The one odd occasion concerned the filling in of our freight reporting sheets. We had all been used to filling in the passenger report sheets and we had got used to filling in the details of the locomotive, load and punctuality of the freight services. The Total Operations Processing System, T.O.P.S. was becoming a feature, and many of these details were obtained by a computer. I will explain this system in a moment.

But there were still some small sidings, where the shunter,

having dealt with and dispatched a train did not see it as a priority to phone in the details to us. We, being unable to contact him, had therefore to leave those entries blank. I think 'somebody from above,' was leaning on Bob, and in his frustration, Bob would mark my freight sheets in red ink, with remarks like 'See me!' or 'This is not good enough!'

The other controllers thought this was hilarious, and I got remarks like, 'Not done your homework again. You'll get detention if you don't do better.'

I challenged Bob, saying that the last time I had been treated like that was at school! I also said that if it kept happening, I would file the sheets in the wastepaper bin. Bob laughed but it kept happening. One day I concealed the sheets. Bob raced in the next day, really worried that no sheets had been received. I told him I had 'filed' them. He was really upset and I had to retrieve the sheets from the draw and give them to him. He laughed in relief. We made a joke about it. No more red writing appeared.

The Total Operations Processing System (T.O.P.S.) deserves an explanation. The system first came to light in the United States of America. There it was used solely for the movement and maintenance of locomotives. British Railways Board Marketing Section purchased the system.

They really developed it, so that, as well as movement and maintenance of locomotives, they designed applications for the movement and maintenance of all passenger, parcels and freight vehicles. Continuing this, they refined the system so that loads and consignments could be monitored at all times. Thus, by the application of a computer enquiry, it should be possible to obtain information on the consist, locomotive and punctuality of all train movements.

It was an incredibly effective system. As well as being able to accurately monitor all train operations currently, there were other side benefits. The system revealed that a large part of the freight fleet was actually surplus to requirements, and subsequently the fleet was considerably reduced, with an accompanying huge saving of running costs. Also, in the past, any parcels or freight supervisor worth his salt, would always have a few wagons, 'up his sleeve,' ready to put in at short notice to supplement a service. While on the surface, this was a laudable activity, in practice it meant that a number of vehicles were always standing idle. I lost count of the number of arguments I had had with supervisors who flatly denied they had any vehicle that I needed.

T.O.P.S swept all this away. It became a very reliable and good system, once the staff outside had learned how important it was to report movements currently. It was such a successful system that the Marketing Section actually sold the much-improved system back to the Americans and made a huge profit for the Railways. That is something else that not many people know about.

One senior officer who would never be taken for granted was Mr H.A. He was the smartest man I ever saw. He appeared punctually every morning at around 8 am. He was always dressed in an immaculate black formal morning suit, with a crisp white shirt and a black bow tie. His black hair was swept back and not a hair out of place. His shoes actually shone brightly. He looked every inch the senior officer – and he was. He spoke with a quiet, almost whispering, voice.

He had an encyclopaedic knowledge of the railway and its

operations. He also had a detached air of authority, which meant that he was, unlike any of the other officers, not a 'matey' sort of person, and he was able, and ready, to invoke discipline without hesitation if it was needed. He was a totally dedicated railwayman and would not tolerate at all, anything that would interfere with its running. I was later to see examples of this, though thankfully I was not responsible.

Each morning, he would come into the Control, nod an acknowledgement to the D.C.C, and walk straight across to me at my panel. 'Good morning Terry,' he would say in that quiet voice, 'What is the situation at the collieries (Betteshanger, Shepherdswell and Snowdown) this morning? Have they got sufficient empty wagons? Have you got enough in reserve at Ashford?' I quickly learned to get all this information from the T.O.P.S. computer and have it on a page on my clipboard ready for him, when he came in.

Then one morning I was caught out. He came in as usual, but instead of asking me about the collieries, he asked if Sheerness Iron & Steel had enough loaded wagons of fuel and were there any reserves at Hither Green. Quickly I went to the T.O.P.S. computer. I was as quick as I could be. He said nothing, but I felt the 'vibes' of impatience as he waited. From then onward I made sure I had the information about the collieries and Sheerness Iron & Steel on the clipboard before he came in.

After seeing me, he would go to Area Two for the Hoo Junction Yard position and other details. Then he would go to the other two Areas for information. He was also very interested in the passenger timekeeping, and anything interfering with it. When he had all the information he wanted, he would then walk over to the D.C.C. and talk to him briefly.

Then, armed with all the information, he would return to his office and summon all the heads of departments, Freight, Passenger, Rolling Stock, etc, one by one, and ask them what their current situation was. He would compare it with the information he had gleaned from us, and if it differed, woe betide the head of section concerned. This resulted in a steady procession of heads of departments coming in around 7.45 am and getting the same information from us.

It was around that time that we began to experience problems with punctuality at Ramsgate. Several trains in the morning rush hour would leave two or three minutes late. Now it may seem strange but if they were five minutes late, they would miss their slot further up the line and they would simply be given a later slot, which sometimes made them later still but did not delay any other trains. But if they were just two or three minutes late, they were too late for their own slot but too early for the next slot, and other trains were being delayed.

This had a snowball effect on other services at Tonbridge and Rochester and thereafter into the London suburbs. It became a persistent problem and the overall punctuality performance suffered as a result. We were instructed to deal with this firmly. If a train was not ready on time it was to be cancelled and the passengers had to be transferred to another train. It was a terrible thing to have to do, morning after morning.

It also meant finding another crew and rolling stock to form the return working from London. Events reached a peak. Geoff, my D.C.C. was unhappy with me. I felt awkward about doing it. The Area Manager at Margate made formal complaints about me, and I was generally unpopular. Then Mr H.A. walked in one morning. He nodded to the D.C.C. then came straight to my panel and asked me how Ramsgate were doing. I told him of the cancellations and the effect it was happening. He said, in his quiet voice 'Carry on exactly as you are doing Terry. You have my support.' Then he left the Control and returned to his office.

I later heard that the Area Manager at Margate received a call from Mr H.A's secretary, inviting him to a meeting at Beckenham in a week's time, where the performance at Ramsgate would be discussed, with the possibility of relocating the current Area Manager, if the situation had not improved. And the situation did improve. Punctuality was restored, and the problem went away.

Six months later I was advised that as part of my training in the Leadership 2000 initiative, Mr H.A. had directed that I was to be relieved of my duty on Area Three for one week and be posted to Ramsgate. There I was to do a project on surveying current communications systems at Ramsgate and proposals for improving the system. I was to meet the very people I had had to deal with during the punctuality problem. I was not enthusiastic.

The first person I had to meet was the Area Manager at Margate. He made it plain that he did not have much time for me, in every sense of the word, but since Mr H.A. had ordered it, he had to submit to being interviewed by me.

I then had to be at Ramsgate by 4 am in order to see for myself the preparations for the start of the morning rush hour on Monday morning. I arranged to travel down to Ashford on the 2350 London Bridge to Dover, Royal Mail Train and thence to travel on the 0233 Ashford to Margate as far as Ramsgate. No-one at Ramsgate made any comment about this. Then I was kindly put wise by another controller, that although the 2350 London Bridge to Dover ran every night, for some reason in the timetabling, the 0233 Ashford to Margate did not run on Monday mornings. Had I travelled on the 2350 London Bridge to Dover, I would have been stranded at Ashford until the first passenger train. I would have been a laughing stock with Ramsgate and I shudder to think what Mr H.A's reaction would have been.

So, having been prevented from making a fool of myself, I drove down to Ramsgate, arriving just before 4 am. I found the station locked up and in total darkness. The gate at the entrance to the carriage sidings was also locked. I had to climb over the wall and walk along the track. In the distance I saw the lights were on in the shunters lobby. I walked up to the lobby, and with great glee, I opened the door, walked in, and said, 'Good morning gentlemen.' I was greeted by good natured laughter, as they realised that I had 'rumbled them' and I was given a cup of tea.

From then on, we got on well. The project was a great success and I later learned that my folder of information was published and was used in at least one later training session with one of my colleagues.

One further story about Mr H.A, was recounted to me by the Station Supervisor at Sevenoaks, who was a friend of mine. Mr H.A. travelled each morning from Tunbridge Wells to Sevenoaks.

There he would change to a train for Orpington, and thence by another train he would travel to Beckenham Junction.

There had been another punctuality purge. If the main line trains were late, connections were to be broken so that the suburban service ran to time. So ran the instruction.

On this morning, Mr H.A's train from Tunbridge Wells was a few minutes late. The suburban train was dispatched on time and the connection at Sevenoaks was broken. Mr H. A. had to wait half an hour at Sevenoaks. He did not criticise the staff for this but used this time to make a thorough inspection of the station.

He found fault with everything, from the platforms not having been swept properly, to fire buckets not ready for action, to waste bins not emptied, to windows not polished, to seats not having been washed clean, and then he went to inspect the paperwork in the office. He listened to station announcements.

At the end of all this and before his train arrived, Mr H.A. gave the station supervisor a comprehensive list of all the things to be rectified and told him to instruct the Station Master to send in a report within three days to the effect that everything had been put right.

At the end of this story, my friend's comment made me smile. He said, 'I don't care how late Mr H.A's train is at Sevenoaks. We will always hold the connection for him.'

My time on Area Three was before the construction and opening of the Channel Tunnel. We therefore handled all the continental freight at Dover, a car train service from Ramsgate and we also had a car train service from Lenham. Trains ran to Willesden for onward transport to the rest of the country, to Hither Green for distribution in South London, and to Paddock Wood, which was just off my patch, for the Transvesa terminal.

Other goods came through Dover but were forwarded on road transport. Then, one day, another transporter of perishable goods for Paddock Wood, contacted staff at Dover to see if it were possible to attach a wagon of their goods to our 2120 Dover – Paddock Wood service. They were referred to us.

I could see no problem, provided that none of the booked traffic for the train was left behind and there was still capacity on the train to take it. I spoke to my colleague on Area Four and he agreed, after a brief conversation with the staff at Paddock Wood. The wagon was duly attached, and the firm were very grateful. Soon the request was coming regularly. The firm told us this was a trial to see if the service worked for them, and if it did, a contract would follow.

This continued for some time. Then one morning Bob (Head of Freight) came to see me. He asked me what was happening, and I told him. Then he advised me that the firm were 'on the fiddle.' They were getting their goods transported freely and seemed to be in no hurry to set up a contract. He requested that no further traffic from this firm be accepted. He would let us know if and when a contract with the firm came into force. We complied with his request and nothing further was heard from the firm.

Another incident involved the 2120 Dover to Paddock Wood. Every night this train was ready to leave an hour early and provided there were no problems we were happy to let it. So it was all one week when I was late turn. But on the Friday of that week we had a fatality. I cannot remember whether it was a suicide or an accident. I had at that time, a new Assistant Controller, and this was his first such incident. He was a very sensitive man and it really upset him. That night, he took a request from the Guard of the 2120 Dover to Paddock Wood to run early. He asked me, and I declined it because the service was running late after the fatal incident.

When he told the guard, he was given a load of abuse. This was quite unusual, because we got on well with most traincrew.

I instructed Dover Town Yard and Archcliffe Junction Signal Box not to let the train out before time. The Guard then telephoned me and started to give me a load of verbal abuse. I told him very firmly that the train would not run before time at all in future if this were the way he behaved.

He then told me he was a Tonbridge Guard and on the next (Saturday) night, he was working a ballast train to Hither Green. If that train were late, he would not take it beyond Tonbridge. Saturday night came and the ballast train was approximately ten minutes late. The Guard telephoned me, reminded me of our previous conversation, and told me he would not take the train beyond Tonbridge.

I politely said, 'Thank you,' and the conversation ended.

I spoke to my colleague on Area Four, advised him of what had transpired, and suggested that he would not want the train in Tonbridge West Yard. He agreed. I then arranged with Ashford Yard and the Locomotive Controller, for the train to terminate at Ashford.

When the train had gone into Ashford Yard, the Guard again telephoned me, demanding to know why I had terminated the train there.

I reminded him that he had advised me that he was not prepared to work the train beyond Tonbridge. We had no-one else who could work the train forward. I said the train could not be accommodated at Tonbridge, so I had terminated it at Ashford.

He then demanded to know how he was going to get back

to Tonbridge. I pointed out that it was a fine night and asked him if he needed directions to the A2O main road. At this he slammed the phone down. Seconds later he had rung the Guards Controller and I could hear him shouting from across the room about 'some tin pot god.'

Fred, the Guards Controller, referred the matter to the D.C.C. and Geoff came to see what had happened. I told him. He was not pleased but he decided he could not argue with the decision. To my chagrin, Doug, the Ashford Motive Power Foreman found the guard a locomotive on which he could travel to Tonbridge.

We had only one notable freight incident at Lenham. The siding there was on a curve. The motor company who were our customers there, were warned not to park the cars too close to the track because of the overhang on the bogie carflats. One day they got it wrong. The class 33 locomotive propelled the wagons into the sidings as normal. One car was parked too close. The leading wagon 'collected' the car, which then, one by one, shunted twenty-nine other brand new cars. The locomotive was fitted with a booster system that overcame the extra weight, and the traincrew were not aware of the incident until they came to a stand.

There was quite a conversation with the customers about the thirty written off brand new cars, but in the end, they accepted that it was their responsibility.

We had one incident at Dover with similar consequences but in this incident the cause was different. The 2238 Knowle and Dorridge to Dover ran most weeknights with twenty double deck carflats loaded with BLMC cars for export. They were strictly instructed that vans, Range Rovers and Land Rovers had to loaded on the lower decks and only saloon cars were to be loaded on the upper decks. The train ran regularly and trouble free most nights of the week.

Then, early one morning, as the train neared its destination at Dover, two things happened almost simultaneously. Canterbury Electrical Control telephoned to say there had been a series of short circuits in Shakespeare Tunnel as the train passed through it. The train, diesel hauled, had continued unaffected.

Then Dover Town shunter rang in. I quote his words. 'I don't believe what I am seeing. The car train has just arrived with forty Range Rovers on the top deck, and they are all convertibles!'

I asked him what he meant.

He told me that forty Range Rovers had been loaded on the top deck, and all their rooves had been smashed off! Forty brand new Range Rovers had been written off without turning a wheel! The train had travelled without incident from Birmingham to Folkestone with the incorrectly loaded Range Rovers. But just before Dover, it had to negotiate Shakespeare single bore tunnel.

Thankfully staff acted very quickly, and the debris was cleared from the tunnel in time for the morning service. But I would like to have seen the insurance claim for the incident!

As I have said before, I always enjoyed going out and meeting the staff I worked with, but one particular visit, not to railway staff, but to the staff who controlled the harbour, was particularly memorable. It is a slight divergence from the railway but there were some fascinating parallels in the way we worked, and I think reader, that you too will be interested.

An exchange visit had been arranged by another Controller to Dover Harbour Control. This establishment is located along, and near the end of the eastern arm of Dover Harbour. Its purpose is to monitor and control all movements in the harbour and all movements crossing the harbour entrances.

It is permanently manned by two members of staff, twenty-four hours a day, seven days a week. It works with the H.M. Channel Control that controls the flow of ships through the English Channel and which is situated in the cliffs above the harbour. The Harbour Control liaises by radio with all ships entering or leaving the harbour and any vessel planning to cross the entrances.

The system of Control is as follows. In either direction from east or west, there is a four mile limit. All ships or craft on reaching this point, must radio in for permission to proceed. If given that permission, they can proceed to the one mile limit. There they must radio in again and not proceed until given permission. This is to protect and keep safe the busy exits from the harbour.

Unlike land vehicles, ships cannot stop easily. All instructions and messages are recorded on a computer in the Control, and by a backup computer that repeats the process. The Harbour Control also strictly regulates each of the berths in the harbour. Any ship delayed in departure can incur for its company charges levied at I believe approximately five hundred pounds a minute.

It is extremely expensive and very inconvenient for motorists queuing for a ferry, to have to be transferred to another berthing park. All this responsibility falls to the Harbour Control.

On the morning that several of us visited the Harbour Control, all was going smoothly. Then – it happened. A ship named 'Tender Carrier' did not stop at the four mile limit. In vain did the Controller try to contact the ship on the radio. A fully laden ferry was about to depart and the 'Tender Carrier' was on course to cross the harbour exit. Repeatedly the Controller called the ship. No response came from the ship's radio operator, and the ship continued to approach the harbour exit. Despite every effort by the Controller the ship continued on its way. Then it passed the one mile limit without stopping. The ferry had now moved out of the berth and was heading for the exit.

There was now a very real possibility of a collision. The Controller radioed the ferry captain and ordered a full 360' turn. This it did and as it did so, the 'Tender Carrier' crossed the harbour exit. Once it had completed its turn, the ferry was cleared to proceed. The 'Tender Carrier' finally stopped clear of both harbour entrances and the radio operator came on the air. 'Tender Carrier calling Dover. Have you been trying to contact us?' The seriousness of their offence, and the possible consequences, was explained to them.

Then the Controller turned to us and said, 'Well, at least it's all recorded on the computer.' Then he gave a cry of dismay, 'Oh. The computer has gone down. Thank goodness we have a backup.' Then an even deeper cry of dismay, 'Oh no. The backup computer has gone down as well!' There was no record of the 'signal passed at danger' by the 'Tender Carrier.'

Suddenly all my colleagues were looking at me. 'What!' I exclaimed.

'It's you. It's your influence that's done this. You've done it again!'

'It's nothing to do with me,' I replied. 'I was just here when it happened.' Needless to say, the story was quickly relayed to Beckenham Control and I was received the next day with much hilarity. But who would have thought that we should experience a signal passed at danger at sea!

Punctuality in relieving your colleagues was treated very seriously in the Control, just as it was in signal boxes. Yet sometimes the most conscientious person suffers from circumstances that are totally beyond his control. I suffered from some of those circumstances.

Because Beckenham was easy to get to by car, it was tempting sometimes to drive up. One week of night duty, I was driving up. It was a week of pouring rain. On Tuesday night, Geoff arrived soaking wet, having had to wait for a late running bus. I offered to pick him up on Wednesday night, an offer he willingly accepted.

That night I had one of the worst runs ever. I got behind slow moving vehicles all the way from Tonbridge to the bypass. Then there was a fifty mph restriction on the bypass. Every traffic light was against me as I drove into south London. I finally pulled up at the bus stop fifteen minutes later than planned, where a rain soaked Geoff was still waiting. As I pulled up a bus pulled in front of me and stopped and another bus pulled in behind me and blocked me in. There we had to sit until they decided to move. I could only apologise and explain that the journey had been like this all the way. I don't think the soaked Geoff appreciated this. He declined a lift home in the morning.

On another occasion, coming in for late turn, I had cut things extremely fine and I was travelling at slightly more than the stipulated speed restriction as I turned into the road outside the Offices. As I approached the entrance to the car park, an elderly man drove out right in front of me from a turning on the left. I knew I would hit his car. I had a split second to realise that if I ran head on into him I would injure him. I therefore swung the car sideways so we hit each other side on, destroying the new offside wing that I had recently had fitted.

We got out, and thankfully my tactic had paid off, because he wasn't injured. As we stood there exchanging details, Brian, the early turn D.C.C, who had just come off duty, and who was known for his dry sense of humour, came over and said, in his broad northern accent, 'Hello mate. Shall I tell them you'll be a bit late mate?'

There was also the embarrassing incident of the Boxing Day and official Boxing Day. I was rostered early turn for the actual Boxing Day and the official Boxing Day. Ivan, who was rostered to be the D.C.C. on both occasions, lived on the outskirts of Pembury, a nearby village. He offered to authorise my being paid for my petrol for both days, if I would pick him up. I would have agreed anyway but the payment was a welcome bonus.

On Boxing Day morning, I got up, at 5 am as usual, did my packing and had my breakfast, then went upstairs to put some shoes on. I sat on the bed to do this – and simply fell asleep. I had no notion of going to sleep. It just happened. When I woke up half an hour later, I immediately realised what had happened, ran downstairs, grabbed my gear, ran to the car and drove as fast as I could to pick Ivan up. We made up time on the run in but I was still twenty minutes late, and worst still, so was Ivan. I promised faithfully to do better the next day.

So to the next day. I got up at 4.30 am just to be sure. I took my shoes downstairs. I did my packing, had an early breakfast, then just before leaving, slipped upstairs for something, sat on the bed – and I was gone. Half an hour later I woke up.

'Not again!' I thought as I raced downstairs. I opened the front door, but couldn't close it. During the night it had snowed and the door was swollen and would not close. I yanked hard. The door closed but the doorknocker came off in my hand. I shoved it through the letterbox and ran to the car. I drove as fast as I dared to Pembury.

There, on the junction with the Tunbridge Wells Road, stood this pillar of snow. He had come to the main road because his side road was frozen over. I turned the wheel of the car, my big old Morris Oxford estate, on the frozen road the car ignored the steering and carried straight on. Gingerly I set back and turned until I was alongside him. He never said a word until we reached Bromley! Once again, we were both late on duty.

But by far the most bizarre incident had it's beginning on the late turn Saturday of the previous week. I had been late turn, and it had not been a good late turn. I had just come in and sat down when the doorbell went. Going to the door, I was surprised to find the people who lived in the flat below, wearing their pyjamas, standing on the doorstep.

They were a lovely elderly couple and very good neighbours, but they were normally abed by this time. The man apologised for disturbing me and asked if I had any trouble.

I said I'd been in trouble all afternoon but had only just got home.

He said, 'Well we've got trouble downstairs. We've been flooded out. We wondered if you'd gone off and left the bath running or something.'

I assured them that I was careful to make sure everything

was turned off before I went to work, and invited them in, and together we looked around the flat. The kitchen and bathroom were fine, and they said perhaps the water had come from the flat roof above. Just before they left, I suggested we check the boiler. I opened the door of the boiler and airing cupboard.

At once the cause of the problem was found. The boiler had sprung a leak in the bottom and fourteen gallons of boiling water had gone downstairs into their airing cupboard. On top of a pile of freshly ironed bedclothes lay a beautiful royal blue candlewick bedspread. They now had psychedelic blue pillow-cases and sheets.

I apologised profusely and offered to pay for the damage, but they graciously declined, saying they were insured, and their only concern had been that I was alright. I rang the emergency number and an engineer promised to be with me on Monday morning. I went to work on Sunday night, and the engineer was very prompt arriving on Monday morning, complete with the new boiler to install.

Although I was tired, I couldn't sleep with him working so I got on with some paperwork. At lunchtime he poked his head round the door and said, 'Well that's it now.'

Surprised I said, 'What, all finished?'

'Oh no,' he said, 'I've got the old boiler out. I'll be back this afternoon to put the new one in.'

'What am I going to do about sleep?' I wondered.

The phone rang. It was my brother-in-law Pete, who was going to leave a message for me on the answerphone. I was surprised he was home, but it turned out he was off work with a heavy cold. Quickly I explained the situation and my need of sleep before I went back on duty. Very kindly, he offered to come over and house sit while I got some sleep, an offer that I gratefully accepted. He came and I duly went to bed. I slept well and never heard a thing.

When I got up, the new boiler had been installed and was working. Pete had even tidied up before he left, sensibly locking the door behind him. I got up, did my packing and had a late tea, before setting off at my normal time. At least I had intended to set off. But I then discovered I was locked in.

When the flats in Whitelake Road were built, they were designed for elderly people, and the doors had locks only on the outside. This was to prevent elderly people from locking themselves in. I knew this of course, but being so tired I completely forgot to tell Pete, who had locked the door on his way out. Although my sister and Pete had a key, they lived about thirty minutes away. I was on the second floor with no other exit.

I telephoned a nearby friend and asked her to come to the base of the flats below my window so I could throw my key down, so that she could come up and let me out. Being a very quick-minded friend, she grasped the situation and wasted no time in getting round and releasing me. While I was waiting, I rang the Control to tell them that I was locked in my own flat, waiting for a friend to come and let me out. Needless to say, no-one believed this, and the news was greeted with derision. I was late, had missed my train and had to drive up, even then arriving late for duty. I told a friend about this and he fitted a proper lock on the door for me.

About six months later, a colleague from the Control visited me, and I showed him the old lock. 'So you really were locked in your own flat!' he exclaimed.

'Yes,' I said, 'so now will you tell the other disbelieving so and so's for me!'

We had very little real aggression to deal with, certainly not on Area Three at any rate. As I have said before, they were professional people who really took a pride in their job. Tempers did flare sometimes in the Control, when we were all working under pressure and sometimes seconds counted in making the right decisions.

I now had another new Assistant. His name was Jim. Jim was quite a character. He was a very big man with a moustache and a thick beard. He very quickly learned the job. He was also a wizard at mental arithmetic.

Ted, our stats and telex clerk, used a calculator to complete the day's statistics. Jim reckoned he could do it quicker in his head. One night a bet was arranged. Jim and Ted were given identical lists of columns of three figure numbers to add up. Ted was fast, but Jim was faster! And his accuracy was one hundred percent.

But, just now and then, on night duty, Jim would come on duty in a mood. Then he would not speak to anyone and would sit staring into space. Nobody, me included, wanted to challenge him when he was like this. One night this was the case. Suddenly several phones started to ring at the same time. I took one, and then another. Jim sat motionless. 'Come on Jim,' I said, 'You take this one and I will take the other.'

Jim still sat motionless and grunted something. I took the calls and then said, 'Jim, if you've got something to say, say it. Don't just sit there mumbling.'

Up Jim came, like a rocket, out of his chair, his big fists clenched. We stood there, face to face. The whole Control fell quiet. It was like some scene out of 'Gunfight at the OK

Corral.' I, for one, was scared witless. 'This is where I get smeared all around the room,' I thought.

Yet I knew I had to face him out. If I didn't, I would have 'lost it' with him. For some moments we stood facing each other. Then suddenly Jim burst out laughing and said, 'You're too nice a guy to hit!' With that he sat down and got on with the job. The whole Control breathed a collective sigh of relief.

After that Jim and I got on like the proverbial house on fire. Jim shared with me his love of Harley Davidson motorbikes, and I saw my first photograph of the Harley Electraglide. When much later, I actually saw one in a showroom, I could see his point. Jim also introduced me to the Spike Milligan books on the Second World War, written with his (Spike's) own madcap sense of humour. They appealed to my sense of humour enormously, and during quiet moments on the night shift on the panel, reading them, tears of laughter would quite literally run down my cheeks.

In the Control, we were not supposed to receive or make personal calls except in an emergency. I had two such calls. The first came one Saturday Night. It was my sister calling to say that our Mum, who had been very ill, had been rushed into hospital at 3 am. We both knew this was the beginning of the end for her.

Ivan was the D.C.C. that night. He came over and asked if I wanted to be relieved immediately to go home. I was very grateful for that. But I could not see that I could achieve anything by going home early. My sister was at home and Mum was in good hands in the hospital, and it would leave the shift a man short. I thanked him, and said I would see the shift out, but I would not be returning for duty for the immediate future.

He understood and authorised me to be on leave for as long as I needed.

I got home and got all the information from my sister, and we supported each other. Our Mum died a week later. Another week passed as we made all the necessary arrangements. Then came the funeral. After that, and once I was sure my sister was alright, I returned to work. My colleagues were really good. No fuss was made but they were all supportive. I could not have asked for more.

The second call could not have been more different. Again I was on night duty. My sister, now married, was expecting their first child. She was in hospital. The baby was overdue and the birth was imminent. It was the 24th October 1978. I had to leave for work at 7.30 pm, and at that time there was no news. I rang just before I left home. I got into work and took over the panel at 9.15 pm. I asked if there had been any calls for me. No, there hadn't. I settled into the night routine as best I could.

Then, at about eighteen minutes past ten, the 'National' phone light started to flash. 'Call for Terry on the national,' called out the D.C.C.

I took it. It was Pete, my brother in law, who told me I had become an Uncle. I had a lovely niece, and both mother and baby were doing well!' I took the details down on my Incident Pad, and I still have that piece of paper today. For the rest of that night I was ecstatic! Point failure? Never mind. Train failure? We can deal with that.

A few days later, still on night duty, I was home in time to meet my sister coming home from hospital with my very new little niece.

It was maybe a year later. I was coming home off night duty

and was standing on the platform at Orpington, waiting for the train to Tonbridge. Suddenly I became aware of an old man on the platform. He was very obviously inebriated. 'How could you get drunk at half past seven in the morning,' I thought, feeling very annoyed.

Then he swayed up to me, grinned at me and said, 'I've just become a granddad!'

My annoyance vanished in a flash. I knew just how he felt. I congratulated him. I also guided him to a place of safety, before catching my train home.

One of the many responsibilities of Area Controllers was the relief of signalmen out of office hours, for example, evenings, overnight and at weekends. At the end of each weekday the Staff Relief people would bring in two books. One was the Competency Book, which contained the names of the relief signalmen, and the names of the signal boxes they were passed competent to work, and the other, equally important, was the Roster book, showing what duty each signalman was on.

One morning the signalman at Buckland Junction, outside Dover Priory informed me at 0615 a.m, that his relief had not turned up. I found that he had been on duty for 12 hours. Buckland Junction was a critical box for the train service. I assured him I would find a relief for him a quickly as possible. I asked if he would like someone to stay with him in the signal box until he was relieved. This was an acceptable procedure, provided that the signalman felt fit enough and was willing to stay on duty, pending relief.

He agreed to carry on working the signal box. I got a member of staff to go to the signal box, and I also arranged for the man to take a hot pie, sandwiches and a hot drink from the station buffet. When asked who was going to pay for this, I told him to get the Supervisor to take it out of the petty cash. I was not sure if I had the authority to do this, but everybody agreed it was a good idea. The signalman really appreciated this, and the signal box remained open for traffic. The other Controllers thought this was hilarious and I got the nickname of being 'the pork pie controller!'

The 0310 Victoria to Ramsgate and Dover Priory newspaper train featured in a number of incidents, the first one being an incredible escape from disaster. Again I was on night duty and the incident occurred in Area Three. As I have said before, we were accountable for every minute of delay to these trains.

On this night the train brakes suddenly came on, bringing the train to a stand between Newington and Sittingbourne. The guard went back to examine the train to find the cause. What he found was that the rear brake hose had come off of its 'dummy,' causing the train brakes to apply. He also found that the tail lamp was missing.

Using his initiative, he replaced the brake pipe on the dummy, and put his Bardic lamp on the bracket to act as a tail lamp. The guard then re-joined his train and after a satisfactory brake test, the train continued on its way. The incident and the number of the vehicle concerned were reported back to me, and I arranged for Carriage and Wagon staff to examine the vehicle further at Dover Priory.

At Faversham, the train was divided as booked. The front portion went forward to Ramsgate and the rear portion went to Dover Priory. All was well, until Dover Priory advised us that they were one van short. The obvious conclusion was that the train had been wrongly split at Faversham and the missing van had gone to Ramsgate.

I contacted Ramsgate, but they assured me that they had only the correct number of vehicles. I asked Dover Priory staff to check that they hadn't made a mistake. No, they assured me, they were still one vehicle short.

Geoff, my D.C.C. was now interested, as was the Regional Control at Waterloo and the Newspaper Association. Geoff suggested I contact Margate to see if they for any reason had detached a vehicle and not told us.

No, Margate assured me that the train had passed without incident. Finally, I went back to Ramsgate to ask them to double check that they hadn't got the missing van.

While this was all going on, the next train came down over the section between Newington and Sittingbourne. It was the 0435 Hither Green Continental to Dover Ferry, running at full speed with a train of long wheel-based four wheeled ferry vans. It passed without incident.

The mystery seemed impossible but could not be resolved. Then suddenly two things happened. By now it was early morning and with daylight an alarming discovery was made. The driver of the first down passenger train stopped it in section between Newington and Sittingbourne and he reported strong evidence of a serious derailment. A large number of sleepers on the track ahead were smashed, although the running and conductor rails appeared to be in place. The train was brought over the section with extreme caution, making it safely, and the line was then blocked.

P. Way staff were soon on their way, and they confirmed that there had indeed been a derailment. They also confirmed that the up line was clear and not affected by the derailment.

At the same time, Kent Police contacted us to say that a farmer at Sittingbourne had reported to them that there was a railway van upside down in his orchard, and what were 'we' going to do about it!

The mystery was resolved, but what an incredible incident. The rear vehicle on the train had become derailed 'all wheels' between Newington and Sittingbourne and had run like that without activating the track circuits, until it came to a check rail. This it had struck at speed and with such force that the couplings had parted, and amazingly the train brake pipe had also parted just at the point where it was coupled to the train pipe on the next vehicle. The derailed vehicle had then somer-saulted up the embankment and finished up, upside down, in the farmer's orchard.

At no time was the conductor rail affected and the track circuits had all cleared as normal after the passage of the train. Thankfully the guard was not travelling in that vehicle. Also thankfully the 0435 Hither Green to Dover Ferry had passed over the damaged track at full speed without incident. The truth really is sometimes stranger than fiction. My relief arrived as the arrangements for the emergency passenger service were being made. By the time I came back on duty the incident had been cleared up, although trains were still running very late as a result of the disruption.

The other incident involving the 0310 Victoria to Ramsgate and Dover also occurred in Area Three when I was on duty. As the train passed Rainham the signalman there, a friend of mine as it happened, reported a possible fire on one of the vehicles. At that time, we in the Control had devised a system of making sure we kept alert during the quiet period on night duty by playing a collection of board games. I was very competitive and determined to win. This particular board game involved a 'Do or Die' card, which, if it looked as if you were going to lose, you could play. It was victory or sudden death. As I was playing the game, my Assistant took the first call from Rainham and called my attention.

Without hesitation I played my 'Do or Die' card (which incidentally won me the game) and hurried straight to the panel to take charge of the incident.

Normally a fire on one of these trains involved a hot axle box on one of the aging vehicles. Not this time! Whatever was the cause of the blaze this vehicle was well alight. The signalman stopped it on the down main line at Newington. Traction current was discharged all lines and the Kent Fire Brigade were summoned.

The van, complete with its consignment of newspapers, was completely gutted right down to floor level. To their credit, the train crew had detached the burning vehicle from the front portion of the train, and after examination the rest of the train was allowed to continue its journey. The rear portion remained trapped and was eventually cleared.

After attention from the Carriage & Wagon staff, the burnt out vehicle was also removed. Geoff, the D.C.C. had another terse conversation with Regional Control.

Another of the characters that I worked with was Ted. Modernisation was slowly catching up with the Control. Hitherto we had to use telephones to advise out our plans for the service. Now suddenly we had a teleprinter. It sat in the corner of the room. Each shift had one man dedicated to operating it. Our man was Ted. He was a short, stocky man, of indeterminate age. On night duty he did he daily statistics fir HQ as well, but on early and late turn his primary responsibility was to the teleprinter.

It was a marvellous improvement. Now all we had to do to send out Circular Twenties (the all Division messages concerning disruption to the service) was to tell Ted. Soon, individual train delays and alterations to the service were going out on the teleprinter. It left the Controllers free to take and deal with incoming calls, and often the cry, 'Telex,' would ring out and Ted would come over with his clipboard and take the messages to be transmitted.

Ted himself was an interesting character. He knew Central London like the back of his hand. He had worked, I believe, as a shunter at Blackfriars during the Second World War and he knew all about the blitz. When it was quiet, he would regale us with stories of the intensive bombing, and how the track engineers would be out as soon as a raid was over, filling in bomb craters, and relaying the track in record time. Twelve hour shifts were common and many men worked eighteen hours a day, only to come back the next day and have to restart all over again.

Ted was also the only man I knew who had actually worked Bricklayers Arms Depot. That was a fascinating yard with connections to the South Eastern via North Kent East Signal Box, on the main line to London Bridge, and North Kent West Box. That was the only double track section I had ever known of which still worked Permissive Block between the two signal boxes.

There was also a connection from Bricklayers Arms to the

Central Division. The yard was laid out like a gigantic fish bone with a main line and lots of short sidings off. Names like Rotherhythe New Road and Mercers Crossing became familiar to us. There was also a railway crane repair depot.

Way back in my early days as Assistant Controller on South Eastern Area One, I had dealt with an amusing incident In Bricklayers Arms. It was 6 am, and I had one hour to go before relief. The early turn shunter at Bricklayers Arms came on the phone to report a buffer stop collision. It involved a 'Queen Mary' brakevan. These were fifty-ton bogie brake-vans designed especially for working unfitted goods trains over the steeply graded South Eastern main line. They were called 'Queen Mary's' because of the extreme length of the vehicles and because that length caused them to sway gently from side to side when crossing over junctions.

I asked what damage had been done to the buffer stops.

He said, 'There are no buffer stops. It's not so much gone over them as gone through them.'

I asked, 'Where is it now?'

The reply was, 'It's the other side of where the buffer stops used to be!'

I said, 'Thank you very much.'

'There's one more thing you ought to know,' he said.

I asked what that was.

He replied, 'It's on its side!'

I asked him when it had happened.

'Don't know,' he replied, 'The night turn never heard a thing.'

One day after early turn, Ted took us down into Bricklayers Arms. Much of it was closed now. But we were able to see some of the sidings. Then Ted took us somewhere I have never seen since.

Walking back on the roads in the direction of Borough Market, we were on a very busy thoroughfare. Then Ted led us down a side turning and then another.

Suddenly we could no longer hear the roar of the traffic and we seemed, from the buildings either side of the street, to have been transported back into 'Charles Dickens times.' Even the lampposts were old. It was quiet and you almost expected to see a horse drawn hansom cab come round the corner. It was quite weird. I have walked that area since, but I've never seen that road again.

Now the signal boxes at North Kent East and North Kent West, and Bricklayers Arms Depot have long been closed. In the last two years, 2009 – 2011, the tracks, which were still visible from a train on the main line, have been lifted to make way for new lines.

Back to Area Three and the Isle of Sheppey with its line from Sittingbourne to Sheerness via Kemsley and Queenborough. In Victorian times this line was envisaged to become a tourist line to the coast, and a terminus was built and named Port Victoria. This never flourished and only the island platform station remains.

But the line did have some points of interest, the first being Kingsferry Bridge. This linked the Island with the mainland, and it was the only link! It was lifted to allow ships to proceed down the River Medway to the estuary and the open sea. Ships sailed on the favourable tides and once a ship had set sail, the bridge had to be raised. The ship could not stop. It mattered not that it might be the height of the rush hour. The authorities would ring us and tell us of the impending bridge lift and all traffic would stop.

Normally we would institute road services when a line was blocked, but there was one other peculiarity, in that this bridge also carried the main road onto the Island. Once the bridge was up, they were literally cut off. Normally, bridge lifts were very infrequent and the time it took to pass a ship was a matter of minutes.

But one day the bridge mechanism failed with the bridge in the raised position. On reflection it was as well it failed in the raised position. I don't exactly know how you would stop a ship on the move if the bridge failed in the lowered position.

But fail it did, and the Island was cut off. The service was suspended. The lift engineers were very efficient. They quickly got to site and as quickly repaired the bridge. The service was then restored. Yes, I have to admit that I was the Controller on Area Three when this happened. Once again came the phrase, 'It was nothing to do with me. I was just there when it happened!' I was to use that phrase quite often.

Another incident, which did involve me, occurred in Queenborough Yard. Had I not experienced it for myself I would have found it difficult to believe that in so densely a populated county as Kent, that there could be such a bleak and desolate place. The ground stretched without feature to the horizon. The sun was not able to penetrate the dense low cloud that day and a bitter wind blew straight off of the North Sea.

Nevertheless I was enjoying myself. I had been given the opportunity of having a ride in a brake-van, hauled by a class 73 locomotive to the Queenborough Iron and Steel Works. The guard talked about his background, and then asked me about mine.

When I told him I came from Control, he said, 'Oh, you're just a pencil pusher eh!' Then he said, 'You wind on the hand-brake, while I go and couple up.'

I said nothing, but as soon as he left the brake-van, I thought, 'I'll give you pencil pusher!' I wound the handbrake wheel on hard. Then I took the brake stick, inserted it between the spokes of the wheel and walked round the walls of that brake van, levering the handbrake very tightly on indeed.

When I had got the handbrake on as hard as I could, I replaced the brake stick in its normal place and strolled out onto the veranda to watch the coupling up. The siding we were on was straight for half the length of the train, then it curved in a great arc to the left. The locomotive had been coupled and was slowly reversing from left to right in front of me. I thought, 'That's real power !' as the electro-diesel moved the wagons slowly back.

Then another, more alarming thought occurred as I realised, 'Hang on, I'm on the end of that lot!' I raced back into the brake-van and just had time to grasp the grab handles before the impact hit me and catapulted the brake-van backwards.

The impact of the shunt actually wound the handbrake on even tighter. Presently I saw the guard strolling back. He heaved himself up into the brake-van and with a little smirk, reached out to turn the brake wheel to release the brakes. The smirk vanished when he found he couldn't move the wheel at all.

'Need a hand?' I asked him innocently. In fact, it took our combined efforts eventually to release that handbrake! On the way back we chatted some more, but the words, 'pencil pusher' were never heard again.

One morning I was on Area Three, when Area One announced that a derailment had occurred at Hayes. It was just one pair of wheels on a set of 8 EPB stock in the sidings, nothing dramatic, but because of its position, the decision was taken that the Hither Green 45 ton crane would attend. I asked the man in charge of rerailing if I could go and watch it when I had been relieved, and he agreed.

Hayes was a very short distance by road from Beckenham and I was soon on the scene. Time to introduce another of the wonderful characters that I worked with. Mr Alan B was the Chief Mechanical Engineer. He had decided to supervise the rerailing himself. Mr B was an expert at his job. His judgements were faultless, and his knowledge of his job was incredible. His staff had absolute faith in him, and as I watched, I could see why.

Holding the radio, which communicated with the crane operator in one hand, and his magnificent brightly polished pipe in the other, he was concentrating on the job, and directing the operator. Yet he still found time to explain to me all that was happening. How for instance, seat cushions were taken from the coaches and inserted between the bodywork and the hauling chains running from the spreader beam high above, to cushion and protect the paintwork on the body sides of the coach.

He explained that once the train had derailed, before any rerailing could be attempted, the coach was examined for any damage done by the derailment. After the coach had been re-railed, the same inspector would once again inspect the bodywork to see if any damage had occurred during the rerailing. If he found any further damage, it would be billed to the

Carriage, Mechanical, and Electrical Engineers (C.M.& E.E) of which Mr B was the head.

I saw the final lift. The carriage rose gently into the air and hovered over the track. The Permanent Way Engineer had examined that track, both for the cause of the derailment and to ensure it was safe for the train to be re-railed. The track was pronounced safe and slowly the coach was lowered. The bogie hovered above the track, while final adjustments to its downward course were made by a group of men manoeuvring the bogie to line it up for the track. When they were satisfied, the signal was given, and the carriage was gently lowered and the wheels of the bogie dropped gently onto the track. The job was done.

The lifting gear was unfastened and the crane, self- propelled, moved slowly away. Its jib was still raised and at one point it overhung the boundary wall of the siding. It was Mr B who saw the lamp post. 'Crane driver stop!' he yelled into the radio. The crane kept moving. 'Crane driver stop!' he repeated, with urgency in his voice. As he repeated the command in an even louder voice the crane jib struck the lamp post with a dull 'clunk,' The lamp post disappeared from view behind the wall. Mr B turned back to me grinning, and with a shrug of his shoulders he said, 'Oh well, they'll never believe that lamp post was hit by a train!'

Sometimes the smallest railway vehicles caused problems, but none caused so much disruption and dismay as the incident with the Wickham Trolley at Folkestone, which became 'the Wickham Trolley Disaster of '78!'

Wickham Trolleys were little vehicles very much used by Permanent Way staff to transport men and materials to and from engineering work sites. They were of much lower height than standard railway vehicles.

For example, they had two windows in the front where the trolley was driven from, but these windows only came up to the level of the buffers on standard locomotives. They could tow another flat trolley, but usually not more than one. They could only travel at a maximum speed of twenty miles per hour. They were popular because they were a much cheaper alternative than a fully-fledged engineering train hauled by a locomotive.

Also they provided a limited sheltered conveyance for the men, who had to work mainly at night and in all weathers.

Just occasionally they had to go to Stewarts Lane for maintenance. This was one such occasion. Obviously a vehicle that can only attain twenty miles per hour running on a busy main line with passenger trains running at ninety miles per hour and very fast fully fitted freight train, and Royal Mail trains, has to be very carefully timetabled and given a specific pathway between passing points.

On this occasion the pathway was 2120 Folkestone East to Stewarts Lane, following the last up service from Ramsgate to Charing Cross, and waiting at Ashford, the first passing point for the passage of the 2240 Dover Priory to London Bridge Royal Mail Travelling Post Office and the 2320 Dover to Knowle and Dorridge (Birmingham) Car Train, with twenty double deck bogie carflats and travelling at around sixty miles per hour.

Everyone was aware that this Wickham Trolley must have a punctual start to enable it to reach Ashford ahead of the two fast trains.

The Wickham Trolley departed Folkestone East at exactly 2120. It was travelling well until suddenly it failed between Sandling and Westenhanger. The crew reported that it had run out of fuel. This was a source of some annoyance because everyone had been made aware of the importance of time keeping. Jerry cans were quickly filled with diesel and loaded on a class 33 locomotive at Ashford. This locomotive ran light engine on the down line, coming to a stand opposite the trolley.

Very quickly the first jerry can of diesel fuel was emptied into the fuel tank on the trolley. The crew were emptying the second jerry can, when someone using a lamp, noticed a dark stain spreading on the ballast. Investigation confirmed their worst fears. In running, the trolley had run over some high ballast and one end of the fuel pipe had been knocked off. That explained why it had run out of fuel! The vehicle was completely immobile. The up line was blocked.

The engineers at Maintrol (Southern House Maintenance Control) conferred with each other, and with us. A new pipe would have to be fitted. The problem was that this could not be done on site because the vehicle was too low to the ground. It would have to go over a pit in a depot. The problem with that was how to get it there.

My Deputy Chief Controller (D.C.C) suggested a length of chain being attached, and having the vehicle towed at walking pace to Ashford. I pointed out the obvious problem that the vehicle was not compatible with any locomotive and should the locomotive have to stop suddenly the buffers of the locomotive would go straight through the driving window on the trolley.

The next scheme Maintrol came up with was to get the Ashford Breakdown Crane out and lift the trolley onto the side of the track. The Permanent Way staff said that was not possible because at the location of the failure, there was nowhere to put it.

Meanwhile the 2240 Dover Priory – London Bridge Royal Mail Travelling Post Office, with national connections from London, was being delayed. It was decided to divert the train via Deal, Minster and Canterbury West. This was not as easy as it sounded because Martin Mill, Deal and Sandwich signal boxes had switched out and closed. Now we had to find from the Staff Relief books, three signalmen who were both competent and available to open the three signal boxes. This was eventually accomplished, and the heavily delayed train was at last on its way.

The 2324 Dover to Knowle and Dorridge was a different problem. The train was formed up in Dover Western Docks station, which has platforms for trains going via Ashford and platforms for going via the Chatham main line. As it was booked via Ashford, it had been formed up in the appropriate platforms. As the line via Ashford was now blocked, the twenty bogie carflats had to be shunted out of the South Eastern platforms, via Archcliffe and Hawkesbury Street Junction signal boxes and back into the Chatham side platforms before being diverted via Chatham. This train was also heavily delayed.

Meanwhile, back at the site of the failure, frantic discussions about how to resolve the problem were continuing. My D.C.C was getting more and more frustrated. It was beginning to look as if single line working would have to be instituted between Folkestone West and Ashford.

Finally at about 3 am, Maintrol came back to us, very

apologetically, to say the only feasible solution was to send a locomotive wrong line from Ashford, attach a thirty feet length of chain, and tow the trolley to Ashford at walking pace. When my D.C.C. heard this, he struck sparks from the carpet as he strode over to me and said viciously, 'I told you to do that five hours ago!!'

The wheels, quite literally, were set in motion. A Class 33 locomotive ran under extreme caution 'wrong line' from Ashford to the site. A thirty feet length of chain was attached and the ensemble then moved at walking pace back to Ashford, arriving there just in time to clear the line for the first up morning train, the 0508 from Dover Priory to Charing Cross. Thus ended the saga that became known as 'The Wickham Trolley Disaster of '78!'

I really enjoyed my five years on Area Three and from the staff on the Area I learned so much about the operations side of the railway. I wanted to take all that experience and use it on the other areas, - and of course, I was looking for promotion. The opportunity came suddenly, and sooner than I had expected.

Chapter Nine - The General Purpose Relief (GPR) Controller Grade C

General Purpose Relief (GPR) and Rest Day Relief (RDR) Grade 'C'

Rolling Stock Control

A Grade 'C' Post became a vacancy when its occupant was promoted to the Rest Day Relief (RDR) Controller Grade 'C'. Not too many people were keen to take the job. In those days, GPR staff could have their duties changed at twelve hours' notice, which played havoc with their social life, and in the summer months they would often find themselves on night duty for several consecutive weeks as their colleagues chose their Annual Leave when they should have been on night duty.

They also had to go to whichever Grade 'C' panel they were sent to, so there was little continuity.

I began to spend some spare time learning about the Grade 'C' panels, looking at the paperwork and talking to the Controllers. From 18th April 1979, when the vacancy first occurred, I began covering the Grade 'C' GPR, at the higher rate of pay.

I was based mainly on the Rolling Stock Panel to begin with, after a short period of learning. When the vacancy was advertised I applied for the job on a permanent basis.

On June 4th, I was accorded an interview. Ron C, the Chief Controller took it, along with a member of the Staff Office. I was warned about the unpredictability of shifts and panels in the GPR position, which I accepted.

On June 11th 1979, my appointment was confirmed. I was given seniority back dated to April 18th. And so, quite literally, a new chapter began in my career, and begins in this book.

"The Doc" and the professional telling off was one of my abiding memories of this early time in my career as a grade 'C' Controller. I had had a very brief spell of learning on the Rolling Stock Control Panel and was still a little unsure of some of the paperwork. So when, on early turn, the Maintenance Control at Croydon gave me a list of unit numbers, I filled in the 'Maintenance Completed' form with those numbers. I made a neat job of it.

The only problem was that the units whose numbers I had been given were actually required for maintenance. They had not been worked on at all. I made a similar gaff with another form. No harm was done but it meant a lot of work for the person who relieved me. That person was 'The Doc.'

By mischance, after early turn on the Rolling Stock Panel, I had agreed to do four hours overtime on my old Area Three Panel.

So I was there when 'The Doc' discovered my mistake. 'Whooose filled all this in,' came the querulous demand.

I owned up at once. Putting my hand up I said, 'I did Doc.'

The words, 'You stupid -**!!, accompanied by the pointing finger, streamed out from the panel. The language went on for some time, and I really believe he did not stop to draw breath or use the same word twice. By the end of it, he was desperately short of breath, blue in the face, and the pointing finger was drooping.

Then he found the other form I had erroneously filled in.

'Whoooose filled all this in?'

Again I raised my hand, and said, 'I did Doc.'

Came the reply, 'You stupid - you know what you are but I haven't got the breath left to tell you.'

In my time on the railway I have been called to account many times, but never has it been done quite so professionally as it was by 'The Doc.' It caused some hilarity among the Controllers, and of course I learned from my mistakes. The Doc and I have laughed about it since.

There were a number of responsibilities on this job but generally it was done in a quiet methodical way. On the night shift each depot and stock siding reported the numbers of the units they had, and the services those units would go out on. Getting information from the sidings was quite quick. From the depots, the information was delayed while the fitters examined the units to ensure they were fit to go out.

Then the shunters would form them into trains and advise us what services they were on. Sometimes units were allowed to run in service to avoid shortages, but had minor defects, which required further attention. Maintenance Control would advise us of them, and we would ensure they were put on services that worked back into depot. These were the numbers I had so erroneously recorded on my first solo day on the panel.

Some work was specialised so special empty trains (ECS) would run from one depot to another, moving the units to where they could be repaired.

The pressure really came during the leaf fall period every autumn, or during our infrequent bouts of snow. So many units were taken out of service for wheel flats. Some had their bogies changed. Some had individual wheel-sets changed, and some ran at reduced speed to the depots equipped with wheel lathes. Then the Rolling Stock Controller and the Area Controllers would work together to decide which trains would run with a short formation.

Sometimes this was difficult because the Area Controllers obviously wanted the heaviest loaded trains to run with a full formation, but sometimes these trains did not end up back at the depot. When that happened some arrangement for swapping them over was made at some point during the working, so that they could end up back in the Depot. The same pressures occurred during our infrequent bouts of snow, with units suffering burnt out motors

It was also obviously important that we be advised immediately of anything that prevented the arrangements from working. I was very embarrassed one evening. I had arranged for a four-coach unit to be attached to a service train from Victoria to Ramsgate, to get a unit back to Ramsgate. This made the train ten coaches instead of six.

Unknown to us, Margate had attached a four-coach unit to the up service that made this train. Victoria did not tell us the train had arrived with ten coaches instead of six. They attached the other four-coach unit to the train, making it fourteen coaches long! This grossly over-length train ran into Bromley South Station, where my D.C.C. and I were waiting for our train. 'Embarrassed' hardly described how I felt! And the train was far too long for the platforms on some of the stations the train called at, so great care had to be taken to ensure all the passengers detrained safely. It could all have been avoided and it was all because two groups of station staff did not tell us there had been a problem.

From my time on the Rolling Stock Control I learned much. One thing I learned was that with roller bearings fitted to the wheelsets, it is impossible to get at hot axle box on the then modern electric rolling stock. I actually proved the exception to that rule, when I was on an area panel and a train came to a stand and was reported to have a hot axle box. Everyone, including my good friend Terry R, who at that time worked for the Rolling Stock Department at Southern House assured me that what I had got was a unit with the gears jammed.

Fitters attended. They examined the unit and reported the gears were all in order. They examined the suspect axle box. With the greatest reluctance they had to admit but could not explain, that it was indeed a hot axle box. In the old days when I was in Tonbridge Box and they ran '5 Pan(try)' stock, during a stock shortage, those units never got beyond Headcorn without having a hot axle box. But the modern stock, equipped with roller bearings, was specifically designed not to fail. I happened to be on the panel when the only known failure of this kind occurred. Of such incidents are legends made.

Locomotive Control

The Rolling Stock Control was an interesting panel, but the Locomotive Control I found an even more interesting one. I had the benefit here of learning from a man who was without doubt the best Locomotive Controller I ever encountered. John C had reorganised the system when he was appointed to the job.

His system was virtually fool-proof. On a large board was an A3 sized worksheet. On one side was a list of locomotive numbers. Next to it each day was recorded at the start of each day, the number of the diagram (the day's work for a loco-motive) allocated to that locomotive. On the other side was a list of diagrams and against each one was the number of the locomotive that was on it at the beginning of each day.

Whenever a locomotive was transferred to another diagram, a forward slash and the number of the new diagram was inserted. At the same time, on the other side of the sheet, a forward slash and the number of the new locomotive was inserted against the number of the diagram. These two entries must always agree. It was important to complete the task without interruption.

As an additional check John would occasionally ask for the number of a locomotive working a train and then check that against the diagram. This information he was able to obtain from the Total Operations Processing System (T.O.P.S) computer. Responsibility for entering this information devolved on the shunter or Inspector in charge.

Where there was a siding with no staff and the crew made their own attachments, John would ask for a visual check somewhere en route. Ensuring that locomotives stayed on their correct diagrams was very important for a number of reasons.

The South Eastern Division was equipped with a number of different types of locomotive and some of them had important restrictions. Should the wrong type of locomotive turn up for a job, the train might have to be cancelled.

The locomotive classes were as follows:

24 class 5,000. These were very powerful electric locomo-tives. They were equipped with collector shoes for the 750 v dc conductor rail, and a pantograph to collect 750 v dc from overhead cables in the yards at Ashford and Hither Green. They were equipped with a flywheel, which was spun at such

a speed as to supply a constant current to the traction motors. They were so powerful that they were dedicated to trains like the Night Ferry, which often conveyed up to seventeen coaches.

They also worked the Golden Arrow services. They could pull over one hundred wagons. It was one of these locomotives that featured in the 'Record Run,' mentioned in chapter two, page seventeen.

Later, with the introduction of T.O.P.S, they were reclassified class 71. A very small number were redeveloped as electro-diesels and reclassified as class 74, but they were not as successful in that role. Only one of the class was preserved and number 5000, in original Southern green livery, is based at the National Rail Museum at York.

Next came the ubiquitous Class 65XX, Crompton Diesel locomotives. They were reclassified by T.O.P.S. as Class 33 locomotives and were subdivided into three classes.

33/0XX could work on all parts of the Southern Region, except between Tonbridge and Hastings, (see below), and indeed onto other regions as well.

33/1XX were equipped for passenger 'push pull' workings and were used mainly on Bournemouth – Weymouth services where the electric R.E.P. units working 4 or 8 car driving trailer units from London, was detached at Bournemouth and the class 33/1 would work the train forward and back from Weymouth to Bournemouth.

The third sub class were 33/2XX. This was a very small sub class with straight sides and a narrow-gauged body, designed specifically for working between Tonbridge and Hastings via Wadhurst.

A quick diversion into history gives us the reason for this.

When the Hastings line was built, several landowners were unwilling to have deep cuttings across their land, so the engineers were obliged to construct tunnels underneath.

Only when the tunnels became due for maintenance was it discovered that three of the tunnels, Somerhill, Tunbridge Wells and Strawberry Hill tunnels, only had two linings of bricks instead of the required number of three. Emergency consultation followed this discovery. It was not possible to open up the tunnels, nor could an additional lining be installed on the outside of them. The only solution was to build another lining on the inside of the tunnels. This was done but it imposed a width restriction on the tunnels.

In steam days, a special fleet of narrow coaches had to be constructed. When dieselisation came, a fleet of 'Hastings Line' diesel trains had to be constructed, and some of the class 33 locomotives had to be designed with a narrow body, and only these locomotives could work the line.

Thus, for example if a train of gypsum 'empties' from Northfleet to Mountfield (Battle), arrived with a class 33/0 or 33/1 hauling it, the train could go no further until a class 33/2 was found to work it forward. Much later the whole problem was resolved by the singling of the lines through the tunnels and electrifying on third rail 750 dc and now all classes can pass unrestricted on the line.

Finally, and in my personal opinion the best, were the 6000 class of electro-diesels. They were equipped with collector shoes for the 750 volts dc conductor rail, and a 1550 horsepower electric engine, but they also had an independent 650 horsepower diesel engine. On the main lines they ran on electric power but in yards or sidings that had no conductor rail, they could switch to diesel power.

The first six of these locomotives were equipped with very solid double conductor shoes on each side. When the conductor rail was iced up, they hauled trains running on diesel power with their shoes down to knock the ice off of the conductor rail. They were numbered 6001 – 6006.

The remaining thirty-six had been developed from these. They had upgrades that improved their performance, but they had lighter conductor shoes.

Under T.O.P.S the first six were reclassified 73/0XX, and the remaining thirty-six were reclassified 73/1XX.

An incident occurred in Stewarts Lane Depot, which was their main base. A shunter attached a class 73/0XX to a class 73/1XX. There was a huge short circuit, which the shunter reported lit up the sky over the whole depot and the two locomotives tried to move in the opposite directions, which being equal in weight and power they were unable to do. They were quickly separated.

Investigations revealed that during the upgrade the wiring on the class 73/1 had been altered and these locomotives would not be able to work in multiple, that is driven by one crew from one of the locomotives. They could be worked in tandem, that is, with a crew working each of the locomotives separately. Brakes would work throughout, but control jumpers must not be attached. A suitable instruction was speedily issued to all parties, including Locomotive Controllers.

This provided an additional complication for Locomotive Controllers because some diagrams required at certain points for double heading of class 73 locomotives, for example, prior to electrification, over the lines between Tonbridge and Redhill.

Then, when it was discovered that two incompatible locomotives were on these diagrams, the Controller either had to ask the Traincrew Supervisors, (T.C.S), or Motive Power Foremen for an extra crew, or he had to find a suitable replacement locomotive for one of them.

These locomotives however, were the most versatile and useful locomotives on the whole fleet. They literally went everywhere and would pull any train. They went into yards and sidings where there was no third rail, and they worked equally well on non-electrified lines and would haul passenger and freight trains with equal ease, and in any weather conditions. It is a tribute to their reliability that many are still in use today, some sixty years after they were first introduced.

The first six locomotives, 6001–6006 have all been withdrawn, but some of these are now running on preserved lines. The remaining thirty-six have been scattered. Some of course have been withdrawn, but I have seen some working Network Rail engineering trains and I have seen at least two converted by Eurostar, with special couplings to move their twenty coach trains.

I can personally testify, from several trips on them in the course of my duties, that these locomotives were also the most comfortable I have ever ridden on.

As well as the fleet on the South Eastern Division, the South Eastern Locomotive Controller was also responsible for the supply of locomotives to the Central Division and for the replacement of any that failed.

From all this, the reader can see that it was very important that the different types of locomotives were kept on their planned diagrams, and a primary responsibility of the

Locomotive Controller was to see that they did.

Certain diagrams were designed so that locomotives on them, went to their parent depot for regular routine maintenance. Again, it was important for this reason that locomotives stayed on their allocated diagram. So, what could cause them to stray from those diagrams?

Well there were several reasons.

It was very important not to cancel a train. So, if a locomotive failed, the Locomotive Controller had to find and take another suitable locomotive off of its booked diagram to replace the failed one. Then the Locomotive Controller had to find another suitable locomotive to replace the one on the diagram he had robbed. He also had to check if the locomotive he had used to replace the failure, was itself due for maintenance. If it was, he had to find a way of changing it over to another diagram as soon as possible to ensure it got it planned maintenance.

Obviously, regular maintenance is important to ensure as far as possible that locomotives do not fail.

Another reason for locomotives not being on their booked diagrams, came from staff outside, having to change a locomotive over, and not telling the Locomotive Controller that they had done so. Depots and Yards were generally very good at keeping us advised, because they also had to update the T.O.P.S system. The problems mostly occurred in sidings.

A driver would know which locomotive he should take but when he got there, he might find one or two locomotives of the same class parked in front of it, with his locomotive next to the buffer stops. Should he cause a lot of delay by starting up and shunting the other locomotives off, then getting his locomotive out, and then shunting the other locomotives back! The locomotives might all be identically the same class, so naturally he would take the one nearest the exit. It might not occur to him to tell anyone he had a different locomotive number to the one on his docket. The trains would run on.

The diagrams would cause the 'rogue' locomotive to work other trains. It might even be changed over to cover a failure elsewhere. Then, suddenly it would all come to light. A depot would report that the wrong locomotive had come in for maintenance. A locomotive might fail and be reported but it would be the wrong number. It was then that John C's system proved its worth. First, he would ensure that he had been given the correct number. I was familiar with John's cry, 'But that locomotive should not have been there!'

Then he would, from his form, find the number of the original locomotive and the diagram it should have been on. Then he would work back through that diagram until he came to a point where both locomotives were in the same place at the same time. From that, he could see the diagram that the 'rogue' locomotive was now working on, and from that he could see where it was currently.

Then, after a phone call to confirm that it was so, he could start making arrangements to change it over onto a diagram that would see it working back to depot. All this had to be done without delaying or cancelling any train. With experience, I learned from John, just where the most likely unauthorised changeover locations were likely to be, and that saved a lot of digging back through the diagrams.

Another thing which caused locomotives to come off their booked diagrams was quite simply that a train might be delayed due to an incident or cancelled simply because it was not required. In the former instance, to coin a phrase, 'what does not come down, will not go back.' If the train were going to be very late arriving, the Locomotive Controller would need to find a replacement to avoid delay to another train.

In the latter instance, providing the locomotive had enough fuel and it was not required for maintenance, it might stay at its current location, and perhaps avoid having to run another locomotive 'light engine' to work a train.

One thing was certain. Every change of locomotive or diagram, for whatever reason, had to be updated on John's Locomotive Board, so that he and the person relieving him at the end of his shift, knew exactly where each locomotive was. The board also contained a section on 'failed' locomotives, with a space for the number and a 'Remarks' column so that details of the failure could be entered.

I learned a great deal from John C and will always be grateful. It was very satisfying to be able to hand over to my relief at the end of a shift and tell him that the Locomotive Board was up to date, to advise him of any outstanding failures, and of any late running trains or other problems likely to affect the locomotives.

But now it was time to move on to another panel which in my capacity as General Purpose & Rest Day Relief Controller. I was going to learn the Guards Control Panel.

Guards Control

The Guards Control was different in many respects to the other two panels. In particular, because whereas Controllers on the other two panels spoke to Supervisors, either Carriage Mechanical and Electrical Managers or Traincrew Supervisors/

Motive Power Foremen, the Guards Controller spoke in almost every case, directly to the train guards themselves.

Guards Controllers quickly learned how to speak to staff in order to get the best out of them. Most guards were very cooperative, particularly once situations had been explained to them, and guards themselves quickly got know the different Controllers who covered the panel.

Difficulties occurred when messages had to be relayed to guards. What started out as a request to a guard to help us out to cover another train and/or work overtime to cover trains, ended up being given to them as 'Control says you've got to do this!' Predictably this resulted in what could be politely described as 'a negative response!'

There were never enough guards to cover all the trains. There would always be at least one, and usually more than one foolscap sheet of duties not covered. It was a matter of pride for the Guards Controller that no train on his shift would be cancelled due to there being no guard. The Guards Controller had to cover all the trains on his shift and also the first two hours of the next shift.

This was to give the incoming Guards Controller a chance to study the diagrams and start covering trains, without losing any trains in the first two hours. Guards' duties would be studied for any spare capacity. Any cancellations for any other reason for example a defective train or a shortage of drivers, could make a guard available for other duties. Of course, if one train had been cancelled, the next booked working for that guard would also have to be covered, unless that train had also been cancelled.

Incidents causing late running also were both good and bad

news for Guards Controllers. Next duties would have to be recovered, but some guards would become spare, and could be reallocated to trains that had not been covered.

One of the problems with Guards Diagrams was they did not match the driver's diagrams, or in some cases the rolling stock diagrams.

I personally experienced many cases where on the arrival of an incoming train at a London Terminal, the guard worked one train back out, the driver worked a different train back out, and the rolling stock formed a third. Thus the late running or cancellation of one inbound train affected the working of three outbound trans from the terminus.

I asked the Guards Diagram Section why this was and was told there were two reasons. Firstly, the guards Conditions of Service were different to those of a driver. The second reason was 'Rostering in the most economic way.' I pointed out that the number of 'traffic incidents' we experienced each day made this style of guards rostering very uneconomic, to which I received the unarguable reply,

'We cannot roster for incidents.'

In the event of severe disruption, caused by snow or a line blockage due to a derailment or other major problem, the Area Controllers would compile an emergency service to give the passengers the best possible alternative service. A copy of this would be passed to the Guards Controller and it would be his job to provide guards for all the trains in the special service. Some of those guards would come from the normal train service that had been suspended. Others would have to be found by juggling the diagrams, persuading some guards to swap trains and some to work overtime, to free up guards to cover the special services.

In addition to the Working Timetable Service there were also 'Q' trains. The C.M.& E.E would request the Rolling Stock Controller to run certain empty trains for them each day, in order to get units requiring maintenance to depots. Guards duties were allocated to these diagrams, but not unusually these duties found themselves on the 'Not Covered' sheet. Sometimes these trains could be run early in order to utilise a guard who might be available then but not later.

Then there were the wintertime de-icing trains. Decisions on whether or not to run them depended on the weather forecast from the Met Office. Again, these duties were often found on the 'Not Covered' sheet, but if they were required, they had to run, if necessary, at the expense of other services.

And there were also requests from the Area Controllers for special trains to be run. Sometimes these were for passenger trains but more often they were for special freight trains.

The Civil Engineers Department ran their own engineering trains. They had staff trained to act as guards for engineers trains only, but there were always far fewer staff trained than trains required, so once again the Guards Controller was required to find cover for those trains where they had not been covered.

The whole subject of engineer's trains could be a minefield for the Guards Controller. Trains ferrying materials during the week were one thing. But trains going into engineering possessions was quite another. Engineering possessions were tightly and exactly planned. The engineers themselves had only a limited time to occupy the track so the trains had to be punctual. They also had to be in the right order.

For example, the lifting of track required that the crane(s) had to be in position with the empty wagons to take away the redundant track nearby and this would be followed by the ballast trains loaded with new ballast. Then the train with the new rails would be required. The trains might not come out in the exact order they went in. Some might be combined, others divided.

So there was no point in running the empty wagons for the old rails if there was no guard to run the train with the crane. If one train was late going in, then all the following trains would be late, and as a result the engineering possession would over run its time and cause disruption to the passenger service and still more work for the Guards Controller to recover that.

Sometimes the engineering possession would run late for other reasons. Perhaps a crane would break down, or the wrong material might have been sent. Sometimes excavators encountered unforeseen problems. If the engineering trains ran too late, the guards on those trains would require relief and the Guards Controller would have to recover their duties.

And if the possession of the line suffered a serious over-run, a special service would have to be arranged and the Guards Controller would be responsible for covering the duties required for the special service, as well as covering the duties of the guards displaced by the blockage.

The Guards Control could be very stressful, and it is sad to relate that while I was a Beckenham Control, two Guards Controllers died from stress related illnesses.

But there were also some wonderfully bizarre and amusing incidents. The one I am about to relate took place on the South Western Division, when we had been relocated to Waterloo and I was working in the Central Division Control (much later on in this story). We were working alongside the other two Controls.

It happened to be a quiet moment and we overheard the following conversation between the South Western D.C.C, Paul S (of course we could only hear one side of the conversation) and a missing guard:

'Hello Guard. We've been looking all over the place for you. There is a trainload of passengers standing in Waterloo Station waiting for you. Why aren't you there? Well where are you now? You're at Heathrow! What on earth are you doing there? Oh, I see. You're being deported – and today is the day! I see. Well in that case you won't be reporting for duty tomorrow, will you? Well, on behalf of British Railways, thank you for all you have done, and best wishes for your future. Goodbye.' The whole Control was writhing with helpless laughter.

Returning to my position a G.P.R Grade 'C' Controller at Beckenham, to which I had been appointed in 1979, the whole Control was subject to reorganisation, and my post and the Rest Day Relief Controller post were regraded from Grade 'C' to grade 'D'. We were invited to reapply for our jobs. I reapplied. On 5th November 1980, I was advised that I had been successful and was now a Grade 'D' G.P.R Controller.

Then, in December 1980, came the opportunity to transfer to the Rest Day Relief Controller Grade 'D' Position. Again I applied. On 28th December 1980, I was advised that once again I had been the successful applicant.

Rest Day Relief Controller grade 'D'
This position gave me a number of advantages. To begin with, Rest Days were only taken on day shifts so there was no

more night duty. Then I had a proper roster, so at last I could predict what shifts I was working, although I could and did occasionally change shifts to assist the working of the Control.

There was one further benefit. I was allowed to cover London Area Four Panel, and I did.

I enjoyed covering the other three panels in my new capacity as Rest Day Relief Controller Grade 'D' but I also enjoyed covering London Area Four, as the next chapter will reveal.

Rest Day Relief Controller Grade 'D' on Area Four

London Area Four was a very complex area, and in 1980 still had the old signal boxes as listed way back on page 32. I won't repeat all that detail but will simply summarise it.

London Area Four covered the Chatham Main Lines from Victoria to Swanley via Beckenham Junction and via Nunhead, from Swanley to Maidstone East and Otford Junction to Sevenoaks, and the South Eastern Main Lines from Chislehurst Junction to Paddock Wood. It also covered the cross London freight routes via the Widened Lines and via Barnes. It had an intensive suburban service to Orpington and Sevenoaks. It also covered the lines from Tonbridge to Hastings and the Romney Marsh Lines from Hastings to Ashford as far as Rye.

It had a Central Division connection on the lines from Crystal Palace to Beckenham Junction and another central Division connection with the lines from Redhill to Tonbridge. It was as I say a very complex area and prone to various incidents - as I was about to discover.

One of the first incidents I was involved in concerned a freight train.. The instructions on time keeping were quite specific. No freight train would leave Factory Junction, the junction leading from other regions onto the Southern, between the hours of 1600 (4 pm) and 1830 (6.30 pm). This was to protect the passenger rush hour service.

The 2000 hrs Widdrington – Southfleet Coal Concentration Depot, two Class 40 locomotives hauling 2,000 tons of coal, was due to pass Factory Junction at approximately 1530. But it was a notoriously poor timekeeper. Every day it would arrive at Factory Junction at between 1605 and 16 10. On four late turns that week, 'the Doc' was the London Area Four Controller. Each day the train followed its usual practice of arriving at about 1605. The signalman at Factory Junction rang the Control to ask what to do, and the 'Doc' answered, 'Yeah, keep her running.' About twenty minutes later the train would thunder at full speed past the Office, both engines rumbling on full power.

The door of the Chief Controllers office would fly open and Ron C would appear, demanding to know who had let it run.

'The Doc,' totally unruffled, would reply, 'Don't you worry yourself about it. She'll be alright.' And 'She' always was.

On the Friday of that week, I was the late turn London Area Four Controller. True to form the signalman at Factory Junction rang me at 1605. 'I've got the Widdrington on,' he said, 'What do you want me to do with it?' he asked.

'Yeah, let her run,' I replied, in my best imitation of 'the Doc.' Twenty minutes passed with no sign of the train. I began to feel uneasy.

Almost thirty minutes had passed from the time of my phone call, before the train came into view. It was not thundering past. In fact it could barely move and from the sound of the locomotives, at least one of them was very unwell! The locomotives had barely passed by the Control window when the train came to a stand and the driver declared one of the locomotives a complete failure.

Where the train stood, in full view of the Divisional Managers Office upstairs, it completely blocked the down main line right in the teeth of the rush hour. The Chief Controller's office door flew back on its hinges, and Ron C came running into the room with a horrified look on his face. 'Who let that train down?' he demanded as he skidded to a halt at my panel.

'I did' I admitted, and sat there waiting for the thunderbolts to fall.

For a few moments Ron stood there breathing deeply in complete silence. Then he said, 'Terry, just remember one thing. You are not 'the Doc!!' Then he went upstairs to the Divisional Manager's Office, which also overlooked the scene, to explain why his instructions had been disobeyed. Two class 33 locomotives were summoned from Hither Green with all speed. They were crossed over and ran wrong line onto the front of the train. They cleared the train down to Southfleet, leaving the main line clear and the train service in tatters.

Another, quite sad incident occurred at Paddock Wood. A lady was found, attempting to commit suicide. She had got down onto the track in the down bay and placed her neck on the rails next to the wheels of a train from Paddock Wood to Maidstone and waited for the train to move off. Thankfully an alert member of staff spotted her in time. The driver was told not to move his train.

The signalman was advised and reversed the signal. Paddock Wood Electrical Control was advised and the traction current was discharged. Police and an ambulance were called, and the lady was taken away. We heard some days later that she had attempted another form of suicide, away from the railway, and she had succeeded.

Another suicide took place at Bromley South, while I was on a late turn on London Area Four. A young student jumped right in front of a train as it was running into the down fast platform. We were later told she was a young Canadian student who was going to have to spend Christmas alone and with no money and no way to get home. We dealt with the incident, relieving the driver and escorting him home, and the train was taken out of service for a full examination, as required by law. The passengers were transferred to another train, and adjustments were made to recover the train service.

I later learned that a friend of mine was on the platform at the time and saw the whole thing. It is something he has never been able to forget.

But now for something completely different, the saga of Shepherds Lane Signal Box. In those days we were still responsible for the cover of signalman, out of office hours. The Staff Relief clerk would bring in the Competency Book and the Rosters at close of work, and we were then responsible for covering any vacancies until the Staff Relief Office opened the following morning.

Shepherds Lane Signal Box controlled the junction where trains from Victoria followed the main line via Beckenham Junction or diverted via Nunhead and the Catford Loop. I was late turn on London Area Four on this day.

The signal box was being covered by two signalmen, each working twelve hours. The day signalman's shift was due to end at 1800 hrs (6pm). He rang me to advise me that his relief, due at 1800 hrs, had just rung in to say he was ill and would not be coming in. I went to the Competency Book and made a list of the signalmen shown competent to work the signal box. As it was being covered by twelve hour- shifts, it was not going to be easy to recover. And it wasn't No-one was available to cover the signal box. Nor could the signalman be expected to remain beyond twelve hours. But if this signal box closed, no train could leave Victoria!

Then I found a solution. Joe J was the signalman at Shortlands Junction. He was marked competent to work Shepherds Lane. If I could find someone to relieve him at Shortlands, would he be willing to go to Shepherds Lane? He was. Joe was always a very helpful as well as a very competent Relief Signalman. I managed to find a signalman to relieve Joe at Shortlands and we arranged for a taxi to take Joe to Shepherds Lane.

The signalman duly arrived at Shortlands and Joe was sent in a taxi to Shepherds Lane. But he never arrived. The early turn signalman at Shepherds Lane hung on for some time after his twelve hours was up. But eventually, reluctantly, he had to close the signal box and leave. Trains at Victoria came to a stand. Where possible, up trains were diverted or terminated short. I, meanwhile, contacted the taxi firm. They admitted that they had picked Joe up but the taxi had been involved in a slight road accident. Joe was unhurt and another taxi had been despatched to the scene of the accident, to pick him up and take him to Shepherds Lane.

Finally we heard from Joe, that he had arrived at Shepherds Lane and would be opening up shortly. We advised Victoria and the trains began to move.

My D.C.C instructed me to ensure that the first down train

must stop at all stations to pick up the stranded passengers.

I advised Victoria of this and asked them to issue a Special Stop Order to the driver and guard of the first train to leave.

But then we heard that the signal box had still not opened. I rang the signal box but could get no reply. My D.C.C was hopping up and down but there was simply nothing more we could do. The D.C.C. reiterated his instructions to me that the first down train must call at all stations. Apart from all the other passengers, the Editor of the Evening Standard was stranded at Kent House station and he was seething with rage and promising a centre spread on the inefficiency of the Railway.

Finally the signal box was reopened. Joe came on the phone to tell me that he had advised us when he got to the signal box, but he had a problem with the door. The box door was locked. The key was tied to a piece of string which hung down behind the dustbin on the platform. As he reached out and grabbed the string, it broke and the key fell down under the platform. He then had to climb down onto the track and crawl along under the platform in all the filth and muck that had collected there, until he found the key.

Finally also, the train service got under way. Despite all our efforts the first train did not call at all stations and flew past the irate Editor at Kent House at full speed. The promised article duly appeared in the next evening's edition!

Not all of our incidents occurred outside the Control. The 'Legend of the Control Kettles' lives on in the history of the now long-gone Beckenham Control. Because we were open every day except Christmas Day and worked round the clock shifts, our kettles were used at least three times as much each

213

day as your average domestic kettle, and they had to be replaced at regular intervals.

One day the Chief Controller decided that kettles with automatic cut-outs were too expensive, and he obtained two ordinary kettles. In vain did we try to tell him that the automatic cut-outs were the only way the kettles would survive, if we were called away to an incident. 'You'll just have to be more careful,' was his response.

The new kettles duly arrived and were commissioned by an Area Controller who went to make the tea. Immediately he was called away to a relatively major incident. It was steam pouring out of the galley door that reminded us that the kettles had been put on.

The Controller concerned raced into the galley, fighting his way through the steam, but alas he was too late. Ceremonially he carried the kettles through the Control and knocked on the Chief Controller's door. When it opened, he said, 'I don't think much of your new kettles Guv.'

'Why not?' demanded the Chief Controller.

'They've both got holes in them,' the Controller replied. He held up both kettles revealing the large holes that had been burned in the bottoms. The door closed to the sound of swearing! We got replacement kettles – with cut-outs!

Another 'Kettle Incident' involved someone not a million miles away from here. Making the tea one day, it was discovered that the socket was dead. The controller instantly improvised by placing the kettle on the stove and switching on the ring. Congratulating himself on his efficiency and improvisation the Controller left the galley with a smile on his face. It was the smell of burning plastic that reminded him of the plastic feet on the base of the kettle. It was rescued just in time before the Fire Alarm went off.

Talking of Fire Alarms reminds me of the time that a new Fire Alarm System was installed at Beckenham. After the sensors, shaped like funnels, had been installed, a test of the equipment was made. A fitter walked along the passage, holding up a pole with a burning rag on it. In vain did he walk up and down the passage holding up the pole with the burning rag. Nothing happened.

Finally, in disgust, he shoved the burning rag right up the funnel receptor and extinguished the flames by suffocating them! We were not over confident of the system.

But one day we did have a fire in the Control. John C was sitting at the Locomotive Control Desk when a light went out above him. The electrical fitters were called and attended. For a while the light worked but then it went out again. Attempts were made to recall the fitters, but they could not be found.

Bill and Ben the Maintenance Men were located and attended. These two men were a marvellous double act. Ben was obviously in charge. He walked round with a hammer and a brown plastic bag. Bill carried a wooden ladder. They worked in total silence. Bill would put down the ladder. Ben would put down the hammer but keep hold of the brown paper bag (we never did find out what was in it).

They would walk away and survey the problem from a distance. Then Bill would move in and place the ladder. Ben would then ascend the ladder and do some work. Then Ben would descend and Bill would ascend. On this day the silence was suddenly broken as Bill took hold of a cable. 'Dooooo dats hot !!' he yelled in a broad Irish accent and shinned down the ladder at top speed.

After another survey of the problem, and still in silence, they went back up and restored the lighting over John C's desk. Then Bill picked up the ladder, Ben picked up the hammer, and silently, Ben still holding the brown paper bag, they departed.

It was about half an hour later that a trickle of smoke was seen coming from the light. It was only the size of that emitted from a cigarette but was it ever pungent! In a very short time indeed the fumes had begun to fill the entire Control. In the end a message was put out on the telex that the Control was temporarily being evacuated. People were coughing and spluttering.

The fumes began to spread next door and soon the Freight Office had to be evacuated as well. The Fitters were finally located. They came and isolated the cable and the light went out. The fumes also stopped. Somebody remarked, 'Typical of the S & T, don't fix it, just isolate it!' Someone else remarked that the Fire Alarm had failed to activate throughout the incident!

Another galley incident occurred when someone else who shall remain nameless, carried a whole tray of teacups into the galley and tripped, dropping the lot. Some cups survived but many didn't. This caused an immediate crisis because there weren't enough cups left to go round. No tea!

An agonised howl came from the galley when Brian G discovered his cup was among the casualties. 'I carried that special Pullman cup safely all around China on my trip, but it didn't survive you, did it!!!

I also had the distinction, whilst covering Area Four, of having both the principal trains of the day in trouble at the same time. The up Night Ferry was running in the 0820 pathway, the ship having been late arriving. The signalman at Orpington telephoned me to say that the train, hauled by a class 5,000 locomotive and comprising seventeen coaches, had come to a stand at Knockholt with the locomotive a complete failure.

As I have remarked before, the class 5,000 locomotives were very reliable, very powerful, being the only single locomotive capable of hauling the Night Ferry, and of very simple construction. But when they did fail, it was absolute. There was no question of a repair on site. They had to be towed to Depot.

T   he Night Ferry being a 'Customs Secured Train,' meant that Kent Police had to be advised and attend on site. This was arranged. Meanwhile two class 33 locomotives were obtained from Hither Green Depot and despatched to Orpington with all speed. At Orpington, they were to be crossed to the up line and run 'wrong line' to the front of the failed train.

As all this was taking place, I received a telephone call from the signalman at Sevenoaks. He told me, 'You won't believe this, but I've got the Golden Arrow standing on the down line at Chelsfield (the next station about four miles up from Knockholt) with the class 5,000 locomotive a complete failure.' I now had the two crack trains of the day facing each other with each of their locomotives having failed.

Quickly I located another class 33 locomotive at Tonbridge. This was manned and departed all speed to Sevenoaks. It was then crossed over to the down line where it ran all the way to the front of the train at Chelsfield, passing as it did so, the two locomotives travelling wrong line on the up line on their way to the front of the failed up Night Ferry.

I do believe that nowhere in the annals of Beckenham

Control is there any other record of the two crack trains of the day having failed at the same time and facing each other. I am told, although I honestly cannot remember, that Bill D, the relief D.C.C. on duty on that day strode over to me, threw his clipboard on the floor and danced on it in frustration!

But things they were a changing. In 1970 the new Area Signalling Centre at Dartford opened and replaced a number of the old signal boxes. Apart from some minor teething troubles the system worked very well. In 1974, after major engineering work over several months, the new London Bridge Area Signalling Centre was opened, and famous signal boxes like Borough Market Junction and Metropolitan Junction among others, closed for the last time.

In 1980 it was the turn of London Area Four Control Panel to be affected when the new Victoria Area Signalling Centre, located at Clapham Junction, opened. There would be no more calls from Factory Junction about late running freight trains and no more sagas at Shepherds Lane. The new signal boxes, or Area Signalling Centres, to give them their proper names, had Regulators whose job it was to oversee the signalmen and arrange for the regulation of traffic.

No longer would we cover signalmen out of office hours because that too was the responsibility of the Regulators. On the whole they system worked well, apart from the one complaint from many signalmen, that with the closure of the signal boxes there were less staff to observe the trains as they passed and note and take the appropriate action in the event of problems occurring on them. That was something I understood and appreciated.

But things were also changing for me. I really enjoyed my

job, but I was always on the look-out for promotion. When an 'E' grade vacancy occurred on London Area One, I applied for it. I was interviewed and verbally advised that I had got the job. But before the paperwork could be issued, the appointment was contested by a senior man, who had changed his mind and decided that he wanted it. His application was upheld. I was sent for and the senior interviewing managers apologised profusely.

I was offered the G.P.R Grade 'E.' I seriously considered it but I had served my time on the G.P.R. positions, with all their unpredictability and constant night duties, and I really did not want to go that way again, so I declined the offer.

On another Vacancy List, I found a vacancy for a Grade 'E' Area Controller of the Central Division. I would have preferred to stay on the South Eastern Division, but I could see no possibility of movement there in the immediate future. I applied for the position but did not get an interview.

Then another vacancy occurred. This was for a Rest Day Relief Controller Grade 'E,' again on the Central Division. I applied for it, not expecting that I would be considered. To my surprise I was called for an interview, which I attended at Waterloo.

At the time, Senior Management had decided that the three Controls, South Eastern, Central, and South Western were to be relocated into one room at Waterloo. I attended the interview. To my surprise and delight I was advised that I had been successful and on 14th September 1984, I was appointed to the Rest Day Relief Controller Grade 'E' post in the Central Division Control.

On this position, I would be covering mostly Areas One

and Two and occasionally Area Three. I might also be asked to step up and cover the D.C.C position. I didn't think that was likely because I was very much a junior member of staff, but when I started working there I was advised and invited to lean the D.C.C's position, and I did, whenever I got the chance.

So it was 'Goodbye' to the South Eastern Division where I had spent all of my working career. It would feel strange. But it was also exciting, learning new areas and working with new people.

There would also be new experiences and new incidents to deal with, as you will see in the following chapters.

Chapter Ten - Rest Day Relief Grade 'E' and MS2 on the Central Division

So here I was, back at Waterloo, but now working for the London Brighton Line and the Central Division. There were three Area Control Panels to learn.

The London Area One Panel (Grade 'E') extended from Victoria (Central) and London Bridge (Central) to East and West Croydon and down as far as Tattenham Corner, Caterham, the Oxted Lines to East Grinstead and Hurst Green, Sutton and Epsom. Most of it was under the control of London Bridge and Victoria Signalling Centres.

It had two major depots, Stewarts Lane, which among other things was home to the Orient Express Stock, and the Snowblower, as well as locomotives and passenger electric stock, and Selhurst Depot that was a major Repair Depot for electric suburban stock.

The Country Area Two Panel (Grade 'E') covered the Brighton Line from below Purley to Brighton, via the Redhill line and the Quarry Line, the Redhill – Tonbridge line, the beginning of the Horsham Branch from Three Bridges, and the east and west approaches to Brighton. It included the Engineers Depot at Three Bridges and the major Electric Rolling Stock Repair Depot at Lovers Walk, just outside Brighton.

The Country Area Three Panel, Grade ('D') covered the east coast from Bexhill via Eastbourne to Brighton, the West Coast from Chichester to Brighton, and the Arun Valley Line to Horsham.

Rolling stock was controlled by the Rolling Stock Controller (grade 'C').

Locomotives were covered by an independent Locomotive Controller.

There was also a D.C.C (Grade MS2) in charge of the whole Central Division Control.

Then, in the middle of the room was a Senior Manager (Grade MS4) who was the Regional D.C.C.

Initially the Central Division Control was the only Control in the room. Soon however, we were joined by the South Eastern and the South Western Divisional Controls.

My new colleagues on the Central Division were an interesting group of characters. On the D.C.C panel were Ken H, Colin M, and Peter C.

Among the London Area One Controllers were Brian E, Brian A, and Roger M.

Among the Country Area Controllers were Dave T, Colin , and Ron W.

Area Three Controllers included Dave C, Brian and Colin.

The Rolling Stock Controller on my shift was another Colin.

Among the Locomotive Controllers was Peter (Ned) K, someone I had known on the South Eastern. His nickname refers to the fact that he was able get most things we wanted, or he knew a man who could. He was excellent at his job and had a good rapport with all the Motive Power Supervisors and Train Crew Supervisors.

I wasn't long in the job before we had our first major incident. A train comprising two three-coach diesel multiple units (DEMU's), had become derailed on a crossover at the exit from the Norwood end of Selhurst Depot, blocking the exit. A lot of electric trains at that time were formed of 4 and 2 coach sets. The 2 coach sets had to be at the right end because en route the train would divide, 4 coaches going one way, and 2 coaches the other. The Tattenham and Caterham branches were good examples of this but there were others. Because all the trains had to go out of the Selhurst end, had something not been done about it, they would have ended up with the 2 coaches on the wrong end.

So all the trains that normally left the Depot from the Norwood end had to have their formations reversed so that once they were out of the Depot, they were the right way round. This was a headache for the London Area Controller, and the Rolling Stock Controller, who had to ensure that this happened and also that no errors were made.

There were also some situations where this simply couldn't be done because of the time element.

Then the Area Controller had to follow up the cyclic working, the diagrams on which each unit was assigned, to see where they could be changed over in order to put them right. Then arrangements had to be made for the stock returning from the rush hour to be diverted to the Selhurst end to be berthed correctly in the Depot.

Throw in for good measure a few units that were required to go to Depot at completion of their work, for programmed or essential maintenance, and you have some idea of the jigsaw puzzle the Area Controller had to sort out. And all this while dealing with other incidents that were occurring at the same time!

I had a busy morning but consoled myself with the fact

that the CM & EE were confident they would have the derailment cleared up and the Depot entrance/exit reopened after the evening peak. There was very little track damage and the P. Way Engineers were likewise confident. I came in the next morning to find chaos.

The rerailing had been successfully completed as expected. They began to move the units back into the Depot. Then, once again, the unit derailed. This time it pulled up a set of points and seriously damaged them, and there was a lot of track damage too. The estimate this time was three days to put it right. It was an ongoing nightmare for me as I was new to the area and had to work hard at what came second nature to the other Controllers.

True to their word, the CM & EE and P. Way engineers sorted it out. The unit was re-railed again, and moved at walking pace into the Depot. The P. Way set about repairing the points and relaying the track, and all was clear at the end of the third day. The Stewards Lane Crane was closed up and set off back to Stewarts Lane. The Brighton Crane had to be reformed before it could go back to Lovers Walk. That was when the third act of the tragedy occurred.

I came in on the Friday morning to find Brian E grinning up at me as I stood by the panel. 'You thought it was all over,' he said. 'Well it isn't. When they were reforming the Brighton Crane, the Tool Van ran away, derailed near the exit at the Selhurst end and fell down the bank, blocking the Selhurst Exit!' Great! Now everything had to come out and go in from the Norwood end, with all the consequences of reforming the stock to get it right.

I came in on Saturday expecting the worst, with the Selhurst Depot problem and the weekend engineering work as well. Brian was raring to go when I walked in. 'It's all squared up and back to normal,' he said. 'There's just the Brighton Crane to work back to Lovers Walk when we can.' I heaved a huge sigh of relief as I took over the panel.

On the London Area Panel there was another thing to get used to, Royal Trains. We didn't have many Royal Trains on the South Eastern, and I was never involved on the rare occasions that they ran. But on the Central Division, although it was quite rare, we did have trains from Gatwick Airport, conveying foreign dignitaries accompanied by a member of the Royal Family.

One such incident concerned the King and Queen of Denmark who were to be accompanied by no less a personage than Her Majesty Queen Elizabeth The Second. All the usual rules concerning Royal Trains were invoked. There was to be a standby locomotive at a strategic point. There was the be a clear pathway of ten minutes ahead of the Royal Train and it was to be monitored for timekeeping at various points along the line.

The plan included that if for any reason it became impossible for the train to run to Victoria, it could be diverted from Clapham Junction to Kensington Olympia. An alternative timetable for this move was issued, but it could not be implemented without permission from the highest level.

The train left Gatwick Airport exactly on time. By the time it came through Purley, it was two minutes early. It was at that time exactly that Victoria Area Signalling Centre reported that a suspect package had been seen on Battersea Bridge. The Bomb Squad were on their way. Phone wires were buzzing in all directions, but no word came to us.

Ken H was D.C.C and I was on the London Area. The train passed East Croydon three minutes early and was approaching Clapham Junction. I consulted with Ken. He had tried to get some response from above, but failed. Victoria regulator came on my phone, advising me that the train was approaching the point of no return. An immediate decision was required.

Again Ken and I consulted. I reminded him that the instructions were explicit. The train was not to be delayed, but should be diverted to Kensington Olympia should Victoria Station become unavailable. Holding the phone to the Regulator in my hand, I said, 'We should go to Kensington Ken.' 'Well I suppose we must' deliberated Ken. Taking a deep breath, I told the Regulator the train was to go to Kensington Olympia. 'Right,' said the Regulator, and it was done.

Almost immediately we got a call from our Senior Manager, telling us to divert the Royal Train to Kensington Olympia. Very shortly after that, we received a phone call from our Senior Manager, asking who had made the decision and acted before it was authorised. Apparently, he had a very senior Metropolitan Police Officer demanding to know who had taken action without his authority. Would the person responsible please go to the Senior Manager's Office at once.

'Well that's me,' I said to Ken, grinning at him. I collected the paperwork and got up to go.

'Oh no you don't, 'he said, grinning back. 'I've been trying to get early retirement for a long time, without much success. This might do it for me.'

Off Ken went. Later he returned doing that little skip that he did when he was pleased, rubbing his hands, and looking very pleased with himself. 'All acquitted,' he announced. Somebody in the Met Police will get the blame for not keeping us informed!'

We later learned that there was indeed a seriously suspect package on the bridge, which was dealt with by the Bomb Squad. With the diversion at the last minute, it was not possible for the horse drawn conveyances to get from Victoria to Kensington Olympia, so Buckingham Palace had arranged for a fleet of limousines to go to meet the Queen and her guests.

Not too long after that, a visit was arranged for those of us who were free, to be at Victoria to see the arrival of a Royal Train. The train was a few minutes early arriving. We watched the Royal Party being escorted from the train to their waiting horse drawn carriages.

I had noticed two things. Beside each carriage was a Footman. As the carriage moved forward, the Footman would march alongside. The other thing I noticed was that one horse did what horses do. Somehow he deposited a steaming pile of faeces right in the path of the Footman. I wondered what would happen when they moved off. I soon found out.

The first Footman stepped nimbly over the steaming pile, then resumed his marching rhythm. The second Footman trod deliberately in the middle of it with his shining boots. The others followed suit, marching through the pile.

Taken all in all, we had very little trouble with the Royal Trains, unlike some of the other regions.

At that time, Railtrack had a motto, 'We're getting there!' The following story was reported to me by a colleague who had dealings with the London Midland Region.

One of the London Midland Region's Royal Trains had

serious problems. The locomotive on the train, which had been withdrawn from service for a week of intensive maintenance and servicing, had failed. The standby locomotive was attached to the front of the train locomotive to save delay.

Sadly the fault on the train locomotive transferred itself to the other locomotive with the result that it also failed. A third locomotive was despatched to haul the two failed locomotives off of the train and then replace them. The whole procedure took some time. The General Manager was summoned to the Her Majesty the Queen's compartment, where Her Majesty is reported to have looked at him with a fixed expression on her face, and said, 'We are NOT getting there!'

And now back to London Area One. I found another frequent occurrence that occurred on Saturday mornings. A single 2 coach EMU ran ECS from Selhurst Depot to London Bridge. In all the points and crossings encountered when leaving the Norwood end of the Depot, there was one spot where there was no conductor rail.

Four coach units had no problem bridging the gap, but 2 coach units had to be driven carefully over the section to avoid becoming 'gapped.' This 'gapping' occurred on three consecutive Saturday mornings. After that, an additional unit was attached to the 2 coach unit, and the problem was solved.

My position on the London Area lasted for a while. Then, as I have said previously, I was advised and invited to learn the D.C.C.'s position, and I did, whenever I got the chance. Although I did not know the Central Division well, I quickly gained experience and confidence. I was soon passed competent to work the panel.

From then on, I seemed to be very much in demand to cover

the panel. I discovered that the regular D.C.C's had a lot of leave outstanding. There had been difficulty taking it because there was a shortage of relief staff to cover them. My arrival and my willingness to cover the panel was a welcome bonus for them. I was shown how to compile the Control Report. I also had a number of weeks of night duty when the Report was completed. I didn't mind that as I reckoned the experience was worth it.

I did ask my colleagues who were all senior to me and more experienced than I was, if they wanted to do it, but they were entirely happy for me to do it, so I did. In the end I was made aware that, as I had covered so many turns, I might be eligible for a personal regrading to Managerial Status Two (MS2).

I made my application to the Personnel Department. It was explained to me that in order to qualify I had to work at least 25% of the duties on the MS2 panel in a year. By that time I had been there for two years, I calculated I had covered the position for 75% of my duties. I filled in the forms, giving the dates, times and reasons, ie Annual Leave, Vacancy, Sick Leave etc. The Personnel Department then began a process of eliminating as much of these as possible.

The dates had to be from January 1st to December 31st of any one year. Anything either side of this was discounted. Then they explained that covering certain long-term vacancies would not count. I protested that if they had filled the vacancies, I would not have been needed to cover them. This was all to no avail. One way and another they whittled the figures down until they stood at 27%. They could not get them any lower. I waited anxiously.

Then John B, Head of Personnel came to me one day and

said, 'Terry, I believe you are right. I will do all I can to facilitate your application.' I waited for a while, then one day I received a letter from Mr Bev W, the Chief Controller, dated 21st August 1987.

It read, 'Dear Terry. With reference to your application for regrading on 2nd January 1987, I am sorry to have been so long in responding, but there were unfortunately some unusual aspects to your claim that required points of principle to be established. I am pleased to confirm that this has now been completed and as a result I am able to advise you that you qualify for regrading to MS2 on a personal basis with effect from 10th November 1986. Please accept my congratulations.' I had done it! I was now an MS2.

One immediate result was that whenever a duty on the MS2 panel was not covered, I was given the first choice in covering it. I now covered the MS2 panel most of the time, only occasionally covering an Area Panel. Looking back, I suspect that one of the points of principle they had problems with, was how to justify the covering of an Area Controller Grade 'E' panel by a MS2 Grade Manager.

Then followed a series of re-organisations. With the arrival of the other two Divisional Controls, the post of Regional D.C.C. had been discontinued, some of those in that position taking retirement. Some became Divisional Operations Managers until they retired.

One morning I had walked up the Control Room to talk to the Locomotive Controller, Peter K. He directed my attention to the window. I need to set the scene a little so that the reader will understand what followed. Our view from the windows was overlooking the viaduct which carried the up and down lines to and from Charing Cross on the approach to Waterloo South Eastern Station. Below the viaduct was the main road and station approach. Behind the viaduct stood a very tall tree whose roots were at ground level and whose branches rose gracefully above the viaduct. Behind the tree was an office block.

Builders had been working on this office block for some time and had at least twice accidentally set fire to the guttering. Now, from this site, a column of smoke was rising. As we watched, the smoke suddenly became thicker and more dense. Then there was a loud 'Boomp!' noise, which shook our building and rattled all the windows. Little bits of a transit van, the largest of them being a wheel arch, rose gracefully above the tree before falling back to earth.

Peter ascertained somehow that the van, containing six gas cylinders had caught fire. By heroic efforts, five of the cylinders had been pulled out of the van but the fire had then really taken hold and everyone had dived for cover. The phones in our Control Room then started to ring incessantly, many people ringing up to enquire if there had been an explosion or had there been a collision or buffer stop collision. We were able to reassure them that all was well. Peter later discovered that police had closed all the roads in the area. No-one had advised the Railway Authorities and trains had run uninterrupted past the site of the fire and explosion.

In due course of time, Ken H got his wish and was able to retire on very good terms. That created an MS2 vacancy. I applied for the position and was delighted to find I was appointed.

Now for the first time I had my own team to manage. It felt

a bit like my first appointment to South Eastern Area Three all those years ago. In the general reorganisation we received the Title of Operations Line Managers.

Operations Line Manager Grade M.S.2.

My team comprised Brian A on the London Area, Dave T on the Country Area Two, Charlie was on the Country Area Three, and Paul W was our Assistant.

It wasn't long before I was in trouble again. One morning Charlie took a call from Brighton The signal box was on fire. I realised that if the fire was on the operating floor, we might get away with it to a certain extent, but if it was the relay room below, we were in real trouble. I asked Charlie to ascertain which it was.

Back came the reply that it was indeed the relay room. This was a major incident. From that moment on, nothing could leave Brighton either on the main line to London, or the east coast branch to Eastbourne and the west coast branch to Worthing. Similarly, nothing could enter Brighton from any direction.

We got every member of S & T and P. Way staff we could lay our hands on. Out they went with the massive point clips. Every pair of points was clipped so that we had one route into and out of Brighton to London. The branch services were terminated short and buses were called in to provide an alternative service. The Special Traffic Department mapped out a special service and the Crew Diagrams Department mapped out co-ordinating diagrams for train crew. This went on for some weeks.

Eventually that day it became possible to bring in one train an hour from each of the branches.

Meanwhile the damage to Brighton signal box had been assessed and the decision was taken not to try to reinstate it. Plans had existed for some time for the eventual takeover of the Brighton Area by Three Bridges Area Signalling Centre. These plans were brought forward. After a period of some weeks we came on duty one bright morning to find that the work had been completed and Three Bridges Area Signalling Centre now controlled the Brighton Area. Normal working had been restored.

Other smaller incidents continued to occur and the typewriter on which the Control Report was compiled was seldom still.

During a later reorganisation on the Central Division, the Country Area Three was merged with Country Area Two and the third panel became the Rolling Stock Control Panel (Grade 'D').

That concentrated the control of the areas into just two areas and at the same time, relieved the Area Controllers of most of the responsibility for Rolling Stock Control.

Then, in October 1987 came another reorganisation. The posts of Operations Line Managers Grade MS2 were going to be replaced by Duty Line Managers Positions (DLM) Grade MS3. One essential difference was that there would now be three regular shifts, each with a Duty Line Manager, then one Rest Day Relief Shift with its own Duty Line Manager, and one General Purpose Relief Shift again with its own Duty Line Manager.

This meant that successful applicants would be allotted their own shift of Controllers and would be responsible for them and for their training and performance. We all had to apply for all of the positions. On 14th January 1988, I was advised that I had been appointed to one of the three regular shifts as Duty Line Manager, (DLM) Grade MS3, with seniority dated from 26th October 1987. I was delighted.

My new DLM colleagues were Micky B, and Dave W as the regular DLM's. Mike M was the Rest Day Relief DLM and Gwyn was the General Purpose Relief DLM. On my shift Brian A was the London Area Controller, Dave T was the Country Area Controller, Charlie B was the Rolling Stock Controller and Paul W was the Assistant Controller.

This once again signalled a new chapter in my career.

Chapter Eleven - Duty Line Manager,(D.L.M.), MS3, South Central Division

It was during this period that the I.R.A. mounted an active campaign in mainland Britain, with devastating effect on our train services. Following a 'coded warning' received by the Metropolitan Police, a device actually exploded in a waste bin on Victoria Station. Thus was a precedent set. All waste bins or similar receptacles were removed not just from London termini, but from every station.

Every time a coded warning was received that explosive devices had been planted in London termini, the Metropolitan Police would require all London stations to be closed and trains to be diverted or terminated short.

At first this came as a total shock. On night duty at 6 am on a Monday morning, the day most often chosen, everything would be running beautifully. Then at 6.30 am, the Metropolitan Police would call, and we would be closing all London stations, terminating trains at Clapham Junction or East Croydon, sorting out the Sutton/Dorking/West Croydon and South London services, working with the traincrew supervisors, and trying to get passengers into London by other means.

Initially we were able to move passengers via the London Underground. But as the incidents continued, the London Underground was also closed. Then the hapless passengers had no choice but to make their way on foot or give up and return home by whatever train they could find. The resulting chaos would last all day, services not being brought back to normal until the next morning.

The arrangements for rolling stock due for maintenance would be thrown to the four winds and it might take days to get that sorted. It was a very effective campaign.

Throughout this troubled time the Control continued to be manned. Then one Monday morning the inevitable happened. The Metropolitan Police ordered the evacuation of the buildings at Waterloo. My shift had been on duty since 8 pm on Sunday night. We were in the middle of trying to co-ordinate the service. We pointed out that it was essential that we remained on site, but this time the Police were insistent.

At around 8 am, a very tired group of Controllers made their way to an office in Friars Bridge Court, which was being prepared for the eventual move of the South Eastern Control from Waterloo. We were equipped with a pencil, a notepad and a single telephone handset each. With this we had to try to bring order out of chaos.

At around 9.30, we were advised that the offices at Waterloo had been reopened. Our early turn relief had been allowed in. Most of the night shift decided to return home straight from Friars Bridge Court, but as DLM, I was required to return to make a proper handover and collect my gear.

It was just before 10 am when I strolled onto the deserted concourse at Waterloo. It was weird. I could see hundreds of rats running along the platform.

Then suddenly, seemingly from nowhere, two armed police officers appeared and challenged me. Being on night duty I was wearing an old three-quarter length jacket instead of my usual suit. I tiredly reached into my pocket for my Duty Pass. This move was misinterpreted, and I saw them reaching for their guns. I called out 'Whoa! I just want to show you my duty pass.' They relaxed as I gave them my pass. 'I've been on duty for fourteen hours. I don't want to get shot now thank you!' They didn't smile. I think they were as fed up with the situation as we were.

My identity established I then had to get home. I did the handover, then, accompanied by Peter K, I set off for home. There were no trains. We caught a bus to Greenwich, and from there, another bus to Hither Green. There, Peter used his influence to secure a place for both of us on an engine running "light" from Hither Green to Ashford. This stopped at Sevenoaks where Peter got off.

We then proceeded to Tonbridge where the final snag occurred. We were required to run via the down platform to set me down. But somehow the message had not reached the signalman, who had set the route for the down main. I offered to get off on the down main, but the crew declined my offer. The signalman was advised, the route was cancelled, and after the 'timeout,' was reset for the down platform, and I finally alighted at Tonbridge. I drove home, arriving there just before 1pm.

The first thing I did was to ring Control, tell them that I had just arrived home and there was no way I could be back for 3 pm for the late turn. I would, however, try to be back by 6 pm. I actually arrived back in the Control just before 6.30 pm. By 9.30 pm I was on my way home again, my relief having come in early because of the chaos on the trains.

The incidents continued to happen. There were a number

of security alerts, although thankfully we were not asked to evacuate the Control again. There were signal, points and train failures, engineering possession over-runs and staff shortages, although the service generally was more reliable.

All the incidents were recorded on the Control Report. This was typed up by the DLM from notes made as information came in. Every night, the night duty DLM completed the Report for the day and arranged for its circulation, and then started the new days Report. All Heads of Department received a copy and one copy went to the Divisional Manager and another to the British Railways Board, (BRB). We always tried to verify the accuracy of the reports. Our reputation stood or fell on this.

It was also used in Enquiries. The original notes we had made at the time of an incident were legally admissible evidence in a court of law. The Control Report was not legally admissible but could be used to support them. We used an old-fashioned manual typewriter. Then, one day we were issued with an electric typewriter. Shortly afterwards this was superseded by an electronic typewriter.

Then, one Monday night a computer appeared. I had had no training on this. I was self- taught on a tiny computer at home, so I knew my way around the keyboard, but that was where my expertise ended. As forcefully as I could I expressed my concern, saying 'I do hope this is not going to be brought into use before I get some training.'

On Thursday night my worst fears were realised. The electronic typewriter had gone, and the computer was up and running. Thankfully it was a very quiet night, so I spent almost the entire night getting to know how to operate it. The Control

Report was completed just before I was relieved.

But I was not alone in my lack of knowledge. Another DLM was presented with a bottle of correcting fluid and told to paint it on the screen when he made an error. There were also the wise guys whose sense of humour was not always appreciated.

One person uploaded a small programme on one of the South Western controller's computer. All of a sudden, as he was typing, the words turned into water droplets that then ran down the screen. He complained that his computer was leaking!

There was fierce rivalry on my panel and efficiency was the name of the game. This was encouraged by our new Senior Manager. It was unfortunate that he had taken a dislike of me, and I had to be doubly vigilant.

One Monday morning, I arrived to find that an insulator pot had exploded and displaced the conductor rail on the down line at Lancing and single line working was in progress over the up line. Preference was being given to up trains for the morning peak service. Engineers were on site and Brighton Electrical Control was keeping us advised of progress.

It was also on that morning that I was scheduled to be interviewed by P. Way Supervisor Pat M, as part of their training for Leadership 2000. We ourselves had completed the first part of this scheme, and they were on the second stage.

The interview was to be filmed. I was later able to obtain a copy of that film and I have it to this day, now in DVD format.

The subject of the interview was the problems between the Permanent Way Department and the Operating Department. Mr M explained that P. Way staff felt the Control was prejudiced against them, that the Control Report showed them in a very poor light, and that they were unfairly blamed when things went wrong. I was asked to explain the problems from the Operating point of view.

I explained that our biggest problem was communication. We viewed the P. Way engineers as very professional men and women, without whose specialist skills we could not run a railway. We also appreciated their work in all weathers. Our problem lay in the matter of communication.

When the engineers take up a planned possession of the line, the train service is re-planned accordingly, sometimes supplemented by buses. This is published, and 'everybody knows about it, nothing can go wrong' (another favourite saying of mine). But things do go wrong. The weather can play a big part in the success or otherwise of the job. Equipment can fail. Engineering trains can arrive late on site.

This latter can be caused by a number of reasons. It may be that the traincrew duty is not covered and can only be covered with a delay to the train. It then becomes a difficult decision whether to hold up or stop other possessions to let the train through to this site, or whether it is better to cancel the train, which will deprive engineers of essential equipment or materials.

This problem became so acute that a clerk in the Traincrew Department was allocated specially to ensure all trains were covered and in the case of traincrew shortfall, to liaise with the Permanent Way Head Office to allow the latter to decide the order of priorities.

So, as I explained to Mr M, we understood their difficulties, and respected them. Sometimes we would be aware that an engineering possession would over-run, and we could work out a plan for the train service, and buses if necessary, to cater for the situation. But no such plans could be made if we were left in blissful ignorance of a problem. Unless we were told in advance, we would assume that all was well, and the possession would be lifted on time.

The worst possible scenario for a controller was to be told, one hour or less, that a planned possession was going to over-run. Even worse if the engineers could not tell us how long the line(s) would continue to be blocked.

Then it would be a mad scramble to re-arrange train services and traincrew and rolling stock to cover the alterations and to retain, if possible, any rail replacement bus services in operation. Inevitably all this would take time and there would be, initially at least, an element of unreliability in the service.

Whilst the cause of the delay in clearing the possession could be justified, the P. Way staff involved would have to take responsibility for the unplanned disruption of the service. It was therefore essential that as soon as the Person In Charge of Possession (PICOP) was aware of a problem that would affect the giving up of the possession on time, he or she must tell the Control, and if possible, give a rough estimate of when the possession would be cleared.

It was whilst I was in the middle of explaining all this, that Charlie came over. He had taken a call from the County Police, requesting permission for officers to go onto the track at Ifield Station to chase suspects.

Now there is a laid down procedure for this, which must be rigidly adhered to, for the safety of all concerned. Firstly the trains in the area must be brought to a stand. This is the responsibility of the controlling signalman, in this case Three Bridges Area Signalling Centre. The controlling signalman is also responsible for requesting the Electrical Control, in this case Brighton Electrical Control, to discharge the traction current.

This is also a complex operation. Some years ago a traction current discharge had been requested to allow firemen to go onto the track. This was done and the firemen went onto the track with their hoses. Unfortunately a train moving on the extremity of that blockage, passed over a junction, temporally bridging the isolation and livening up the isolated track. Though it was only momentary, it was sufficient. Sadly a fireman was electrocuted and killed. From that time onwards, new regulations were introduced, that whenever such a blockage was requested, traction current on neutral sections of conductor rail either side of the blockage had to be discharged, as well as the affected section. This affected more trains and it took longer to bring them to a standstill.

This was the case in this incident. By the time all trains had been stopped, and traction current, including neutral sections, had been discharged, some fifteen minutes had elapsed. This was very frustrating for the Police, who saw their suspects gleefully disappearing in the distance. I had spoken to the Electrical Control to warn them of the impending request and save time, while my Area Controller had spoken to the signalman. But it still took fifteen minutes. In that time the suspects were in danger at any time of being electrocuted.

We then had to wait for the Police to advise us when they and the suspects were clear of the line before traction current could be restored and trains were allowed to continue their journeys.

All this was being filmed by the P. Way cameraman, as our

interview had to be temporarily suspended. Light relief was provided by the advice from the police that the suspects they were chasing were 'handbag snatchers.'

I was also overseeing the clearance of the possession at Lancing, which was due imminently. Brighton Electrical Control advised me that traction current had been restored. I noted the time and advised my Area Controller. We now awaited the lifting of the possession by the P.Way Staff.

This also gave my interviewer an opportunity to see the entries being made to the Control Report. Resuming our discussion, I explained the importance of truth and accuracy in compiling the Control Report. There was no place for bias of any kind and any inaccuracy would be quickly shown up.

The interview ended well, and everyone seemed happy with the outcome. The problem at Lancing was resolved, though sadly the handbag snatchers at Ifield escaped. And occasionally I enjoy watching my copy of the film.

Chapter Twelve - Purley

I was Rest Day off on the 12th December 1988. I saw the television news, which broadcast that a serious train accident had occurred at Clapham Junction that morning. It was indeed a tragic triple collision, caused by a signalling fault, which resulted in thirty-five people losing their lives and around five hundred more being injured.

I immediately changed my plans and went to work to assist the South Western DLM. This was not an unusual or exceptional act on my part. Other controllers did exactly the same. My job, when I got there, was to take on and deal with the other incidents, leaving the DLM free to deal with the major incident. It was a steep learning curve.

But little did I know that in less than six months, I myself would be involved in a major incident on my own patch.

On Saturday 4th March 1989, I was early turn DLM. It was a 'mucky' day. We had been beset by technical failures. The worst of these came at approximately 10 am, when Three Bridges Area Signalling Centre Regulator advised me that they had lost all track circuit indications in the East Croydon area. The Signal and Telecomms engineers (S & T) were in attendance, and arrangements were being made to provide hand signalmen.

Three Bridges Area Signalling Centre was a modern installation and trains were identified on the signalling panels by their four- digit individual train descriptions. But in a failure of this kind, the train descriptions had frozen in the last known position, so each train had to be identified. Thankfully the failure was quickly rectified.

Then at 1.40 pm, Three Bridges Regulator reported loss of all track circuit indications in the Purley/East Croydon Area. 'Here we go again,' I thought. But this was immediately discounted as we received simultaneously two reports, one from Brighton Electrical Control that all traction supply and control in the same area had been lost, and my London Area Controller Brian A was advised by Purley station that there had been a train crash.

Just for one moment, I froze. This couldn't have happened. The system did not allow it. But then a voice inside my head seemed to say, 'It has happened! Now get on with it and deal with it as you have been trained to.'

Station staff at Purley reported that one train had gone down an embankment and overturned. I knew there were casualties, and almost certainly fatalities. I immediately informed the Emergency Services that a major train accident had occurred at Purley Station, and casualties including fatalities had resulted, but details were as yet unknown..

The Electrical Control advised me that the train that had gone down the embankment, had carried away the traction current control cables and it was impossible to say which conductor rails were still 'live.' We had to warn the Emergency Services to stay clear until we could ensure their safety. Thankfully Purley has a P.Way Depot and staff were quickly on site with test mats, thick rubber mats with a lamp in them. The mats were placed on the conductor rail and if the lamp lit up the rail was live.

Again thankfully we quickly proved the entire area was isolated by the accident. The Emergency Services were allowed on site.

The next task was to ascertain how much of the area was affected. We were able to establish that the boundaries of the affected area were Penge West, Star Lane, Upper Warlingham, Tattenham Corner/Caterham, Waddon and Streatham. Armed with this information, the London Area Controller began planning the immediate re-arranging of the services, assisted by the Assistant Controller. Cover over such a wide area could not be achieved with special bus services but arrangements were made with London Transport for all buses in the area to accept passengers with rail tickets.

Later, as this incident was going to last some days, the planning sections came on board to plan a daily emergency service.

Meanwhile I also advised the Maintenance Control at Southern House, the Senior On Call Officer, the British Railways Board, and the Press Office. The railway breakdown cranes at Brighton and Stewarts Lane were placed on standby. All this was achieved by the team within 10 minutes of the moment of collision.

It was established that the 1217 Littlehampton – Victoria, running fast to East Croydon, had descended Stoats Nest Bank at line speed, reportedly under clear signals until finding signal T168 on the London end of Purley up fast platform, displaying a red, stop, aspect. As the driver reacted immediately to this, he saw ahead of him, the 1250 Horsham – Victoria which had just left the up slow platform and was crossing to the up fast line, a correctly signalled and regulated move.

The 1217 Littlehampton, despite all the efforts of the driver, who remained at the controls, passed the up fast signal T168 at danger and collided with the rear cab of the 1250 Horsham.

The impact derailed the 1217 Littlehampton and deflected the train down the embankment. All the coaches of the leading unit and two of the four coaches of the second unit, fell down the embankment, deflected by trees, which prevented them from hitting a house in Glenn Avenue. The second coach passed the first coach. The seventh coach was derailed but stayed upright. Only the last coach remained on the track. It was in this coach that my relief , Phil, was travelling. He was uninjured, and being unable to get to London, he assisted on site.

The emergency service was arranged as follows.

Thameslink services (now First Capital Connect) were diverted to and from Moorgate.

Shuttle service Horsham to Redhill.

Bognor/Littlehampton services were diverted via Horsham and Dorking

Shuttle service East Grinstead/Uckfield to Oxted.

Railair services diverted from Gatwick via Three Bridges, Horsham and Dorking.

Temporary accommodation and lighting were arranged as this incident was going to be ongoing for several days.

The driver of the 1217 Littlehampton was injured and was taken to hospital He was conscious, and he was interviewed as quickly as possible.

Once the Emergency Services were fully alerted and arrangements for their safety were in place, we then began monitoring the services, and as a team, examining them to see if there was any way we could improve them. We liaised continually with the Electrical Control to ensure that neutral sections were maintained to protect those on site, continuing to rescue trapped passengers, and ensuring their safe removal to hospital.

For the subsequent enquiry I had to obtain the details of all the crew's duties that day and the previous days. This was necessary to identify any possible cause of distraction, or lack of rest between duties. I also had to ensure that our Press Office was kept informed of every development. Under no circumstances were any of us to talk to the Press ourselves.

The Signal and Telecomms Department came out in force and examined every piece of equipment on every signal painstakingly to establish if there was any possible cause of malfunction. If the signalling system was working correctly the driver should have had visual, and audible warnings (Automatic Warning System, AWS, 'sunflower') and the upcoming signal aspects should have warned the driver that he was approaching a signal showing a red 'stop' aspect, and allowing him time to reduce the speed of the train accordingly.

In order, the signals before T 168 should have shown aspects as listed here. The first in rear of T.168 one yellow aspect, the next in rear two yellow aspects and the last a green aspect. The task incumbent upon the Signal & Telecomms staff was to examine and find any possible fault, and this examination they carried out thoroughly and with real dedication. After some days they later reported back that they could not say that there was no fault, but they could say they were unable to find any fault with the system. The AWS system was also examined.

I managed to get a communications van to site, which proved a great help to us as many of the normal telephone lines were inundated with calls.

Brighton Crane was ready just before 3 pm. Stewarts Lane Crane was being readied. London Underground Limited, (LUL) were providing heavy lifting gear from their Neasdon Depot.

While all this was going on, we continued to monitor the service, making improvements where we could. Brian A, London Area Controller advised at 3.50 pm that traction current had been restored between East Grinstead and South Croydon. His relief arrived and he was thankful to be allowed to go home.

Other incidents also continued to occur, although thankfully they were minor. The South Western D.C.C continued to assist me and made notes of other incidents for me to add to the Control Report later. Some of the minor incidents were taken care of by staff on site where they happened. They understood the circumstances and went out of their way to help us in this way.

Staff on site, and notably the Duty Officer and the Emergency Services kept us well advised. We in turn, made sure the Press Office and our passengers were kept informed. All the notes I made I kept safely in one place, because I knew they might be called for and used in the Public Enquiry that inevitably would follow. I continued on duty until relieved by Phil at about 6 pm.

Then it was time to gather up all my notes and begin to compile and type up the Control Report. That done I had to compile a Report for the Transport Police, and another Report for myself, for reference and information. I eventually left the Control Room at 2200 hours, fifteen hours after taking duty.

Sadly, five passengers lost their lives in this incident, and eighty- eight people, including the driver and two other members of staff, were injured.

The succeeding days were hectic as can be imagined. To lift the coaches that had gone down the embankment was an impossibility for rail-mounted equipment. Messrs Greystone Sparrow provided a huge crane with two hundred tonnes lifting capacity. To site the crane, it was necessary to demolish a newly built garage owned by the residents of the house, which the falling train had so narrowly missed.

Eventually the coaches were removed and taken to Selhurst Depot. Six months later, almost to the day I was taking my shift around Selhurst Depot on an accompanied educational visit, when rounding a corner, I saw the unit that had been the rear unit of the 1250 Horsham - Victoria. The rear cab had been stove in. It was a reminder of the tremendous forces at work in the collision. It also had another effect. I felt chilled for the rest of the day.

Also, day-by-day, we were able to clear lines and restore facilities and thus improve the service. This sometimes meant that Controllers had to amend all the arrangements that had been so carefully put in place by the Planners, and this meant revising and recasting traincrew duties and rolling stock provisions. It was a stressful time for the Controllers, and I was very proud of the way they coped. The planners too adjusted their plans, which included revising traincrew rosters.

It is not within the remit of this little book to discuss the possible causes or the details of the subsequent Internal, Public, and Police Enquiries. Other publications deal with the matter in much greater detail. I have a copy of the Public Enquiry Records. But incidents of this kind affect everyone involved, and those effects often come out a lot later. I was very grateful to the team on duty that day for the great job they did. I was very proud of the fact that we were complimented by the Police on the amount of detailed information we were able to gather at the time, which made their job so much easier.

I was also very grateful to Brian G, the South Western DLM, who came down to assist me in the first hours of the incident.

And, even in the midst of tragedy, some humour can be found. I was advised by a member of staff, who was at the scene at the time, of the following incident. I cannot vouch for its accuracy, but I believe it was true.

A passenger on the train, realising that the brakes had been severely applied, prayed, 'Please Lord don't let the train derail.'

As it derailed, he prayed, 'Please Lord don't let it turn over.'

As it turned over, he prayed, 'Lord please let me survive.'

The train came to rest and the dust settled.

As the passenger gathered his wits, he heard a voice. It was a passenger in an adjoining bay who said, 'Excuse me. I believe you have lost your spectacles.'

Finally, I have one souvenir of the occasion that I really appreciated. It was a letter from Mr Jim G, Operations Manager South Central, dated 6th March 1989. It read:

'Dear Terry, Purley Crash. Just a note to thank you for your efforts in dealing with the above over the weekend. Whilst we should not gain any satisfaction from such incidents, I am mindful of your efforts in providing a service for our customers. Yours Sincerely, Jim G.

UPDATE ON PURLEY TRAIN COLLISION

My personal belief, based on my own experience of signalling and operations, had always been that the driver, an experienced man with a good record, had not made any mistakes, and that he had been seriously mislead by a fault in the signalling system, which had resulted in preceding signals showing "green" clear aspects.

I considered his conviction had been grossly unfair. But it was only my own belief. I had no way of proving that. Nor could I have any say in the matter then or now. All I was able to do was present the known facts. You can imagine my delight when I saw the following headlines.

Purley Train Collision 4th March 1989
Additional Information 12th December 2017

On the 6pm London News tonight, it was announced that, following a subsequent Court of Appeal Enquiry, the Judge said that there had been admitted infrastructure problems, which had been identified as the cause of the accident on 4th March 1989, and the Driver of the 1217 Littlehampton to Victoria had been acquitted of any and all responsibility, and that his conviction had been quashed. The Driver was interviewed and simply said how thankful and relieved he was that the shadow of blame, which had lain so heavily, had now been lifted.

I could not have been more pleased!

Chapter Thirteen -
Life goes on at Waterloo

And now, from the sublime to the ridiculous. We, as a company, were at the time becoming part of a new organisation known as Network SouthEast. The sign on the side of the footbridge from Waterloo South Eastern to Waterloo Main Line, proudly displayed a huge sign to this effect. Except that what it actually read was Notwork SouthEast. I would like to have shaken the hands of those responsible. It was there for a number of days before arrangements were made and it was altered, by those in authority.

It was quite rare on the night shift to have many serious problems with passenger services, but on the night of 28th January 1989, we had a potentially very serious incident. Our first reports indicated that an engineering train conveying a small crane that had departed from Three Bridges Yard just before midnight bound for an engineer's possession at Balham, when the jib of the crane broke loose and struck the wall of Merstham Tunnel.

It then rebounded, fouling the offside track just as the 0015 Victoria – Gatwick RailAir service was passing at full speed. The jib struck the coaches of the Gatwick Express. It was a high speed impact and a number of windows on the offside of the Gatwick Express were broken. Several passengers were slightly injured by flying glass. Thankfully too there was no derailment.

Later the full story became clear. What had broken loose was in fact not the jib of the crane that was being conveyed but some signal gantry structures that were also being conveyed. It also transpired that prior to the accident the overhanging structure, then fouling the nearside of the engineers train had struck a ground shunt signal at Redhill, damaging it and knocking it over.

This had pulled the load further off of the wagon, so it was foul of the tunnel wall as it entered Merstham Tunnel. This had caused that structure to rebound to the offside and then strike the 0015 Victoria to Gatwick. Around six passengers were injured by flying fragments and were conveyed hospital, their injuries reported as not serious.

As a direct result of that incident, the instructions for the inspecting engineering trains before departure were revised extensively and a Safe Loading Certificate was to be completed and signed by the Inspector. This sometimes caused delays but I do not recall any similar incidents occurring after that. Up to my time of retirement that instruction was still in force.

On 11th September 1991 another major incident occurred, this time at Barnham. I was early turn and we had a relief controller on the country area. I had not been able to remember the order in which Woodgate and Woodhorn Level Crossings at Barnham came. After this incident I never forgot them.

I had a call from the West Sussex Police to say that a motorist at Woodgate Level Crossing had reported a passing goods train had the two rear tank wagons bouncing off the track. I rang the signal box myself and advised the signalman, who at once blocked both lines.

Almost immediately I had another call from the Police to tell me that a motorist at Woodhorn Level Crossing had reported the same train derailed and the rear two tank wagons were on fire. The Emergency Services were called and attended. The incident sounded really serious, but in fact the wagons were filled with wax oil. Sparks from the derailment had ignited the gunge that had collected under the tanks over a period of time.

The firemen extinguished the fires and released the pressure caps. A great cloud of smoke was discharged, and that, as far as the Fire Brigade were concerned, was that. Of course, that was not that at all. Thankfully, because both we, and then the signalman, had been promptly advised, no other train was involved. But the down line had been badly damaged and single line working was imposed over the up line for several days while repairs were effected.

One other result came from this incident. Several years later I was talking to an Area Inspector and he asked me if I remembered the incident.

When I said I certainly did, he asked me if I had seen the photographs of it.

I replied that I didn't know that photographs had been taken.

He said that they had, and he obtained a set for me. They certainly did look dramatic and I have had them enlarged and framed.

One day our shift were 'spare,' that is, we were not required for duty in the Control. I arranged for my shift to meet me at Tonbridge and I would take them in my old yellow transit van, nicknamed 'The Yellow Peril,' to the Channel Tunnel Exhibition at Folkestone. We had a great day there.

The exhibition consisted of a lot of photographs and displays and an 'N' gauge model of the line. It was divided into three sections, the first being the English terminal at Folkestone, then a middle section representing the actual tunnel, and finally the French section at Coquelles.

We watched this impressive display for a while. Enter a cleaner, equipped with a 'hoover.' No he didn't suck a train up. But as a twenty-coach model train approached, he completely forgot the power lead trailing from the hoover. Twenty coaches went, one after the other, up in the air. The whole train ended up scattered all over the model. Roars of laughter greeted this incident and the story spread far and wide that Terry couldn't even visit a model railway without a major incident occurring.

There was also a sting in the tail. Most of the team lived on the Central Division so it was agreed I would run them back to Tonbridge in time to catch a train to Redhill.

Arriving back at Tonbridge, we found we had missed the train to Redhill by a matter of minutes.

As the next train was not for some time, I offered to run them to Redhill in the van. As we were driving along the A25, a lorry passed us. A bolt flew off from its bodywork and smashed my windscreen. I happened to have an emergency windscreen, so I dug it out. Unfortunately it was for a Ford Cortina, not a Ford Transit van, so it didn't quite fit. Charlie B was sitting in front beside me, and he ended up holding the bit that didn't quite fit, all the way back to Tonbridge. And then it began to rain !

The next day, I found that the whole story had preceded me. Great was the mirth that greeted me. Brian, a Relief Controller from the South Western Division came down and said, 'Terry, you are a lovely bloke and a good operator. But I'll tell you something. If I was sitting on a plane at Gatwick Airport and saw you get on, I would get off.'

On the 8th January 1991 I was night duty DLM or the Central Division. Gordon M, the Operations Manager South Eastern Division came to me with a request. Several days before, there had been a buffer stop collision at Cannon Street. A suburban train comprised of either eight or ten EPB stock had run into the station and had been unable to stop before colliding with the buffers. The leading cab was damaged, and the shock waves had travelled through the train causing an overriding and slight telescoping between the fifth and six coaches.

The train had remained in the platform for several days, firstly for the investigation and then for repairs to be made in order to make it possible for the train to be worked away to depot. These repairs had been completed and the train was now ready to be moved. It was essential that this move be made as soon as possible to free up the occupied platform, which had caused delays to the working at Cannon Street, as well as being an embarrassment to the Company.

It was also essential that the move be monitored throughout. The problem was that due to a shortage of staff in the South Eastern Control, there was no night duty DLM. So Gordon asked me if I could be South Eastern DLM for that night as well as Central DLM. I was very pleased to be asked and agreed at once.

As it happened it was an unusually quiet night both on the Central and South Eastern Divisions. The move from Cannon Street was accomplished exactly a planned. I was able to close up the Control Report for both Divisions and set up the new ones for the next day. I also compiled a report for Gordon on the moving of the stock from Cannon Street, and paged him before going off duty to advise him of its success.

Chapter Fourteen - 'The South Eastern Division - a Model of Complexity'

Gordon also involved me in another of his projects. He discovered that one of my hobbies was making video films. I had made around a hundred films, some for schools (including one for the child of a colleague of mine), amateur dramatic shows, charities, the occasional weddings etc. He asked me if I would make a film of the South Eastern Division with the above title. His intention was to use it at a special presentation for Senior Officers and influential people from outside the industry. It was a wonderful and challenging project.

Almost all of it was filmed on my Rest Days or after shifts and Gordon arranged the appropriate payments for this.

We met to plan the sequences. Gordon wanted an aerial view from Charing Cross to Waterloo East, a view of Borough Market Junction from ground level, a session in London Bridge Area Signalling Centre, a view of the St. Johns, Lewisham, Parks Bridge complex, a drivers eye view of the line from Charing Cross to Tonbridge, and some other clips that he had. To all this, my own Operations Manager reluctantly agreed, because it meant I was not available for overtime on the Central Division.

And so the project got under way.

My first challenge was the view from Charing Cross to Waterloo. Years before, I had helped school children with a Railway Project, and as part of that I had been able to take one of them right up onto the roof of the main line station at Waterloo. This gave a birds eye view of Charing Cross and Waterloo East.

It was perfectly safe. Access was gained by a lift to the top floor and then via a fire escape passage, protected by strong guard rails. It was a very impressive view. So to this site I proceeded with my video cameras one weekday afternoon after early turn. I set up the cameras and waited. I began filming at the beginning of the rush hour. The weather was perfect, and I was able to shoot a very good film.

Next, I had to find a suitable location for the filming of Borough Market Junction. This is the junction just north of London Bridge Station, where four lines go to and from London Cannon Street diverging from two lines going to and from London Charing Cross. It is the busiest junction in the world. During the rush hour there was a train movement every twenty-one seconds.

Going back to my days at Orpington Control, it was the only signal box we were forbidden to ring, except in an emergency because of the intensity of the service. The signal box there had long since gone, its work being done by the signalmen at London Bridge Area Signalling Centre. The actual signal box itself complete with its equipment is now preserved in the National Railway Museum at York.

Obviously it was too dangerous a place to film from the trackside. Even getting there and back would be hazardous. With the agreement of the Area Manager at London Bridge, I was located in the tiny observation cabin on the end of one of the platforms at London Bridge Eastern Station. This afforded an excellent view of trains negotiating the junction and another happy afternoon after early turn was spent filming the trains there.

The next part of the project involved a visit to London Bridge Area Signalling Centre (ASC). Again permission had to be negotiated by Gordon, because nothing I was doing must be allowed to distract the signalmen from their very intensive job. I have briefly described elsewhere in this book, the area covered by the ASC, but very briefly, the ASC comprised several operating panels with entry/exit buttons, each manned by a signalman, and the whole operation overseen by a Signal Box Regulator, who oversaw the entire operation and liaised with us in Control.

The ASC covered an area comprising Charing Cross, Cannon Street, and the Blackfriars route from Apocathary Street Junction down to Metropolitan Junction, Borough Market Junction, through London Bridge South Eastern station with its six platforms, through to North Kent East Junction, where the Greenwich Line diverges, on through New Cross, down to St Johns Junction where the North Kent Line diverges, through the St. Johns, Lewisham, Parks Bridge, Mid Kent lines complex, on through Hither Green and Grove Park and down to Chislehurst Junction.

The ASC also covered from London Bridge Central all suburban routes to the outskirts of Norwood and Selhurst. Again a fascinating afternoon and evening was spent there.

The next part of the project was probably the most challenging. The St. Johns, Parks Bridge, Lewisham Junction complex is one of the most complex junctions. In the old days it was controlled from two signal boxes at St Johns and at Parks Bridge Junction.

The four up and down fast and up and down local lines from

Charing Cross and Cannon Street to Tonbridge and beyond run through this complex. At the St. Johns end, the up and down North Kent and Lewisham lines diverge to the left. A flyover over the main line tracks brings trains from Blackfriars to Dartford via Nunhead and the North Kent lines, with a further junction to Lewisham, and a fly-down from the flyover, bringing trains from Dartford onto the up fast main line.

The Parks Bridge Junction end comprises the four main lines, the Mid Kent lines to and from Lewisham to Ladywell, with a spur rejoining the main lines and a separate junction from the up and down fast lines to the up and down Mid Kent Lines, joining the spur from Lewisham to Ladywell below the main lines.

These were the junctions I had to film. Gordon tried to get me a helicopter to film from. But here even his considerable influence failed. The British Transport Policed did not own a helicopter and the Metropolitan Police would not allow a civilian to travel in one of theirs because of insurance problems. To hire a commercial helicopter was prohibitively expensive, something like three hundred pounds a minute I believe.

Not to be defeated, Gordon found an alternative. The Citibank Building very near to Parks Bridge Junction was a twenty-one storey building with a flat roof. This provided an ideal vantage point from which to view and film the junctions, albeit it was straining the efficiency of the cameras to their limits.

On the day of the filming I was Rest Day so I had the whole day to work on the project. Optimistically I drove to the building, where parking had been arranged. I unloaded two cameras, the television monitor, the extension cables and microphones and earphones and some other assorted gear. This I loaded onto a trolley and made my way to the entrance to the building.

I was met there by the security man. He was expecting me and let me in, but when he saw the trolley load of equipment, he looked at me and said in a concerned voice, 'Where do you think you are going with all that lot?'

'Up to the top of the building,' was my confident reply.

'I don't think so,' he said, 'Have they told you about this building?'

I said they hadn't.

'Well,' he said, 'for the first twenty-one floors you will travel in a lift. But you are then going onto the flat roof via a fire escape ladder. You will just have to take the essentials and I will look after the trolley and the rest of the equipment until you come down.'

And so I had to select only the essentials, the two cameras, the extension power leads, which were to run from a socket in a room on the twenty-first floor (thankfully they were long enough) and the earphones. The monitor and the other equipment all had to stay behind. So up we went. At the twenty-first floor the Security man guided me to the fire escape and kindly helped me up with my equipment. Once again it was a beautiful day and the view was phenomenal.

There was just one slight snag. The roof was indeed flat. There was no protective balustrade around it. From a view near the edge I could see all the tiny figures and the 'Dinky Toy' vehicles in the streets below. It was a reminder not to go too near the edge. But the weather was really good, bright and sunny and with not a breath of wind at all.

I set up the cameras on their tripods so the filming would

be as smooth as possible. One camera covered the northern junctions and the other the ones to the south. I was fascinated by the view and spent some time just gazing out. The sun was hot and I became thirsty. I remembered a cold drinks dispenser on the twenty-first floor. Leaving the cameras running, I negotiated the fire escape and purchased a can of drink.

I retraced my steps back up onto the roof. When I had first surmounted this ladder I was a bit concerned at what I might find, but this second ascent, knowing what it was like, did not worry me.

Inevitably, after my drink I needed a toilet. There were no such facilities on the roof, so back down the fire escape I went. By the time I was making my third ascent, I was quite relaxed about it.

After several hours up there, I began to look around me. On one corner of the roof I noticed what looked like gigantic instruments including one shaped like a large kettledrum. Being curious, I ensured that the cameras were working and that I would not get into the view, I wandered over to have a closer look.

I was examining the kettledrum, when I heard a shout from behind me. A man's head appeared above the fire escape and he yelled at me, 'Get away from there quickly!'

I rapidly obeyed, asking, 'Why - is it going to explode?'

The man emerged from the fire escape, and came over to me. 'No, no,' he said, 'It's not going to explode. But these are our electronic communications systems. When you stood near them, you cast a shadow over the transmissions and blocked our communications with the whole of northern Europe!'

I apologized profusely and promised not to go near them again.

The man smiled and returned to the fire escape.

Some time later, Gordon himself appeared from the fire escape. He had come to see for himself how things were going. He took a look around and turned a light shade of green. As I stepped backwards, I tripped on a very low ridge. 'For goodness sake Terry, don't fall over the edge,' he said. 'It wouldn't look good in the Accident Book!'

The filming was completed, and Gordon kindly helped me to dismantle the cameras and equipment and helped me down the Fire escape with them. On the ground floor I was reunited with my trolley. Gordon and I discussed the next stage of the project, a driver's eye view of the line between Charing Cross and Tonbridge.

And so it was arranged. One afternoon, equipped with my trusty camera, I joined Gordon and the driver of a service that ran fast from Waterloo East to Orpington, - or at least it should have done. The first part of the journey went according to plan. But after London Bridge we caught up with a late running stopping train and followed it all the way to Orpington. By the time we had got past it and run to Sevenoaks, Gordon ruefully said, 'I think we'll have to give up on that one. It really would not impress the audience. I have a film of a cab ride from Sevenoaks to London. It wasn't quite what I wanted, but it was a good run and it will have to do'

So the filming was completed. Gordon took a copy of the tape of St. Johns/Parks Bridge, and using a programme of his own, speeded up the tape. He then returned it to me, and I was entrusted with putting all the clips together and imposing the titling and music. This was a complex task and I had no more rest days off. The date of the presentation was later in the week after the completion of filming.

I had to go to my Operations Manager and ask for two days leave in order to complete the film in time. He was not happy at all about this, but eventually granted the leave. I worked all of one day and half of the next on the film. It was completed to my satisfaction at around midday on the day of the presentation. I had just time to make two copies and then set off to Waterloo with a copy for Gordon. I gave it to him at 2.30pm and it was shown at 5 pm. Apparently it was a great success. Gordon was very grateful and I was very pleased.

Then it was back to the Control and business as usual.

Chapter Fifteen -
Farewell Waterloo - Hello Croydon

Incidents continued to occur, as indeed they do each day, but there were no more major incidents in my time at Waterloo. But once more things they were a changing. The South Western Division Control was moving to Wimbledon. The South Eastern Control was moving to Friars Bridge Court, and we on the Central Division were to move to Croydon. The South Western and South Eastern Controls moved, and we said goodbye to our colleagues who in future we would deal with only by telephones and computers.

However, Stephenson House, nicknamed 'The Rocket Shop' (a reference to Stephenson's famous locomotive 'The Rocket') was not ready for us, so we remained in splendid isolation at Waterloo. The planning Departments for each Division had also departed, so we were very much on our own. Contractors had been brought in and they were changing all the inside of the building. Because it was a listed building the outside could not be touched.

Whose fault it was I do not know but the setting off of the fire alarms became almost a daily occurrence. This also resulted in a full attendance by the Fire Brigade with up to seven tenders and a Turntable.

At first this caused consternation among the many passengers, especially at peak times. But as days passed the travelling public got used to this and in the end became quite blasé about it all. Representations were made continually about our moving to Croydon, but still there were problems, the details of which we didn't know and we could not move.

I was off duty when the incident happened and can only relate it as I was told of it. One Friday night a pipe that was three parts paint and one part rust was punctured. All over the weekend water dripped through the ceiling, until by Monday morning it reached the three four foot square electric air conditioning plants in the false ceiling. In the subsequent explosive short circuits the false ceiling was brought down. Thankfully no-one was hurt.

I was long weekend off and came in on early turn to find a metal framework where the ceiling had been and where someone had hung a set of Christmas tree lights. There was a fresh emphasis on our desire to move. Not many days later, the move finally took place. So the chapters on Waterloo end, and a new chapter at Croydon begins.

On our arrival at Croydon we found things very different. Stephenson House (known to all as 'The Rocket Shop') had a specifically designed Control Room. All of the other South Central staff had moved to Stephenson House some time before and were well established.

We had to get used to a lot of new equipment. Each of the Control Panels had initially five computer screens, worked from two keyboards with a switching device.

The first was a telescreen telephone system. On its first page were the most frequently used numbers. For other numbers, you scrolled down, using the keyboard. To call a number, you simply touched the appropriate square and the number automatically rang. You then picked up the receiver to speak.

This was an excellent system and very reliable. But it had to be kept up to date. One of the DLM's with a much greater knowledge of computers than I have, volunteered to take responsibility for this. He did a good job. But at least on one occasion a number 'slipped the net.' This was unfortunate because a very senior officer, who had moved on in his career, was rudely awakened by me in the wee small hours, as I attempted to advise the On Call Duty Officer of a serious incident. His response to being so rudely awakened was expressed in one, (unprintable) word before he slammed the phone down.

Next to this was the screen on which the Control Report was compiled. This was very simple to operate. It was also connected to a printer, so the Report could be printed off each night.

Next to that was a Total Operations Processing System (TOPS) screen. We used this to obtain details of any locomotive, passenger or freight rolling stock involved in any incident.

Next to that was the teleprinter screen. Now all the Controllers were able to send their own telex messages.

Next was a screen upon which we could call an image of each signalling panel in our major Signalling Centres at London Bridge, Victoria, Three Bridges and Ashford. We could even access the Channel Tunnel Screens from Coquelles to Folkestone!

Finally we had the Automatic Train Recording (ATRE) screen.

Our five rotating teams initially comprised nine members, including the managers. This was subsequently cut to seven and finally to five, during the many reorganisations that followed. I won't bore the reader with the details of all these re-organisations but will just mention three that were significant to us.

In 1992, privatisation was looming. The Organisation called Railtrack was formed. The three Area Traffic Controls, (signalling centres) were merged into two. The London Area was signalled exclusively by London Bridge and Victoria Area Signalling Centres, as far as the outskirts of East Croydon.

The Country Area was signalled, from East Croydon, by Three Bridges Area Signalling Centre and the myriad small signal boxes that existed and still exist today.

We also gained a new name. Firstly Network SouthCentral Service Centre, then, much later as the first private company took over the franchise, Connex South Central Service Centre. Duty Line Managers became Service Centre Managers

Maintrol, our CM&EE contact, was removed and returned to Southern House, Croydon.

With all these changes, our responsibilities also changed. Initially we were all individually given the choice to go to Railtrack or to go to the commercial companies.

After a very great deal of consideration I elected to go to one of the commercial companies, Connex South Central.

This surprised some of my colleagues because they knew me as an operator rather than a commercial man. It surprised me a bit too, but I had grave doubts about Railtrack and the new commercial companies were an uncharted territory for me. Long term, the operating side might have been the better choice, but short term I definitely felt I had made the best decision.

So, finally things settled down and we got used to our new

routines. One thing that did not change was the number and variety of incidents that occurred in each twenty-four hours. On the night shift there were a number of people who accepted being 'On Call' as part of their job.

Contrary to popular opinion, at the time, we tried hard not to call out people un-necessarily. But by the nature of the job, some people got more than their fair share of callouts. One of those people was a member of the Permanent Way staff. He was renowned as an excellent engineer, but he was also renowned for being a very heavy sleeper. On a number of occasions, we had tried to call him out but invariably the taxi firm we sent out returned to say they were unable to wake him. Then we had no alternative but to call out his opposite number, who very philosophically came out without complaint.

One night however, I was determined to get this man out. We sent the taxi firm to his home. They returned with the expected answer, - no reply. I instructed the taxi controller to send his man back, telling him to knock on that door until either the engineer answered it or the door gave way. After half an hour, the taxi firm rang me. They told me their driver had walked into the room, placed a door knocker on the table, and walked out again without saying a word. The other engineer came out.

When we had to call someone out, my approach varied. If it was someone who was awkward, had made life difficult for us or was generally uncooperative with the Control, I was very cheerful. 'Good morning. I hope I haven't disturbed you too much.' I would then explain the situation in detail. I would usually end with the remark, 'By the way, it is raining very hard so you will need protective clothing. Thank you for helping us.'

If on the other hand it was someone who was conscientious and always trying to help, my approach would be very different. I would ring them, and when they answered, I would offer to ring them again in a few minutes, to give them time to 'come to' before I explained the problem to them.

One of the latter was one of the Movements Inspectors,(formerly Area Inspectors), who were always called out to late running engineering works or serious incidents, which, left unattended, would adversely affect the morning rush hour services. This person once advised me that when they knew I was on night duty, they went to bed with their clothes on, ready for when I called them. But they always went out, and I don't remember any incident or problem that they did not sort out completely and in time. We became good friends, mutually respecting each other's abilities and capabilities.

One day, I invited the Inspector to visit the Control. To some people this had all the appeal of a visit to the dentist. A deal was struck that I in turn would go to meet the passengers at Oxted, during the evening rush hour. On the day in question, I was early turn. The rush hour was over and it was fairly quiet. I suddenly became aware of a 'presence' behind me. I turned round and stood up to greet a tall unsmiling figure in an immaculate uniform. We had a cup of tea and I introduced the people on my team and showed how the job was done. That visit was the beginning of a friendship that has lasted to this day.

In due course I made my visit to Oxted station in the rush hour. To my friend's frustration, it was also a quiet day, and a very pleasant evening was enjoyed.

Much later, this friend, in the course of their duties, enabled me to gain some experience of engineering work, that I really appreciated. I really wanted to know exactly what I was asking people to do, particularly with engineering work. It was on area I knew little about. I had the agreement of my Management to go out on the track.

But first I had to pass my Track Safety Exam and get my certificate. I had walked the track for years in the course of my jobs, but I recognised the need. The railway environment is a very dangerous and unforgiving one and I was happy to improve my safety.

The training was in two stages. Firstly, I had to work in areas where there were conductor rails at 750 v DC. I had to know how to walk safely in these areas, keeping a sharp lookout for any movements of trains, while learning how to cross safely over running rails and conductor rails, in all weathers.

Having passed that exam, I was then taken to Wembley Freight Operating Centre (WFOC) where I had experience of walking under the overhead wires running at 25.000 v AC. Trains in that area passed at speeds of up to 105 mph. At one point I was directed onto a bridge over running lines. The overhead cables were crackling like a log fire due to the misty rain falling at the time.

Then I was asked to look over the bridge. Below me were wires running at the same voltage as those above me. When asked how I felt, I replied that I felt a bit like one of Bernard Matthew's turkeys in an oven! My Certificate, when I received it, became a prized possession.

On another occasion, I was invited to do some point winding at South Croydon, during an engineering possession.

Normally, points, the devices that change the direction of track and therefore trains, are mechanically and electrically locked to the signal box that operates them. In order to wind these points, the electrical locking has to be disconnected. This is done with a special key. When this is done the indication of the position of the points is lost to the signal box.

Then the mechanical locking must be disconnected. This is done with a large metal key. Finally the point winding handle has to be inserted. This is a large heavy piece of equipment. I was fortunate in that it was located in a line side box. (I remembered back to my South Eastern days when the signalman at Chislehurst had a point failure. This same type of handle had to be collected from the signal box there and carried half a mile up the track before the work could start.)

The points then have to be wound over. It's a bit like a pump as the handle is pumped back and forth. At first nothing seems to happen, then suddenly you can see the point blades moving to their new position. Once the points are in their new position, a point clip has to be inserted on the underside of the rail to hold them in place. This is something like a 'G' clamp. This procedure has to be followed every time the points are to be moved. Nothing must ever be foul of the top side of the rail as this would cause a derailment.

Finally, when the work is done, the points are wound to the normal position, the mechanical locking is reinserted and the electrical locking is reinserted. Then the person doing the work has to contact the signal box and ensure that the point indication is showing correctly. Then the points have to be moved several times until both the signalman and the engineer are satisfied they are working correctly again.

All the time I was working I had the Inspector as my lookout. If I was told to move to one side I did so immediately because the adjoining tracks were 'open,' that is trains were running past me on them.

Working on engineering trains was also fun. I learned to couple up trains and to operate the change couplings on the class 73 electro-diesels. For this it is a matter of balance, to swing the heavy coupling up on its pivot, with one hand, and insert the metal locking pin, like a large rolling pin, in with the other. If you did not get this right, you had to let go the coupling and start again. Trying to hold the coupling up while inserting the pin was a sure recipe for a bad back.

Then I had to go underneath, beneath a crane and a wagon, to couple them up. The tiny space was incredible. It had to be done in exactly the right order. First the coupling hook had to be swung up from the crane to the wagon. Now they were physically coupled, the brake pipes had to be connected. First turn off the brake taps. Then remove the brake pipe on the crane from its housing and couple it to the brake pipe on the wagon.

'Take the brake pipe off its housing before turning off the tap, and the brake pipe will come up between your legs and lift you over the top of the wagon by your tender parts,' I was told. I always remembered that. Once the brake pipes were coupled, I could then turn on the brake taps.

Then the brake had to be tested for continuity, ie that the brakes worked on every wagon. If they didn't, the weight of the train could push the locomotive forward, regardless of the signal aspect. So the brake test was essential. I remember watching the first train I coupled, slowly moving off. As it went past,

I thought, 'I coupled that!' Then I thought, 'I hope it stays together!' It did.

Another bundle of fun was unloading wagons of ballast. These wagons contained between forty and fifty tons of track ballast. I always thought that looked easy, just undo the hatches and let gravity do the rest. But no, like every other job, there was a correct procedure. Get it wrong and you could have a nasty accident, or at the very least give yourself several hours of backbreaking digging.

The wagons had a platform at one end. On a vertical frame there were three large metal wheels, a bit like large steering wheels. The hatches under the wagons were opened and closed by turning these wheels. The first wheel opened the nearside hatch, the centre wheel the centre hatch and the offside wheel the offside hatch. Sometimes ballast was needed in the middle of the track but at other times it was needed on one side or another.

If more than one hatch needed to be opened, it was usual to make a second or third run over the section with the train. The ballast lay as a heavy mass in the wagons, especially if it was wet from rain. To loosen it, you had to turn the wheel slightly back and forth until you could feel the ballast loosening.

Timing was absolutely essential. The man in charge of the work would mark the start of the drop, usually by standing at the point. A P. Way man, (track engineer), would stand on the platform of the wagon, ready to turn the wheel when told to do so. The train would move very slowly forward. As the wagon reached the exact spot of the drop, the signal would be given and the wheel turned, opening the hatch. It took several turns of the wheel to open the hatch and this time had to be allowed for.

Similarly, at the end of the drop, time had to be allowed to turn the wheel to close the hatch. The signal would be given, and the hatch closed exactly at the right spot. It was a fine art with these forty or fifty ton wagons, working in the dark, because most engineering jobs were done at night, and often in bad weather. The drop had to be exact. Get it wrong and you would have to move the excess stone by hand with shovels. You could not just leave it, because it would be laying 'high' in the track and could cause a derailment.

Also it would leave insufficient stone in the wagon to drop it where it was needed. Under no circumstances should you open a hatch while the train was stationary. The force of the mass of stone falling would lift the wagon right off the track and it would derail. You then had to re-rail it, - after you had dug all the stone out from under it.

One day I was enjoying this activity, being supervised by the Inspector. I was at the centre wheel and my companions were on either side. At a moment prearranged without my knowledge, each jumped from their side of the wagon. As they dropped safely to the ground, the train started to gather speed. 'You're right away to Three Bridges,' they called out, waving goodbye to me. There was absolutely nothing I could do. The rapidly accelerating train was going too fast for me to bail out.

My imagination ran riot. I was seeing myself on the platform of this wagon as it ran through soot laden, filthy dirty Balcombe Tunnel. It would do my complexion no good at all! Thankfully it was only going to another part of the sidings, where I safely dismounted and joined my grinning companions.

During the course of these exercises, I had to take a track

knowledge assessment. Another Movements Inspector met me at Redhill Yard. I was asked to demonstrate the use of the emergency track circuit operating clips. These clips looked rather like jump leads. When fastened to the running rails, they activated the track circuit on that section and put the signal in rear to danger. They had to be fastened on the conductor rail side of the track first, (but not on the conductor rail). This was because when the cable was stretched to fasten onto the other side of the rail, if I slipped, I would not touch or fall on the conductor rail.

I was not asked to demonstrate the short-circuiting bar, used to cut off traction current in an emergency but I had to demonstrate that I knew how to. This bar is a long, heavy piece of metal with a 'v' shaped end and an insulated handle. It would hook under the conductor rail. Then you turned your face away, to avoid flash burns or flash blindness, and dropped the handle so that it connected the conductor rail to the running rail. There would be a blinding flash and a bang and the traction current would be isolated.

Sometimes the flash would be so violent that the bar would be welded to the running rail. The Electrical Control would try to recharge the traction current three times, but with the bar in position they would not be able to and the traction current would be left off while the incident was investigated.

The reason for three attempts to recharge was that sometimes an insulator pot would blow, or a short circuit might occur for no serious reason. Delay would be saved. But if the traction current could not be recharged at the third attempt there was obviously a more serious problem and it would then remain isolated. It was rather like the domestic trip switches in a modern house. I was later to experience it being used in earnest just once, in a tragic accident.

I also had to demonstrate that I knew how and where to place detonators. These are explosive devices, circular in shape and with a metal strap to fasten them to a running rail. The passage of train wheels would crush them, causing them to explode but with no risk of derailment. A driver, hearing the loud bang, would know that he was being warned of danger ahead and he would reduce the speed of the train accordingly. These devices had to be placed one a quarter of a mile from the obstruction, one at half a mile, and three, 10 yards apart at one and a quarter miles.

At the end of the test, my assessor was very surprised and quite impressed that this man who had come down from head office had passed 100%. I was rather pleased myself.

There was one occasion when I was out on the track on my own and a somewhat disturbing incident occurred. I had obtained permission from my Senior Manager to do this. I was on a different patch, the main line from London to Brighton, between Coulsdon South and Merstham and the Inspector who had accompanied me previously was occupied with an engineering possession in the London Area. I had been invited by a P.Way Supervisor to join him on the possession there.

I drove to Coulsdon South and parked my car there. Using a signal telephone on the end of the down platform, I spoke to the Regulator in Three Bridges ASC. I identified myself and advised him of my intention to walk down the track to the engineering site and asked him to confirm that both lines were still blocked by the Engineers Possession. He confirmed that both lines were blocked. We agreed that I would telephone him before I entered Merstham Tunnel, and again when I had reached the other end of the tunnel.

Thus assured, I set off down the track. I was wearing all my high visibility clothing as required. It was a dull day but dry and the walk was not unpleasant. I noticed a number of obstructions, tree branches etc, on the walk-way and was glad I was doing this in daylight.

I had passed under Skew Bridge and the northern entrance to Merstham Tunnel was in sight, when to my surprise I heard a locomotive warning horn sounding on what I believed to be a blocked line. Turning round, I saw an engineering train coming towards me on the down line. I raised one arm to show the driver that I was aware of him and stepped well clear.

As the train approached it slowed down. The driver leaned out of the window and called out, 'Do you want a lift?'

I explained why I was there, and he said, 'Oh the engineering possession has been cleared.' Once we are clear of the line it will be reopened to passenger trains.' Those trains travel over that section at approximately 90 mph and I was so grateful that I had not entered the tunnel.

I gratefully accepted a lift and climbed up into the cab of the class 33 locomotive. The driver took me to Redhill, where I was able to catch an up train, which called at Coulsdon South. Before catching it though, I telephoned Three Bridges ASC to advise them that I was clear of the line. The next day, back in the Control I asked a few questions. I could not establish whether or not the traincrew had been advised and cautioned to look out for me. I did not pursue the matter further.

I thoroughly enjoyed all my experiences out on the track, and I learned so much. Now, when I had to ask somebody to do these things, I knew what I was asking them to do. I felt that was very important in my job. But all good things must end eventually. In a discussion with my new boss it was explained, quite understandably, that they could no longer afford to pay me overtime to continue learning. I was welcome to continue in my own time but without pay.

I would have done it for nothing because I so enjoyed being out on the track with real professionals doing a physical job. The problem was that, if I had an accident while doing unpaid work, the Company insurance would not cover me, and I would not receive any compensation. In any physical job, or indeed just being on the track itself with moving trains, there was always the possibility, even with the most professional people, of having an accident.

I actually have in my possession a special card issued to all employees on 15th July 1994, marking 365 days known when no staff had been killed on the tracks. It was the only year there were no deaths. I could not take the risk for myself or for my family, that I could be injured, lose my job and receive no compensation. So, with great reluctance, I agreed that the learning activities would cease.

Another person I had a great respect for was the shunter at Redhill. This lady, slightly built and standing a little over five feet tall, was able, very competently, to couple and uncouple passenger and freight trains and did so regularly. I marvelled at the fact that she could easily raise or lower the couplings on a class 73 locomotive, something I had found very difficult to do.

We had at that time a regular train of aggregate stone running from the South Eastern Division to Salfords Aggregate Sidings. A shunter was booked on night duty to receive this train and see it in. For some reason, he was unreliable and sometimes failed to turn up. Twice the train was approaching Salfords when the signal box advised us that the shunter had not turned up. I had to ask the Redhill shunter to attend, and each time she did so without complaint.

However, during a conversation with her after the second time, I discovered that in order to accomplish this, she had to walk down the trackside on her own in the darkness and pass a lineside gypsy encampment. She never experienced any trouble, but she was always wary. When I found out about that I insisted that she would not do it again.

The next time the shunter failed to turn up, I had the locomotive run round the train, and returned to Redhill where it was stabled in the yard. The resultant complaints from the Aggregate Company ensured the matter was resolved locally.

(left) Paul dealing with an incident
(right) John A seeing the funny side of it!

Chapter Sixteen -
Meanwhile, back in the Control

I was not on duty when, due to a driver's error in braking, a set of empty coaching stock collided with the buffer stops at Tattenham Corner at around 6 am one weekday morning. This was a perfect, if unintended, test of the design structure of the new sliding door type of carriages. They did exactly what they were supposed to do in such extreme circumstances.

The wheel bogies and running gear were left behind on the track and the tubular bodies continued upright and in line across the concourse. No one in them would have been injured. They collided with the station building, demolishing it and coming to rest with the roof of the building resting on the roof of one of the carriages.

Sadly, a member of staff who was in the building died instantly. We never minded clearing up a mess provided no-one had been hurt, and this was a very sad outcome. This cast a shadow over the proceedings for all those who were on duty.

I was on duty however on the night when the train was recovered. It was a complicated operation. The building had all but collapsed, and it was very difficult to extract the carriage from under it. There was also a bit of a panic on. Tattenham Corner Station was traditionally used by her Majesty the Queen, on her visit to Epsom Racecourse for Derby Day. This date was fast approaching.

It was also, or had been, a listed building. When somebody

pointed this out to us, the response, from somebody who shall remain nameless was, 'Well its listing now, - all over!'

Given all the complications the operation that night went very smoothly. The remains of the roof were removed. The carriage was loaded onto a road transporter and taken to Selhurst Depot.

The rest of the building was demolished, and the station was reopened in time for the morning. In a remarkably short space of time a new brick built station building was erected and was open in time for the Queen's visit. Someone pointed out to me that its new position was sideways on to the station and quite a distance from the concourse. I wonder why.

Many of the incidents we dealt with were complex, challenging but satisfying to tackle and rewarding when we won. But we had our tragedies too. Sadly the railway was often chosen by people as a certain means in which to end their lives. They had many reasons for doing so.

One young Canadian girl student was on her own at Christmastime, had no money to get back to her own country and was desperately lonely and depressed. She ended her life by stepping off of a platform into the path of a fast moving train. This ended her life instantly.

The driver was badly affected by the incident that he was powerless to prevent. I was on duty at the time and I know it affected me. It always seemed to me to be such a tragic waste of life. I often felt it would be good to meet these people and try to show them that life could be so good. But we don't know their circumstances or their state of mind at the time. Unknown to me a friend of mine was on the same platform at the time and saw the whole thing close up. It is something he has never forgotten.

Another tragic incident occurred in a tunnel on the South London Line. In most incidents, death is instantaneous, but this is not guaranteed. Again, it was a young girl. She had walked into the tunnel to be sure of not being seen. In due course she was struck by a train and terribly injured, but she did not die. The impact flung her across the tracks and conductor rails, where she lay in terrible agony until a train coming the other way struck and killed her.

When her body was discovered, both the trains had to be taken out of service for a full incident examination, and reports were prepared for the police and the coroner by all those involved.

We did not have to submit reports as a copy of the Control Report contained all the details that we were advised of. The drivers I believe were thankfully unaware of the incident, until they were stopped and questioned.

The most tragic incident that we were involved in was not a suicide but the accidental death of a child. It was, notwithstanding the collisions at Purley and later at Cowden, the worst incident that I have ever had to deal with in any Control, and it is something I have never forgotten.

Because the driver and relatives and friends of the child concerned are still alive and may one day read this account, I have deliberately been very vague about the details.

It was a Sunday afternoon, when my team and I were on duty. On an unmanned station on the South London Line, two little girls, aged about eleven years, and with no adult present, were playing. One was on one platform and the other was on the other platform on the other side of the tracks. They were throwing a ball to each other.

Inevitably one girl threw the ball short and instead of reaching the other platform it fell onto the track. The other girl jumped off the platform down onto the track. She came into contact with the 750 volt DC conductor rail and was electrocuted and died horribly. The other child was hysterical on the other platform. This was the scene found by the driver of an approaching train.

He immediately made a full emergency application of the brake. As the train stopped, he grabbed the short -circuiting bar (a device for cutting off the traction current in an emergency by causing a short circuit) and the track circuit operating clips from the cab and got down onto the track. He applied the short-circuiting bar to the conductor and running rails. There was a big flash and the traction current was isolated.

The driver then placed the track circuiting clips on the opposite line, which had the effect of turning the signal in rear to danger. He then removed the child from the track. Then he got in touch with the signalman and arranged for the Emergency Services to attend. They did so and the child was taken to hospital. Sadly she was pronounced dead.

We had called the on-call Duty Manager, who attended. Between them, he and the Police arranged for the child's parents to be advised. The Train Crew Supervisor was advised, and the driver was relieved of duty and accompanied home. A relief driver was arranged to take the train forward.

We had kept the Electrical Control advised. When the Police had completed their investigation and were clear of the track, the Permanent Way engineers were allowed to check that the track had not been damaged by the use of the short circuiting bar, and when the signalman was advised that the line was clear, he arranged with the Electrical Control to restore the traction current. The train, which had stopped short of the station, was allowed to continue its journey and the normal service was resumed. I ensured that all my senior officers were advised. We also made sure that our Public Relations Officer was advised.

The Area One Controller had rearranged the service, so that crews and another train was substituted for the heavily delayed train at the incident. When all was done and everyone who should know about it, had been advised, I took my notes and used them to compile the incident report on the Control Report.

Many questions were asked. Why was the station unstaffed? Did the girl's parents know where their children were and what they were doing? But these were questions for other people to deal with. We had done the best that we could, especially all those on site, and particularly the driver, for whom I have the greatest admiration.

Everyone was affected by this tragedy. It was the only time everyone in the Control was very subdued, even when they went home. Thankfully this type of incident is very rare.

And now for something completely different. Sometimes, actually quite rarely, I was asked to head up an interview panel for new applicants to work in the Control. One interview I remember particularly.

We were looking for a new General Purpose Relief, (GPR) Controller. The General Purpose Relief DLM was not available so I was asked to take the interviews instead. My partner in crime was Chris, who at the time was the Rolling Stock

Controller on my shift. Of the applications received we selected three likely candidates.

The qualifications we were looking for were a reasonable knowledge of railway operations and a willingness to learn more, someone who would be a team player, and someone who would remain calm under pressure, all essential qualities especially for a GPR Controller who would be working more than one panel, and round the clock shift work, including weekends.

Our first candidate was a man called Andy. My colleague Chris said that he knew the man and thought it only fair to tell me that. Andy had worked in the CM & EE department, was knowledgeable and a hard worker. The other two candidates were something of an unknown quality.

Chris gave an undertaking not to let his prior knowledge of Andy influence him or my decision. Andy was the first candidate to be interviewed. He was called, came in and sat down. Then he stood up. He said, 'I'm sorry but I really do not see the point of continuing. I know I won't get the job. I don't want to waste your time. I'm sorry.' With that he got up, turned and walked out.

We called the other two candidates in. We interviewed them in turn. Afterwards we discussed the interviews. The other two candidates were a bit lack-lustre. They had a basic knowledge of railway operation, but we agreed that neither of them impressed us greatly. It was important to get the right person for the job, because in a crisis, everyone depended on everyone else to do their own job well and help out others as necessary. My comment was, 'It looks as though we will have to re-advertise the job.'

Chris agreed. Then he said, 'You would have found Andy

so much better. He really does do a good job and he knows what it is all about. The only problem is that he can't take interviews. I don't want to interfere with your decision, but if I could persuade him to come back, would you still be prepared to interview him? I will leave it entirely up to you.' I agreed that, if Andy was prepared to be interviewed, I would give him a second chance.

During the lunch break, Chris went to talk to Andy, and he came back to tell me Andy had agreed to be interviewed. We interviewed him and were able to ask him a lot more questions than we had been able to ask the others, because he did have a much greater knowledge and experience than the other two candidates. With the interviews finished, Chris and I were able to discuss the outcome.

I was firmly of the opinion that we would have to search a long time to find someone else with Andy's depth of knowledge and experience, and I voted to select him. Chris said, 'I'm so pleased you feel that way. I promise you it was the right decision. You will not regret having Andy in the Control.' And so it proved to be. Not only was he efficient, but also worked very quietly.

I quickly learned that I could give him a job to do and it would be done, efficiently, thoroughly and quietly. I was so impressed that I tried to persuade him to take a regular position on my shift. He thanked me, but said he preferred the variety of being on the relief, covering different panels, and he didn't mind the irregular shift patterns. His standards never dropped, and it was always good to have him on my shift.

Speaking of the different panels, I had made a point as DLM of knowing and being able to work all the panels in the

Control. Most of them I had worked during my career, and those panels I hadn't or panels which had undergone major changes in responsibility, I took time to relearn. I really believed that a DLM should know and be capable of working every panel.

Another challenge that I faced was learning about the Snowblower. Some years before a very heavy fall of winter snow occurred, particularly affecting the South Eastern Division of British Rail. The Sheerness branch on the Isle of Sheppey was particularly badly affected. The single line was blocked and even the snowplough got stuck. This machine called a Snowblower, was based at Inverness, where the lines are regularly affected by heavy snow.

As it happened Scotland was experiencing a comparatively mild winter, so the British Railways Board decided to move the Snowblower from Inverness to the Isle of Sheppey. The machine did its job well and the line was very quickly reopened.

So successful was this that the Railway ordered six of these machines to be based at various parts of the country, one being based at Selhurst Depot on my patch, to be available for the South Eastern and the South Central. We were rivals to see who would be the first to use it. But first we had to learn about it.

A day was arranged that we would all convene at Stewarts Lane Depot, Battersea, and the fitters would take us around the machine and show us its uses. I was asked to come in on my Rest Day to take part in this. On the day in question I went to Tonbridge Station, armed with my video camera, the idea being that I could take a film back for my team, who were not able to be with me, to learn about it.

However, things did not go smoothly. I arrived at the station to find total chaos. There was a major signalling failure between Tonbridge and Sevenoaks. Only approximately one train in four was getting through. All the others were being diverted. I quizzed the station staff, but they could not tell me anything. This annoyed me because they were equipped with monitors that displayed where the trains were.

I tried to ring Control but was unable to get through. I faced the choice of catching a train that was being diverted via Paddock Wood, Maidstone West, Strood and Dartford to London, and which was about to leave, or let it go and wait to see what happened. I chose to go on the train.

As it pulled away, I saw one of my colleagues who was also going, walk onto the platform. It was the wrong choice I had made, for the very next train was allowed through to Sevenoaks, and my colleague arrived more or less on time, whereas I was two hours late.

When I finally got near to Stewarts Lane Depot, I had to get a taxi for the last part of my journey. More problems, even the taxi driver did not know where the Dickens Gate, the entrance to Stewarts Lane was.

He dropped me at Battersea Dogs Home. From one of the staff there I found out where the Dickens Gate was and walked the rest of the way to it. Now, if you have never visited Stewarts Lane Depot, you will have no idea how vast it is. It is a gigantic spiders web of tracks diverging in all directions to all points of the compass.

The Depot has berthing points for South Eastern and Central rolling stock that stable there between the morning and evening rush hours. There are sidings for units under repair, there is a large Locomotive Depot. There is also a large collection of sidings holding stock and locomotives that are due for preservation.

The Orient Express stock and the spare Pullman cars are stabled in a large shed there. There are also Breakdown Crane sidings where cranes and their ancillary vehicles are stabled and repaired. There are the Engineers Sidings that hold assorted long rail trains and other rail mounted equipment. The de-icing and leaf clearing trains are also stored there.

Somewhere in this massive spider's web, the new Snowblower is also stored. The equipment was so new that many of the people I asked did not know what it was, let alone where it was. Suddenly across one set of tracks I saw our party. But I was unable to cross the tracks to join them because a train of empty electric coaching stock was approaching, and I must wait for it to pass before I could cross.

The train comprised twenty coaches. By the time that had passed, my party, electing not to wait for me, had disappeared. Eventually I found the shed and was able to listen to the last hour of the lecture. My Senior Manager totally ignored me. When the lecture was over and the others had departed, I remained behind.

I briefly explained the problems I had had in getting there and asked the fitters if they would be kind enough to explain it to me. I also asked if I could film it and them in the process. They were very pleased to help me.

It was an incredible machine, capable of blowing huge drifts aside, but also, with the correct gear on it could work on third rail electrified lines and clear low-lying snow. It had a crane facility and it had other track maintenance equipment, so it could work on engineering jobs as well.

It was also self-propelled at a slow speed, so one it had been hauled to a site it could work independently of the locomotive. I spent all afternoon with them and made quite a film, which on the next quiet night turn I was able to show my team. It was a fantastic machine and very expensive but worth every penny.

It stayed untouched for some time until that winter we had a very heavy fall of snow in the London Area. I immediately ordered the Snowblower to Selhurst Depot where they were experiencing great difficulty. The South Eastern were also experiencing difficulty and also ordered out the Snowblower, but we just pipped them to the post. Triumph was short lived, for it arrived at Selhurst Depot with the wrong equipment.

Chapter Seventeen - Emergency Exercise
Hawfinch 31ˢᵗ October 1993

Another person, also called Terry, was a colleague and friend of mine. His background was the Carriage, Mechanical, and Electrical Engineers, (CM & EE). He was also an expert with computers. He became the last DLM to be appointed to the position of Duty Line Manger before the coming great divide between Railtrack and Network South Central and finally full privatisation.

One of his first real tests as a Duty Line Manger was Exercise Hawfinch. On Sunday 31ˢᵗ October 1993, a scheme that had been devised by our Senior Managers, in cooperation with the Emergency Services, to simulate the derailment and collision of a passenger train, was put into action. The operation was called 'Emergency Exercise Hawfinch.' My colleague Terry was the Duty Line Manager, and I was required to be on duty as an observer in the Control.

My Senior Manager gave me very strict instructions. Under no account was I to speak to, advise, or in any other way help my colleague. I was there only to observe and make and record the notes required by the scheme for later assessment.

An Engineering Absolute Possession of the Lines between Lewes and Keymer Junction (just above Burgess Hill on the London Brighton line) had been taken after the last train on Saturday night.

The scenario was that a stolen motorbike had been thrown

over a road bridge onto the up line at a location between Keymer Junction, where the Lewes lines diverge from the main lines to Brighton, and Plumpton, on the line to Lewes. A closer location was just the Keymer Junction side of Folders Lane Bridge.

2Z30, 0854 Eastbourne to Victoria, comprising 2 x 4 coach emu stock with unit 5409 leading, had collided with the motorbike and been derailed towards the down line. 6Z30 0857 Redhill – Newhaven was approaching on the down line and collided head on with the up train. 6Z30 was at first reported as conveying dangerous goods, but this was later discounted, and the load was confirmed as being ballast.

To make the incident as realistic as possible, the engineers actually arranged to physically derail the front coach of unit 5409. The comment went round that we would all have red faces if we were not able to re-rail it before Monday morning's rush hour!

Knowing that I myself would be closely observed on the day, in carrying out my duties as Observer, I arranged with Terry a short time on the previous day, to give him some tips and warnings of pitfalls to avoid. Two things in particular I remember telling him, one being to summon the Signal & Telecomms Emergency Communications Vehicle to the site as normal telephones would be swamped with calls and make contact difficult.

Not too many people knew about this facility but it proved invaluable on the site of the major accident at Purley and again later on at the site of the major accident at Cowden. The other thing was to ensure that he spoke to the relevant people and relayed his instructions to them as a priority, ignoring incoming calls in order to do so. I warned him to leave incoming calls to his staff, because if he started to take the incoming calls, he would be swamped with calls and be completely unable to do his job.

The day itself dawned bright. The passenger train had been successfully derailed and the down freight train was stabled in two parts adjacent to the derailed coach, suggesting that the derailed train had gone into the side of the goods train.

At 0931 two controlled explosions were set off, simulating the noise of the collision, and we were off. I won't go into details about the whole incident, but I found the initial sequences were interesting.

The first report was from Brighton Electrical Control at 0932, of an each end tripping of traction current between Keymer and Ditchling Track Paralleling Huts (TP huts) at 0931. An each end tripping out of the traction current usually means some more substantial problem that simply a blown insulator pot. It is something that requires investigation.

Three Bridges Area Signalling Centre, (ASC), confirmed this a minute later. Traction current was isolated from Folly Hill to Burgess Hill TPs and from Ditchling to Plumpton TPs. Three Bridges ASC reported two trains in the affected section and believed to be derailment and collision.

Sussex Police advised 0935

West Sussex Fire and Rescue advised 0935.

Group Pagers to all Senior Officers were activated at 0935.

Rolling Stock Manager Brighton advised 0936.

At 0943, Three Bridges ASC reported location of the accident was at Folders Lane Bridge.

At 0945, Three Bridges ASC reported identity of trains. Up train was 0854 Eastbourne – Victoria, comprising 2 x 4 EPB, and down train was 6Z30 Redhill – Newhaven freight train.

At 0950 the Mobile Operations Manager reported that his mobile phone was not working.

At 0950, Rolling Stock Manager (RSM) was on site but was denied access by the Police as he had not got a permit for the Exercise. Had this been an actual live incident, it could have a serious effect on the investigation.

The RSM looks for immediate evidence of the cause(s) of the accident. He needed for instance to see how hot the wheels are, indicating that the brakes had been applied, and how hard they had been applied. Obviously, any delay would allow the wheels to cool and so give inaccurate or no information at all.

There were other things that he needed to see immediately, but we won't go into that. As I said at in my introduction to this little book, it is not a technical treatise. The RSM was advised to wait for the On Call Officer to arrive and seek assistance from him.

At 0950 the London Area Controller produced a detailed map of the site.

At 0953 it was found that no full consist had been entered on the Total Operations Processing System (TOPS) and it was suspected that they train might be conveying dangerous goods. All that was shown on TOPS was Locomotive 37009 and eleven empty vehicles.

Urgent enquiries revealed that in fact the train comprised locomotive 37009 and twenty-two empty vehicles and two brake-vans. The enquiries also confirmed that there were no dangerous goods on the train. This inaccurate information could have delayed rescuers accessing the passenger train.

0958 – Sussex Police advised by Control that there was no asbestos present in the passenger stock and no dangerous goods on the goods train.

At 1005 an Incident Room was set up in an adjacent field.

At 1011, Brighton TCS reported information from the Area Traction Inspector on site, the names and condition of the traincrews involved in the accident, and confirmed that replacement traincrews were on their way.

At 1012, map reference TQ 332 181 was given for the site of the accident.

At 1017, temporary accommodation was requested.

At 1018, after consultation with Retail Senior Managers, it was agreed that a telex message would be sent to all points, explaining that Emergency Exercise Hawfinch was simply an exercise and not a live incident. This should reduce the number of telephone calls being made by staff not involved in the incident, who were trying to get information for their passengers.

Also at 1015, SWD DLM advised that Brighton Heavy Lifting Breakdown Crane had been put on standby and the BRUFF Road/Rail utility vehicle was being manned. It was later discovered that this latter had departed Brighton at 1005 to go to site.

This vehicle was an extremely useful tool. It contained jacks and heavy lifting gear and tools. It could be driven to the nearest rail access to the site, then be driven onto the track. Rail wheels would be lowered, and it could then proceed to site. It even had a traversing gear that would raise it from the track, turn it right round and lower it back onto the track facing the opposite direction. This completely solved the difficulty of getting road vehicles to site.

While the incident was in progress there was a real emergency call by Sussex Police that information had been received to the effect that an explosive device had been planted in Balcombe Tunnel. This was a real incident and not part of the exercise. This also had to be dealt with by the Control at the same time. Trains were stopped and the tunnel was searched. Happily, there was no device and trains were soon on the move again.

It reminded me of the accident at Purley (Chapter 12) where I had agreed with my London Area Controller that I would take full control of the major incident and leave him to deal with any other incidents that arose on the Central Division. The system worked well, but you had to have a good man on the Area whom you could trust.

The incident management continued almost to plan apart from those first few difficulties. All the 'casualties' were removed to hospital. To everyone's immense relief, the train was finally re-railed without incident.

The Permanent Way Engineers inspected the track and were able to declare it undamaged. The trains were removed. All the Emergency Services left the scene. The traction current was restored and the blockage of the lines was lifted. Normal working was resumed after a very worthwhile Exercise Hawfinch.

A few days later a 'Debrief Meeting' was held, which was also very helpful.

There was one final aside. The whole operation including the debrief, was filmed on video by Ron, a good friend and colleague of mine. The videotapes were then passed to me to edit and compile three short films. I had completely forgotten this when I got out the notes for this book.

I retrieved the original videotape and transferred it to DVD and there at the end were the titles, 'Filmed by Ron -. Video edited and compiled by Terry Collins, Terryvision 1993*.' I had to smile. Fame at last.

*I had been an amateur film producer since my early teens, making films for charities, schools, professional shows, the occasional wedding, and other organisations, including the Railway, see chapter 14.

I always maintained my amateur status, not making any films for profit but simply for the challenge and enjoyment factors. Initially I made them under the name of TC Films, but inspiration struck and I called them 'Terryvision' and that really caught on.

Chapter Eighteen - Cowden

1994 also saw the final split between Railtrack and the Commercial Companies that held franchises to run the trains. Network SouthEast and Network SouthCentral were dissolved. The rolling stock went to three newly established Rolling Stock Companies, who leased them to the Commercial Companies.

We, the staff in the Control were given the choice of going with Railtrack or going to one of the Commercial Companies, in this case Connex. It was a very difficult decision. I was first and foremost an operator and not a commercial man.

On the other hand, I held a personal belief that the way in which Privatisation had been set up was flawed. This belief was strictly personal to me, having no connection of any kind and with no reflection on management or Board.

I personally believed the fragmentation of such a complex industry was bad for passengers and staff alike. But this is not a political book and we will leave the matter there. Suffice it to say, I eventually made my decision and became a member of the commercial staff of Connex.

From being a Duty Line Manager, I became a Service Centre Manager. I was allocated a small team. I had a Train Arranger Inner (London Area) a Train Arranger Outer (Country Area) a Rolling Stock Arranger and an Information Manager. My Train Arranger Inner was Paul, My Train Arranger Outer was John, my Rolling Stock Arranger was Chris, and my Information Manager was another Paul, nicknamed 'Orson' because of his penchant for wearing a cloak and a large hat, which always instantly reminded us of Orson Wells.

This was probably one of the best and most professional team it was my pleasure to work with. I was also pleased that others, including reluctantly the other rival teams (although they would never have admitted it) thought so too.

The old Senior Manager had gone. His place was first taken, on a temporary basis, by a gentleman called Brian, and later by the permanent appointment of another gentleman called Clive, both of whom were a breath of fresh air to me.

Our team occupied the left side of the Service Centre and the Railtrack Duty Manager and his Assistant occupied the right side.

One of the major changes that came from privatisation was that, as a commercial company, we were no longer allowed to talk to signalmen, that being the prerogative of Railtrack. We were no longer allowed to talk to the Permanent Way Engineers, or the Signal & Telecomms Engineers.

Our staff were not allowed to go onto the track, even in an emergency, and it was made very clear to everyone that if they contravened these new regulations, went onto the track, and subsequently sustained injuries, not only would there be no insurance compensation at all, but they would also lose their jobs!

It was against this privatisation background that my team and myself faced the last major incident during our working time together.

Saturday 15th October dawned a very foggy day. I drove to

Croydon that morning for early turn Service Centre Manager.

I had actually driven quite near to the area affected later by the accident and noted that visibility was down to fifty yards in places. I arrived at the Service Centre in very good time and relieved my night duty colleague. My normal shift came on duty, except that Paul, was away and Brian was on the Inner Area, and John on the Outer Area. Memory eludes me who was on the rolling stock panel. 'Orson' was our Information Manager.

On the desk on my right was my good friend and colleague, Ron. He was now a Railtrack Duty Manager and was assisted by Keith. The Railtrack Control shared our accommodation at that time.

It was a comparatively quiet morning. A train had been delayed at Purley for thirteen minutes while Police dealt with eight youths without tickets and caught smoking on the train. There were some minor station staff shortages. Everything else was going well.

Now, when it was quiet in the Service Centre on a Saturday morning, it was the unofficial custom for one of the team to be released to go to the galley and cook us all a full English Breakfast (and it was a full breakfast too!).

Off he went, and soon the lovely smell of breakfast was wafting into the Service Centre. In due course Orson reappeared, laden with full plates. Mine was put on the desk beside me. The time was just before 0830.

Suddenly Keith (from Railtrack) ran to our desks. The time was 0831. He told us that the 0804 Uckfield to Oxted had passed signal OD58 on the up Ashurst Loop at danger, run through no' 532 points and entered the single line section, with the 0800 Oxted to Uckfield already in the section.

The two trains were rapidly approaching each other in thick fog and there was nothing anyone could do. Both trains were of old stock, with no built-in radio communication.

The traincrews were equipped with mobile phones but these were unreliable, and there was also a peculiar effect on mobile phones in that area. I myself had once experienced a problem when my own mobile phone started to ring itself and could only be stopped by removing the battery.

The signalman at Oxted, someone else that I knew, had tried everything he could think of but in the end, he was as helpless as the rest of us. We could only hope that the traincrews might glimpse each other through the fog and by braking hard, miti-gate the force of the collision.

At 0841 I advised my On Call Officer, Clive, that we had a problem. I explained that the up train had passed a signal at danger, had gone into the single line section above Ashurst, that the down train was approaching and that a collision was imminent. I then paged all the Senior Officers.

One thing I forgot. Our Director was no longer included on our Senior Managers Group Pager. So he was not initially advised.

I made sure that our Public Relations Officer was told and updated. Then I got onto the Traincrew Supervisors and obtained details of the two traincrews involved. I also asked (remembering from the Purley crash) for details of the duties of those traincrews for the previous two days.

Part of the investigation involved ensuring that they had had adequate rest between duties so that fatigue could be eliminated from the possible causes.

We also quickly obtained the details of the units and coaches involved. The formation of both trains was identical, two x 3 coach units formed of motor coach, trailer coach, driving trailer coach, then motor coach, trailer coach, driving trailer coach.

This meant that on the down train the motor coach was leading, while on the up train the much lighter driving trailer coach was leading. It would be these two coaches that would bear the brunt of the collision.

The Area Traction Inspector was advised and was arranging replacement traincrews.

I was also able to give some assistance to my Railtrack colleague, Ron. I advised him to make sure the Emergency Services were advised immediately. I also advised him to get the Signal and Telecomms Mobile Communications Centre Van to site as a matter of urgency.

One sad thing aside from the main problem was that the leading unit on the down train was 205029, which was the only unit restored to the original British Railways Southern Region green livery. Even the interior had been restored to its original condition by a group of students as a college project. It was this unit that was one of the two to bear the worst of the damage.

At 0849 we heard the news we had dreaded. A passenger had telephoned the Police from a nearby farmhouse to confirm that the collision had taken place. From 0850 a number of calls were received from members of the public reporting the train crash.

At 0858, Railtrack advised us that a passenger had walked to a farm half a mile away to report the accident.

Thankfully, as this was a non-electrified line, no traction current was involved.

By 0911, all our staff had been advised and responded.

At 0921, Railtrack reported there were two fatalities.

At 0925 the Depots were advised to have all heavy lifting gear crewed and on standby for the anticipated call.

At 0930, I confirmed with Telecomms Fault Control that the Mobile Communications vehicle had been activated and asked for an estimated time of arrival, e t a, on site.

At 0932, Railtrack confirmed heavy lifting gear definitely required and Fire Brigade requested it be sent with all speed.

At 0945, Railtrack advised us that there were four fatalities.

At 0955, it was discovered that our Director had not been advised. He had heard the news on the radio and had come into Stephenson House. He was on his way up to the Service Centre.

I had compiled a timed incident report with all the messages we had received right up to date. This was on the desk beside me.

I also suddenly saw my breakfast, as it lay untouched on my desk. Quick as a flash I slid open a drawer and slid the laden plate in. Staff later told me that the sight of me hiding my breakfast completely broke the tension for them and they had to work hard to hide their mirth as the Director walked in at 1001.

I apologised to the Director that he hadn't been the first to be advised and explained I had forgotten that he was not on the Senior Group Pager. He said I was not to worry, he would attend to that, and asked for a situation report.

I ran through the list with him so that he was right up to date. He patted me on the shoulder and said, 'Well done Terry. Carry on.' I felt much better. Then he left the building to go to site.

At 1005, acting on information from Railtrack, I advised our Welfare Department that traincrew were suspected of being among the fatalities.

At 1010, the Train Arranger Inner advised that casualties were being removed from the site to the Kent and Sussex Hospital, Tunbridge Wells. This was confirmed by Railtrack, who advised us that there were four fatalities, thirteen slightly injured and one person unaccounted for.

At 1047, Telecomms Fault Control reported that the Mobile Communications Centre Van would be on site in fifteen minutes.

At 1055, with little news coming from site, we were advised that our Director was now going on site.

I won't continue with the minutiae of all the calls we received but, with the reader's forbearance will step back and take a strategic view of the incident.

The two trains involved were the 0800 Uckfield to Oxted and the 0804 Oxted to Uckfield. The trains were booked to pass each other where the single track running line diverges into two lines at Ashurst.

The 0804 Oxted to Uckfield had started out a few minutes late. Ordinarily that time would have been made up but because of the fog making it impossible to make up time, it had not reached the passing loop when the up train arrived. Most of those minutes would have been recovered by the driver but for the thick fog we were experiencing.

The Repeater Signal for signal OD58 was at "Danger," a warning to the crew of the up train, that the actual signal, situated beyond the up platform and towards the junction with the single line, Signal OD58, was also at "Danger." The condition of this signal was examined as part of the investigation. The lens was found to be dirty, which slightly reduced the output, but it was still clearly visible.

Inexplicably, despite all these warnings and the cab warning equipment, the up train, had stopped at Ashurst station, then left the station, passed the signal at danger and proceeded onto the single running line section The down train meanwhile had left Cowden station as normal, and was some three hundred yards south of the station when the collision occurred. Sadly, both train crew of the up train died in the collision.

At 1138 our On Call Officer reported that the leading coach of the up train was derailed all wheels, but in line with the track. The bodywork of the entire coach had been demolished above sole bar level. The leading coach of the down train had been completely derailed and had gone sideways down the embankment.

At 1155, my Senior Manager, who had also gone to site, reported the leading motor coach of the down train was on its side with very severe leading cab end damage.

Again, I will not go into all the details as the day progressed. The casualties were identified, but I do not want to poach on the official Enquiry Documents. It eventually was established that the missing member of the traincrew was among the fatalities.

Some four hundred and fifty gallons of diesel fuel had spilled from the ruptured fuel tanks and this was another task that the Fire Brigade dealt with very efficiently.

While all this was going on a bus service had been established between Uckfield and Oxted to connect with East Grinstead to London services.

When my relief arrived, I was able to type up the Service Centre Report. There were a number of minor incidents besides the major one. There had been a train failure at Wimbledon causing cancellations between Wimbledon and West Croydon, another train failure at Norwood, and on the coast, "fog block" signalling was brought into force between Hampden Park and Polegate due to thick fog. All these items were duly entered on the Report.

Then, as I had done at Purley, I compiled a separate report for my Senior Officer, another for the British Transport Police, should it be called for, and finally a copy for myself. Then I retrieved from the drawer the solidified remains of my breakfast, and with it suitably concealed under some papers, returned it to the galley and disposed of it. Then I went home.

With all the casualties removed from site and finally accounted for, the site became an Engineering Possession. It was eventually decided that even our heaviest lifting gear was insufficient to lift the derailed vehicles, and a two hundred ton lifting device was hired in from Mssrs Hewden Stewart. Before it could be erected on site, a special mat had to be laid as a temporary road to transport the equipment across fields to the site.

It took a very long time to recover the derailed vehicles and remove them from the site. The engineers then had to make repairs to the line. The Uckfield line was not reopened to traffic until 1840 hours on the 18th October, four days after the accident. The results of the first part of the Public Enquiry were released on 23rd May 1995.

It is always terribly sad when people die or are injured in a railway accident. That day two passengers and three members of traincrew had their lives brutally cut short, and thirteen people were injured. But we must always also be aware of the invisible injuries, the effects on the minds of those involved, the things seared on their memories by what they have seen and had to deal with. These effects go on long after the physical injuries are healed.

When a train is derailed it becomes an obscene sight. It is something that should never happen and yet the physical evidence is there before our eyes. When the dreadful collision took place at Purley, it was almost instantaneous. One moment all was well and the next, the terrible accident had happened, and we were thrown into the situation.

That was not the case at Cowden. Those on the ground, having done everything they could to prevent the accident, had to sit there helplessly for around five minutes, waiting for the inevitable collision. It must have been terrible for them.

Nor was it much better in the Service Centre and Railtrack Control. Each one of us there knew with a dreadful certainty, what was about to happen deep in the fog shrouded countryside, that people were going to die or be terribly injured. I know of staff who have never recovered from that day and one of my own team had to receive counselling.

The Public Enquiry was held in two parts, and there were also the Internal Enquiries. Many questions were asked. One subject that came up for discussion, was the flank locking. This is a little-known subject outside of the industry, and with the reader's forbearance I will give a short explanation of this.

It has been good practise when planning a line, that it should never be possible to signal two trains onto a collision course. Where two lines cross or as in this instance, two lines become one reversible line, the design includes mechanical and/or electrical controls that do make it physically impossible for trains to be signalled into the path of each other. That has been standard practise for many years.

But what provision is made to protect a train that is travelling from a double track onto a single reversible passes a signal set at danger? In almost all cases, trap points are installed, that always set the route for the trap, usually a diverging line or a sand drag, and are only reversed to allow safe passage of a train, when the signal is cleared for the train to proceed. Thus, should a train pass a signal at danger, it is safely diverted away from a collision situation.

When the Uckfield line was singled with passing loops, no such provision was possible at Ashurst. In this case it was actually physically impossible, because the ground fell away either side of the station.

I am not qualified or experienced in the redesigning of railways so I do not feel I can make any further comment on this.

As I have stressed before, this is not a political book, nor does it seek to apportion blame. It simply reveals that, in the case of this accident, as with many accidents, there was no single cause. It is when all the factors come together at the same time, that accidents happen.

Chapter Nineteen -
The Final Divide and accountability

It was not long after this accident that the Railtrack Control was relocated to Friars Bridge Court. From then on, all liaison was only possible by telephone and fax machines. In my personal view this was not a good move.

The next thing to happen was that Railtrack assumed authority for all movements on running lines. A series of charges was levied for every possible movement of trains. Each Train Operating Company (TOC) had to submit its timetable to Railtrack, who would then agree it and bill the Company for it.

This would be the arrangement for the standard service. Any movement in addition to this had to be signed for and faxed to Railtrack for approval. Only when the fax with Railtrack approval was received could the move take place.

Thus, when empty coaching stock was required to run additionally to the timetable working, a request was faxed to Railtrack and Railtrack would approve it and raise a charge with the company concerned. In an effort to avoid this, companies attached empty rolling stock to passenger trains for which the fee had already been levied.

This was not entirely successful because Railtrack had separate rates for 2, 4, 6, 8, 10, and 12 coach trains, because a longer train used more electricity. Thankfully, in the Service Centre we had minimal involvement with these matters, only becoming implicated when we juggled the empty rolling stock.

Something else also happened with the system of accountability that was brought in. I will try to explain it. As a corporate railway, whenever incidents had occurred, we had recorded the delays and reasons and that had been the end of the matter. Now as a private company all delays had to be accounted for, and the costs calculated and attributed to whichever company was responsible.

My boss, Clive, instituted the NART system. The initials stood for Not Arrived Right Time. The daily form had several columns, relating to problems with Traincrew, Rolling Stock, Station Staff, Signalling, Track, and Other Causes.

Our Operations Manager suggested an extra column for me when I was on duty because of my reputation for having incidents. I thought he was joking! My original saying came to the fore, 'It was nothing to do with me. I was just there when it happened.'

A typical incident that occurred on a late turn shift when I was on duty, will I hope, show clearly how the system worked. At 1605 hrs on a weekday afternoon a fire broke out on the track on the down line approaches to Brighton Station. Delays were accounted to be at the rate of £500 per train per minute. As the evening rush hour was about to begin it became obvious that some company was going to receive a big bill.

As the problem was a fire on Railtrack property, I decided it was a Railtrack bill. Railtrack disputed this, saying that the fire involved a cable. 'Fine,' I said,' the cable is yours, the fire is yours and the bill is yours.'

'No' argued the Railtrack Manager, 'The fire was caused by rubbish on the track, which has damaged our cable, and so the bill is yours.'

'No,' I argued, 'The rubbish is yours, the fire is yours, the cable is yours and the track is yours, so the bill is yours.'

The Railtrack Manager did not agree, 'The rubbish came out of one of your trains, therefore the fire, the cable damage, and the delays are down to your company.'

'No,' I retorted 'The rubbish was blown onto the track from your embankment, you cannot prove that it came from one of our trains, so the responsibility and the bill are yours!' We could not agree, so the matter was referred 'upstairs' where all TOCs and Railtrack each had a Department dedicated to the resolving of these disputes.

Personally, I felt these disputes were not a matter for the Service Centre, our job simply being to record the facts and let others make the decisions on accountability. We still had plenty of incidents to manage.

Our responsibilities and our titles may have changed, but the railway and its incidents remained unchanged. One of the things that still affected everyone was the weather. Never more so than one winter, when we had a heavy fall of snow. The electric trains were disrupted and now there were no locomotives to haul them, as had been our way of dealing with it before.

I was booked early turn Service Centre Manager. Knowing how bad the train service was, I rang my late turn colleague the day before and suggested that I take the Late Turn, stay overnight at the Service Centre, finding somewhere to sleep, and then do the Early Turn the following morning. For some reason my colleague was not keen on this.

So, on the day, I set off in the morning. I quickly discovered the route from Tonbridge via Redhill was blocked. I rang in and warned my colleague that I was going to travel to Croydon via

Sevenoaks and London Bridge. He already knew the situation and was expecting this. There was one other problem in that due to a cold, I had almost lost my voice. However, this was no time to give up when everyone else was struggling.

The service to London Bridge was disrupted, but eventually I got there. However, the services to East Croydon via New Cross Gate were also severely disrupted. I was travelling in one of the old slam door trains. We left London Bridge, with the train arcing severely due to ice on the conductor rail.

We had only got to New Cross Gate when the fuses on the London end four car blew, leaving the front four car struggling and hauling the rear four car unit. We were travelling on the down through line and we just made it to Sydenham, when with a big flash, the fuses blew on the front unit and we came to a stand.

I went forward and spoke to the driver and guard, identifying myself as a railwayman and showing them my Personal Track Safety Certificate, and offered my services, which were gratefully accepted.

It had been decided to terminate the train at Sydenham and evacuate the passengers. The only problem was that we were standing on the down through line with no platform adjacent, so the passengers would have to be evacuated by the use of ladders.

We established that both the down through and the down local lines had been blocked. We also established that the traction current had been isolated. Then the traincrew and I began the slow process of bringing the passengers down the ladder, helping them across the tracks and then helping them up a ladder onto the down platform.

Arrangements were made for another train to run via the down local platform and pick up the passengers and I tried to announce this but in the cold weather and with my cold, my voice was almost gone. The passengers got the drift of what I was trying to say and were most grateful as well as sympathetic.

At the traincrew's request, I rode with them to East Croydon. I crossed the tracks to re-join the train. As I climbed back up the side of the train I was only just in time. The compressors started working and I knew someone had restored the traction current without checking first that everyone was clear of the track. That is how accidents happen!

The traincrew were very grateful for my help and wanted me to travel with them to Brighton now that the train had been made fit to run. I would have loved to have gone with them, and said so, but I had to relieve a colleague who had already been on duty fourteen hours, so I had to leave them at East Croydon.

There was one other occasion when I was very late on duty. My shift had been changed three times, to fit in with the sickness of colleagues. I was convinced I was on late duty. I awoke at 5 am, the time I would normally get up. But I turned over and went back to sleep.

I was awakened by the phone at 6.45 am. A voice with a strong Yorkshire accent addressed me.' Good morning. Are you suffering from a sticky mattress? Has the Saab failed to start? Are you going to grace us with your presence this morning?' I'm late turn, I protested. 'No you're not. You're early turn and you should be here.' said the voice. I didn't argue. 'I'm on my way,' I said.

Leaping out of bed, I made my ablutions, dressed hurriedly

and dived out to the car. There wasn't even time for a cup of tea. I drove as fast as I legally could and arrived in the Service Centre just after 8 am.

Jockey and the team had very ably been holding the fort for me. A neat pile of incident reports lay on my desk for me to type onto the Service Centre Report. 'Mr E, (our Director) has been in,' said Jockey. 'He asked where you were, and I told him you were in another office getting some paperwork. He asked how the service was running and I told him everything was on time and it was all going very well. He said he could live with that and went out.'

I was, and still am, very grateful to Jockey. But for his competence and the loyalty of my team, my career could have come to an abrupt end.

A new initiative had been announced by Connex. The new Connex Metro service was to be introduced. On the Central and South Eastern suburban areas, the aim was to provide a frequent and regular service. To quote the advertising of this service, 'At least four trains an hour each way. Just turn up and go. Fast, frequent and convenient.'

I was tipped off by our Press Office that a certain London daily newspaper had picked this up, and that representatives were going to stations on the South London Line between Victoria and London Bridge to see how good it was.

It so happened that I was talking to a Station Manager on that line. He had just mentioned that one or two stations were currently unmanned due to staff shortages. I told him what I had heard and was just suggesting that he might like to revisit that, when the phone appeared to have been snatched from his hand, and a very peremptory voice came on the line.

He introduced himself as a senior officer and told me that station staffing came within his remit and not that of the Service Centre. I tried to explain my concerns, but he interrupted and reiterated that it was not the concern of the Service Centre. I acknowledged his seniority and the conversation ended.

However, I did make an entry concerning the unstaffed stations, on the Service Centre Report. Although I said nothing and did not include it in my entry, I had in mind the dreadful accident involving two children that had occurred on an unmanned station on that very line.

As a precaution, I asked for the telephone conversation that had been recorded (as all conversations involving the Service Centre automatically were) to be downloaded and made available to me.

As anticipated, I was summoned to that senior officer's office at lunchtime the next day. He had seen a copy of the Report. I was not invited to sit down. I stood to attention. I listened, as he raised his voice to me. My only response to his complaints was to say, 'I see sir.' At one point I politely reminded him that our conversation had been recorded. When he had finished, I said, 'Will that be all sir?' I was told to leave.

This all happened at about the same time as the Watergate scandal was rife in America. When I got back in the Service Centre, I found some wag with a distorted sense of humour had been busy, and in various parts of the Service Centre were advertisements for 'Terrygate' tapes at one pound each.

A little later that day, my temporary Senior Manager passed me in a corridor. 'What did you do to him?' he asked me.

I said I had been very polite and asked why.

'When he passed me, he was very, very angry!' he replied laughing.

In conclusion I have to say that the Connex Metro Service did live up to its promises and ran very reliably. As to the staffing level, I had done all I could to raise the profile of the matter

Chapter Twenty -
Liaison with Emergency Services

Because I had had the experiences of Purley and Cowden, and many other incidents that involved liaison with the Emergency Services, Senior Management chose me to represent them at various Emergency Services Training Meetings. I really appreciated their confidence in me, and I did my best to justify that confidence. I also enjoyed meeting many of the people.

My first meeting was with the Association of Chief Police Officers (ACPO) at New Scotland Yard. It had an inauspicious start. I duly arrived on time at the imposing entrance that we all see on television. I was met by a uniformed officer, who escorted me into the building. After that impressive façade I was expecting a streamlined super centre but was surprised to find the offices looked just like any other of the many offices I had seen.

The officer escorted me to the lift. We ascended to the first floor, where the officer got out of the lift. As I tried to follow him the lift doors whipped shut and I rapidly ascended several floors before it stopped. I managed to negotiate my way back to the first floor.

As soon as the lift stopped, I shot out, only then just getting clear before the lift doors snapped shut again.

A rather embarrassed officer greeted me. 'Sorry about that,' he said, 'Those lift doors are a bit urgent!' He led me to a big room. Inside, on a semicircle of chairs, sat more senior police officers than I had ever seen. It was quite imposing.

My task was to explain to these senior officers, the dangers faced by their staff when they had to go onto the railway tracks in pursuit of criminals, and the problems we had.

I explained that when we receive a request from the Police to allow them onto the track, we have to take every precaution to ensure their safety. In addition to the fast moving trains, we had on the Southern area of the railway, the conductor rails which fed between 650 and 750 volts to the traction motors of the trains, and these conductor rails were always 'live.'

Upon receiving such a request, the first task is to stop trains. This is not as easy as it might sound, and sometimes takes a few minutes.

Then we have to arrange for a responsible person locally to ask the Electrical Control to discharge (switch off) the traction current. It has to be done locally, preferably with someone on site, because when the time comes to recharge the traction current, the only person who can ask for the current to be restored is the person who asked for it to be off.

Therefore, if possible, it is always better to have someone who can physically see that the lines are clear, before asking for the traction current to be restored. If an incident goes on for some time and the person who asked for the traction current to be discharged, has to be relieved, the person being relieved and the person relieving them must speak to the Electrical Control and come to a clear understanding who is in charge of the request for the isolation.

Then neutral sections of the isolation have to be established. Some years ago, a Fireman was killed after traction current had been discharged through a section, because a train travelling over a junction and going onto a different route, momentarily livened up the 'dead' section. From the time of that incident, great care has been taken, by discharging neutral sections either side of the incident, to ensure it never happens again.

But doing this can create havoc for the railway. I gave the meeting a prime example of this.

The police requested to go on the line at New Cross to pursue suspects. Traction current had to be discharged on all six of the main lines. The neutral sections could extend back as far as London Bridge, Borough Market Junction and Metropolitan Junction, affecting trains from Charing Cross, Cannon Street, and the line from Blackfriars. The other end of the isolation would extend down to St. Johns Junction. I asked them to imagine how long it might take to stop all the trains in that area, before discharging traction current.

I should point out at this point that with our modern trains these days there is a system of immediate communication between signalman and driver, including an option to stop all trains, the message being transmitted simultaneously. But in the days of my lecture, that system did not exist. Only once all this had been done could we give permission for the Police to go onto the track.

Sometimes the frustrated policemen could see their suspects gleefully making their escape and be helpless to stop them.

However, it is worth mentioning that the suspects were equally at risk from very severe burns, electrocution, or being run over by a fast moving train, until the lines had been made safe.

When we gave the police permission to go onto the tracks, we always added a proviso that they must tell us when they were clear, so that we could restore traction current and reopen the lines to traffic. Sometimes an incident might involve more than one police force. Then we must have assurance from both forces that their staff are clear, before traction current can be restored.

One final safety aspect I stressed. Once the police had declared themselves clear of railway tracks, under NO circumstances must they return to the line, because traction current would have been restored and trains would be running again. If they needed to return to the tracks again, they must go through the proper procedures again. Frustrating we knew, but infinitely better than someone being killed or seriously injured.

The Senior Police Officers listened to all of this and occasionally made notes. They seemed to understand our position very well and there were no questions. Then I added the sting in the tail. With the arrival of Railtrack, there were Track Access Charges. Any incident that caused delay would result in a Track Access charge being levied by Railtrack.

For example, if a Train Operating Company train was delayed by a passenger taken ill or a stock defect, Railtrack would levy the charge for that delay and for the delay to any other company's trains that were delayed, to the Train Operating Company whose train it was.

Similarly, if there was a fault on the track or with the signalling, Train Operating Companies, whose trains had been delayed, would levy a Track Access charge to Railtrack.

Track Access Charges also extended to the Emergency Services. If the Emergency Services were summoned to an incident or accident on the tracks, then obviously there would be no charge levied.

The same did not apply however to police chasing suspects.

In this instance, Railtrack would consider the incident to be external to the Railway and would levy the Track Access Charge to the force concerned. This generated renewed interest from my audience.

When I advised them that depending whether it was a week-day or weekend, the location and the time of day, ie peak hours, the charge could be £500 per minute per train, the interest was further heightened. I explained that Railtrack had a complete department for deciding liability and levying charges, and that the Train Operating Companies all had similar arrangements.

This I suggested was a very good reason for officers to advise us immediately as soon as they were clear of railway lines. It also enabled us to restore services and minimise as far as possible the delays and disruption to our customers.

I was thanked for my presentation, and there being no further questions, I thanked them and took my departure. From feedback I gathered the presentation was well received and I was pleased.

My next assignment was to West Sussex Fire Brigade and a meeting was arranged at Littlehampton on 9th September 1994. I was invited to take a guest and I took my sister, because I knew she would be a good and honest critic. She was given a ticket to travel with me.

We duly arrived at Littlehampton where we were warmly welcomed, and I began my presentation. I started with a very brief explanation of the origins of the signalling system. The purpose of this was to explain flank locking, which I have mentioned before in this book.

I explained that in modern signalling systems, when a route

was called and set, any points that would cause a conflict would automatically be reset away from the route being called. The point of this was that even when a line had been blocked to trains and traction current discharged, point-work could move automatically when a route was called, so under no circumstances should their staff tread on or walk across or place equipment in the point-work.

I went on to explain, just as I had with the Police, the safe procedure for stopping trains and isolating traction current. The Firemen particularly appreciated the need for isolating neutral sections of traction current.

I also explained to them the Railtrack system of Track Access Charges and the importance of telling us when they were clear of the railway. Again, since incidents could happen anywhere, sometimes more than one Brigade was involved and it was imperative we were advised by each Brigade involved, when they were clear of the track.

I reassured them that of all the three Emergency Services, in my experience the Fire Brigade was usually the best at doing this. This was for two reasons. Firstly, the Fire Brigade was run on military style discipline, which required each stage to be completed satisfactorily, and secondly, when the Fire Brigade left the scene, by and large their job was done.

When the police left the scene, their first priority was to get any detained suspects safely into custody, and similarly the Ambulance Service first priority was to get injured people to hospital. So sometimes we were temporarily, and understandably, overlooked. However, the Railtrack Track Access Charges made an impact on this.

Again, I enjoyed my time with the West Sussex Fire Brigade.

I was thanked and I believe I was appreciated.

But my best critic was my sister. She said, 'They obviously realised that you weren't a "divvy" and they saw you knew what you were talking about. It was good. Well done.'

Arrangements were made for me to give a presentation to the Ambulance Service, but this was not taken up, which was a bit of a disappointment.

However, that was more than made up for by my final assignment, which was to go to the London Fire Brigade. I was sent to give my presentation to their Southwark Training Centre.

There I was warmly welcomed. I gave the same presentation to them, so I won't repeat it here. Suffice it to say it was well received. But there was a bonus. They wanted to know if it was possible for them to see our heavy lifting gear and emergency equipment. I assured them it would be possible and that I would make the arrangements and get back to them.

On my return to the Service Centre, I contacted the authorities at Brighton, Lovers Walk Depot, explained what I wanted and asked if they could help me. They were very willing to help and made the necessary arrangements.

On the day, we travelled to Hove, where we all met up. Brighton had done us proud. They had got out their biggest breakdown crane, which I believe was a seventy-ton lifter. They let us all explore the cab and the controls. Once again, I was amazed as I always was, at the tiny control cabin that I could barely fit myself into.

The Brighton staff explained that when the crane was working, the person in charge of the job would be the only person to communicate with the crane operator. Communication could be by spoken word but was often by a series of hand signals.

Various things had to be taken into account when lifting. The crane could lift its maximum load when it was lifting head on. As soon as the jib had to be traversed, the weight that the crane could lift was reduced. Outriggers would be pulled out on either or both sides to stabilize the crane, but often lifts would have to be made in several stages.

Then the vehicle or object being lifted would have to be propped up so it could not move, the stabilizers would have to be retracted into the body of the crane, the crane would then move under its own power or be moved to a new position and the whole process started again. It mattered not whether the move was a few inches or several feet, the process was repeated each time.

Those huge machines and the skill of their operators fascinated me and I always enjoyed watching them at work. Sadly in this modern age almost all of the cranes have been withdrawn. When such work is required, contractors are brought in. It was said that the cranes were not accurate enough, but they did their job very satisfactorily for over a hundred years.

As well as the crane, the staff brought out the BRUFF road rail vehicle. This had played a big part in Emergency Exercise Hawfinch, see chapter seventeen. This was and indeed still is an amazing vehicle. The size of an average lorry, it contains lifting jacks, supports, tools, and all the associated equipment for responding to derailments.

As seen in Hawfinch, the equipment carried can lift and traverse the front end of a coach. If a vehicle or vehicles are displaced away from the track then a crane is necessary to effect rerailing but for comparatively minor derailments or lifting jobs, the BRUFF is ideal, and saves all the expense and delay in preparing a full sized crane.

But its most amazing feature is that as well as the normal road wheels it also has a set of wheels to run on the railway. So this vehicle can travel by road to the nearest rail access to the incident, then drive onto the track (taking care with the conductor rail) and run along the track.

When it arrives at the scene, if the lifting beam is the wrong way round, it simply raises itself up and swivels round, then lowers itself back down onto the track. Obviously care has to be taken in moving it by rail. The signalmen concerned must always be kept in touch regarding any such movements.

Our friends in the Brigade were very impressed with all of this.

As a finale, the Brighton crew raised the jib on the crane to its maximum height. Then they moved it along the track under its own power. They got very close indeed to the footbridge spanning the tracks through Hove station. My comment, 'If you hit that bridge I'm not going back to the Service Centre!' was greeted with wide grins. They stopped just short of it.

When all the equipment had been stowed safely away, we all adjourned to a local hostelry and enjoyed a very nice meal. I was presented with a letter thanking me for the presentation.

Then Simon, the Fire Chief said, 'We've got something else for you.' They gave me a large paper bag. I opened it and drew out a magnificent shield with the London Fire Brigade crest and the words, 'London Fire Brigade' engraved upon it. It is proudly displayed on the wall of my lounge to this day. Simon said, 'That makes you an honorary member of the London Fire Brigade Southwark Trainers'.

That was the last of my presentations to the Emergency

Services, but I was asked to do one more presentation, to the Public Relations Department, on the subject of 'Railway Operations and the part played by the Service Centre.' That was very well received.

Chapter Twenty-One -
Horsham and Streatham Hill

After the presentations, which I had thoroughly enjoyed, I returned to my normal duties, which I also enjoyed. The incidents continued to happen with great variety.

Another form of Track Access Charges came to light. If people were delayed on our Division and missed ongoing connections from other London Termini as a result, we had an obligation to get them to their destinations if at all possible.

We could ask the other regions if they would hold trains for these displaced or delayed passengers (sorry – customers) and we would if necessary, arrange taxi's for them across London. Our opposite numbers on the other regions would require a fax request to do this and subsequent delays to their trains would be debited to our Service Centre. This would have to be agreed between us before they could help us.

We never saw the amounts that were involved, those facts were relayed to the appropriate Connex Department for them to negotiate. But we had to start the process, by agreeing in writing that we would accept responsibility. Then, if the cause of the delay was found to be due to track or signalling, we would notify Railtrack by fax that in due course, Connex would be reclaiming the debited amount.

If it proved not possible for these delayed customer to be taken to their destination by train, we had to compare the costs of getting them to their destination by road or finding hotel accommodation for them overnight and arranging for their tickets to be honoured on the first available service on the following day.

The stations involved would do the local arranging of taxi's or accommodation, our part in this being to fax our acceptance of responsibility for the delay, to the appropriate Service Centre, who would then liaise with the stations. I fell foul of these arrangements early on in the setting up of the system.

The last train from East Grinstead to Victoria was delayed at Oxted, waiting connection with the last train from Uckfield to Oxted, which in turn had been delayed by slippery rails due to the leaf fall. A family arrived at Victoria for a destination on the Midland Region. The train from East Grinstead was in excess of thirty minutes late, and it proved not possible to hold the connection from Euston.

We therefore arranged with the Midland Service Centre to get them as far as possible by train and then provide road transport to their destination. On advising my On-Call Officer, I was told that it would be better to get them as far as they could by rail and then arrange for them to stay in an hotel until the next morning.

Of course, I should have contacted my On-Call Officer before making the arrangements. I then rearranged the matter with the London Midland Service Centre and sent a fax to Railtrack to advise them of the change of plan.

After the matter was settled, I gathered my team together and we discussed the incident and the best way to handle such incidents in future. It was a good object lesson for me and for them.

The next incident I am about to describe occurred at Horsham and it took me right back to my earliest days in my first signal box. I will try briefly to describe the layout at the country end of Horsham. There is a up main line, from which trains can be diverted to the up platform loop, platform one, or remain on course and run to up platform two.

There is also a siding on the up side of the main line which runs parallel with the up main and which runs into the up loop platform one. Thus a parallel move can be made, bringing a train out of the siding into platform one while at the same time signalling a train from the up the main into platform two.

At the exit from the siding there is a set of trap points. In the normal position they are set to route a train from the siding into a sand drag. They are only reversed to allow a train to run from the sidings to platform one when the exit signal is cleared for them to do so. As soon as the signal is returned to danger, the points revert immediately to route a train from the sidings into the sand drag. It is a very efficient form of flank locking.

I was early turn one morning, when at lunchtime the Railtrack duty Manager advised me that a train in Horsham up siding had passed the exit signal at danger, run into the sand drag and one pair of wheels had become derailed. I started the usual procedure for these incidents. I advised the Traincrew Supervisor (TCS) of the incident.

I had established that the train had no passengers and both driver and conductor were uninjured. I asked the TCS to get the name of the driver and his duty number and to get as report from him of what had happened.

Next, I obtained the number of the unit concerned. I advised the Maintenance Control and asked for a fitter to attend to assess the damage and consider and advise us of the best way to re-rail the wheels. Railtrack was arranging for Permanent Way staff to attend to assess any track damage.

The train that the unit should have formed had to be cancelled because no other rolling stock was available to replace it. My Train Arranger Inner was arranging for a traincrew and stock to be provided from London for the next working of the cancelled train.

Because of the flank locking, the train had derailed away from the main line so it was possible to continue safely running passenger trains on the up main. Then I got a phone call from the TCS. His driver reported that he had rung the train out from the siding, the signalman had signalled him into platform one, and after releasing the brakes, he moved off.

But as he came up to the starting signal, it suddenly went back to danger in front of him. He saw the points go over but was unable to stop the train in time and it ran into the sand drag. The promptness of the driver in applying the brakes was evident from the fact that only the first pair of wheels had derailed.

Suddenly light dawned. I remembered as a learner signalman at Wadhurst, being so keen to do the job efficiently that as a down train passed each signal, I quickly put the signal back behind it. So keen was I that I almost put the starting signal back in front of the train and would have done so but for the restraining arm of the signalman who was supervising me!

Reg said quietly, 'I shouldn't do that if I was you. The drivers don't like that sort of thing.'

I was so grateful.

The driver would have had to stop suddenly, passengers

would have been upset, and the interlocking meant that I would have had to send the 'Signal Cancelled,' to Stonegate and re-offer the train before I could signal it away, all very embarrassing.

I telephoned the Railtrack Duty Manager, who as it happened was an old friend I had worked with before. I asked him what moves had been signalled at Horsham when the derailment occurred. He told me that a train had been signalled on the up main and was running into platform two and the empty stock had been signalled out of the siding to platform one.

I told him what the driver had reported, that as he was about to pass the signal it had gone back in front of him and he was on the points before he could stop. I said I believed I knew what had happened, that the signalman was putting back the signals behind the up train, and had accidentally put the siding signal back in error, causing the points to move and divert the train into the sand drag.

I asked him if he was prepared to ask the signalman that question.

He said he would. A few minutes later he called me back, and told me the signalman, who was a learner under supervision, had admitted doing exactly that. The supervising signalman at Horsham was nowhere near as good as Reg had been with me. I put only the facts on the Control Report, the driver's report and our actions in response.

A little later I was called to a senior manager's office. He invited me to sit down. He said he wanted to talk to me about the Horsham incident. He assumed it was driver error and we would have to foot the bill for rerailing, track and stock repairs, a tidy sum.

I advised him that I didn't think we should take responsibility.

I told him of the signalman's error, and because of my sympathy for another learner, I emphasised that he was a learner signalman under supervision. That made the matter the responsibility of Railtrack. I was thanked for my help.

The next incident I am going to describe, occurred at Streatham Hill sidings. Again, I will ask the readers patience as I explain a few technical details. The sidings at Streatham Hill, used to stable five twelve coach trains between the two peak hour services, were equipped with the normal conductor rails.

But in the sheds, where the stock was stored, a different system was employed. Thick cables called 'Jumpers' and connected to the power supply, were suspended from the roof of the shed. When coupled to a bracket on any driving cab of the train, they provided the traction power that enabled drivers to release the train brakes and drive the train forward until it came onto the conductor rail at the exit from the shed.

Then of course the jumpers had to be disconnected before moving forward. Having the power from the jumpers enabled fitters to work on the trains under power without the threat of coming into contact with a live conductor rail.

My team and I were on late turn duty one weekday afternoon when my Train Arranger Inner advised me that Streatham Hill Shunters had reported the jumper system had failed at 1430. A quick call to the Electrical Control confirmed that we had indeed got a problem.

The five trains were stuck in the shed with no power even to release the brakes.

We discussed the options. One solution would be to detach units from trains in London and use those units to replace the ones in Streatham Hill. This would avoid having any delays, but all the trains would run short of the booked number of coaches, as would the trains we had robbed to make them up. I wasn't satisfied with this. I thought we could do better.

It all depended on several factors being favourable. I made a phone call to Redhill Train Crew Supervisor. Did he have a class 73 locomotive available?

Yes, he did.

Then, did he have a traincrew available?

Yes he did.

As a matter of courtesy, I asked Jockey if he would let me take this incident on and keep an eye on other things for me.

He readily agreed.

Then I spoke to Selhurst Electrical Control and explained my plan. I asked them (a) was it possible and (b) would they be happy for me to do it.

Their reply was yes it was and yes they would.

Then I spoke to Streatham Hill shunters, explaining what I was planning to do and asked them if they were willing to help. They said they would, even though it would make a lot of extra work for them.

My plan was this. Send the class 73 locomotive light engine all speed from Redhill to Streatham Hill. It had to be a class 73 because it had a flat front cab. The class 33's had a curved front cab so to attach them to electric rolling stock would have meant extending the buffers on the coaches and then retracting them when the locomotive had been detached. This would take far too much time and the job would be impossible.

When the Class 73 got there, attach it to the front of the first train, pump off the brakes, then in a suitable gap between trains, haul the train out onto the main line.

The Electrical Control said they would have to take an isolation of the traction current while the train was brought out onto the main line but they could do that. Also the train would have to run out on the down main and then cross to the up main to go to London.

Finally I had to talk to the Railtrack Duty Manager. Thankfully Robin was another of my former Central Division colleagues and a friend. I explained the problem, and the solution I had devised. I needed his approval to run the locomotive light engine from Redhill to Streatham Hill and then for all the shunts of the five trains.

I would not have time to fill in all the permission forms as it happened, but I gave him my guarantee that all the permission forms would be faxed to him for him to sign and return to me before I went off duty.

I asked him to tell the signalmen to give the locomotive 'a fine day.' That was a phrase from the very old days in the signal box. It meant give him a clear run. The adrenaline was running high. Success depended on a lot of people all being prepared to work together. One failure would see the whole plan collapse and the rush hour in ruins.

Having got the approval of Railtrack I went back to Redhill TCS, told him what the Electrical Control had said and that we were 'GO!' As soon as the locomotive was ready it would be given preference over everything else.

He told me the traincrew were already on the locomotive.

We were 'GO!' My enthusiasm must have been infectious because everyone involved seemed really keen to make it work.

The locomotive set off. The driver said afterwards that it was the fastest and clearest run he had ever experienced.

It was about then that my manager Clive rushed into the Service Centre. Somehow, he had heard what we were doing. 'It won't work,' he said, 'and the rush hour will be in ruins! And we'll get the blame for all of it.'

I quietly said, 'I think it will work. We have everybody in position, and they all know what we want them to do and they are ready to do it. The locomotive is on its way and will soon be there.

Clive departed looking very worried.

The locomotive arrived at Streatham Hill and was attached to the first train. In due course it moved to the exit to the sidings. It then had to await a gap in the service. As soon as that occurred the traction current was discharged, the train was pulled out onto the main line. The traction current was restored.

The stock crossed to the up line and departed for London Bridge with the booked crew aboard. The locomotive returned to the shed to attach to the next set.

The first train from London Bridge was twenty minutes late start but had its full complement of stock, as had all the other trains that we would have had to run short of stock.

The next train came to the exit. A slot was found between service trains, and the traction current was discharged. The train was hauled onto the main line and the locomotive was detached. The traction current was restored, the train crossed to the up line and departed for Victoria.

The locomotive went back into the shed for the next set. The train that went to Victoria arrived there in time for a right time start with its full complement of stock.

And so it was for the remaining three trains, one to London Bridge and two to Victoria. All arrived in time for a right time start with their full complement of stock and the booked crews. And no train was delayed at Streatham Hill while the trains were shunted to the main line. I was ecstatic.

I thanked Jockey for his help in keeping other things going. Then in turn I telephoned Redhill TCS, Selhurst Electrical Control, Streatham Hill shunters and my friend Robin at Railtrack to thank them all for their willingness, and their help to make the job such a success. I also kept my word and filled in and faxed all the permission forms to Robin for him to sign and fax back.

Clive came back into the Service Centre. He still looked a bit worried, but he was smiling and very relieved. He came up to me and said, 'Terry, I never thought you'd get away with that!'

I got on very well with Clive, so I was able to say to him, 'Well Clive, that was the way the job used to be done – before the great divide.'

That operation was a major success, and as it turned out, it was the last major incident to occur before my time came to step down and take early retirement. I couldn't have wished for better.

Chapter Twenty-Two -
Time to say goodbye

This final chapter is probably the hardest to write. All the other chapters deal with the myriad incidents that occurred, the wonderful characters, dedicated, skilled at their job and with a definitive railway sense of humour, a humour that I shared. These were the people I worked with to resolve all the problems that we encountered. Over the years I had been compelled to make many decisions. It was what the job was all about.

But this decision was certainly the hardest one to make. I took a long time to consider all the aspects and I don't mind saying that I prayed for wisdom. For me, although I didn't see it at the very beginning, the Railway had become a way of life. It was never just a job. The shift work encouraged this.

Working around the clock, in all weathers, dealing with every kind of situation, the major accidents, the sad incidents, the frustrations when plans went wrong, the security alerts, and the times when we won, like the Streatham Hill incident, or being the Guards Controller for eight hours and managing to cover all the vacant duties without one train being cancelled, all these things bring about close working relationships.

Then especially there was that definable railway humour. Most of the jokes were 'in house' and would fall flat outside of the situation we were in at the time. But some still come to mind that can be shared, like the delay to a train in an intensive rush hour service at Charing Cross after a lady's shoe came off as she boarded the train.

The shoe was retrieved from the track and returned to her quickly, but that train and others were delayed. When I asked what reason I should show for the delay I was immediately told, 'Late start due to Cinderella!'

There were also my two favourite phrases, often used during incidents and always resulting in laughter and breaking the tension. The first was, 'Everybody knows about it. Nothing can go wrong!' The second, when it had gone wrong, was, 'It was nothing to do with me sir. I was just there when it happened!'

But I was looking to the future. The railway was changing, and the changes were dramatic. If I stayed, it was never again going to be the same job. The job as I knew it was going. It would cease to exist. Privatisation was in full swing. I had had two years' experience of it and I didn't like it.

As I have said before this is not and will not be a political book. I speak only from personal experience. There are issues about the railway system needing funding, and the subcontracting of staff, but that was not my primary concerned. I was seriously concerned about the fragmentation of a very complex industry, in particular in relation to Traffic Control/Service Centres.

Most jobs on the railway are clearly defined. A signalman, or signaller, to use the modern term, deals with signalling. A driver deals with driving. But a Traffic Control/Service Centre deals with multi agencies.

Sadly it is a fact of life that from time to time major accidents will occur. One very senior manager for whom I have a great deal of respect, once said to me, 'There is no such thing as a safe railway. The only safe railway is one that doesn't move at all! It's our job to make it as safe as we possibly can.'

It shook me at the time when he said it, but he was right. When major incidents do occur, my belief, backed up by personal experience, is that they must be dealt with by a centralised Control Centre, whatever title you give it.

The Emergency Services have long recognised this and although all three may be present at a major incident, overall control is usually given to one of the services, usually the Fire Brigade, which is best equipped to do the job.

The recovery and investigations at Purley worked well because all the threads of the job, signalling, CM & EE, Permanent Way, Electrical Control, the Public Relations, and Welfare Departments, and facilitating and protecting the Emergency Services, were fed to and co-ordinated by one agency, the Traffic Control at Waterloo HQ.

Cowden worked very well because of the close working relationship between the Service Centre and Railtrack Control, with colleagues from both sitting next to each other and co-ordinating the rescue, recovery and initial investigation

But how well will future major incidents be worked, when Network Rail and the Train Operating Companies are physically separated from each other, only in contact by telephone and with every movement of trains regulated by contracts that have to be signed, and with staff only able to talk to other staff of the same company because of confidentiality issues?

That was the new system as I saw it and it made me very uneasy indeed. When a major incident occurs, it usually happens without warning. Staff and customers are often injured and certainly suffer extreme shock. It is at these moments immediately after an accident or incident has occurred, that a centralised co-ordinated response is essential, in order to deal with it safely, swiftly and competently.

It was with all these issues in my mind that my decision was finally made. I made a formal application in June 1996, to receive early retirement/voluntary redundancy. It was suggested that I transfer to Railtrack, taking my experience with me, but grateful though I was, I declined the invitation.

I was interviewed and asked for my reasons. I shared my concerns. Those involved understood my reasons although they might not have agreed with them, and they respected them. My name was put forward for selection, and along with applications from three thousand others, it was accepted.

Friday 2nd October 1996 was my last shift. I was early turn and it was a remarkably quiet shift. I had all my own team with me on that last shift, Jockey, John, and 'Orson.' I took advantage of the lack of incidents to clear my desk and return any Railway equipment.

At 1430 my relief arrived. I shook hands with the team and with my relief. Then I picked up my bag and left the Service Centre for the last time. It was the end of my career with the Railway and the end of a way of life.

Unknown to me until later, my team sent out a message on the telex and pager systems to all stations.

The telex message read, 'After 34 years of service, Terry

Collins, Service Centre Manager has just completed his final shift for Connex SouthCentral. We wish him a long and happy early retirement. From all his shift (the Brownies).'

The pager message, which also went to all senior officers as well as all stations, read similarly, 'Terry Collins has left the building! After 34 years of service, Terry Collins, Service Centre Manager, has just completed his final shift. We wish him all the best in his retirement. (Service Centre Staff).' END.

I don't remember any other Duty Line Manager/Service Centre Manager being saluted in that way. It was the finest accolade I could have wished for.

I also received a very nice letter from David Sawyer, Production Director for Connex SouthCentral. I have retained the original letter and with it a fine reference. The letter read:

'Dear Terry

I am very sorry to have missed seeing you before you left on Friday. You know that I have very much admired your support, hard work and achievements over the last two years. My task will be much harder without you.

I am sure, however that you will soon be putting your talents to work again in some way or another, in the very near future.

Enjoy the rest while you can.

Yours sincerely
David'

His Reference read:

'To whom it may concern

RE; Terry Collins

I have known Terry Collins for over two years, during which time he has been accountable to me for the efficient provision of our train services. During this period Terry has proved conscientious and able to work well under extreme pressure.

He has a record of honesty and reliability and I have no hesitation for recommending him for employment.

Yours sincerely

David Sawyer

Production Director'

And so, on November 4th 1996 we had a celebration meal at Stephenson House to mark the occasion both of my retirement and the retirement of others. My boss Clive and another manager Mark were there to wish us well.

Mark came up to me, shook my hand and said, 'You picked up some big ones Terry!'

Clive walked over to me, shook my hand and said, 'I never thought you would get away with Streatham Hill!'

Smiling I replied, 'Well Clive, that's how the job used to be done in the old days.'

He nodded in agreement, smiled and shook my hand.

David Sawyer was also there to shake my hand and wish me well.

A week later, I had to return to Stephenson House for some minor paperwork. I still had my Identity Pass that worked all the security devices on the office doors, but I needed to gain entry to the building. I pressed the buzzer and a voice responded. I explained who I was and asked for a door release.

'Oh no. Don't worry. I'll send someone down to escort you,' said the voice.

'But I don't need an escort. I was working there last week,' I said.

'I am afraid we must escort you because you are no longer a working member of staff. I will get into trouble if I let you into the building unescorted.'

I didn't want to get anyone into trouble so reluctantly I agreed and waited for my escort. It was a strange feeling. One day I worked there and had a desk of my own and the next week I was a visitor who needed an escort. I didn't belong there any more.

It is now seventeen years since I retired. The railway has changed dramatically in that time. The big super panel Area Signalling Centres like London Bridge and Victoria, which replaced so many of the smaller boxes that I knew, are now themselves soon to be replaced.

Soon almost all of the former Southern Region will be controlled from just three super-sized computer controlled signalling centres. Points are fitted with heating devices as standard in wintertime.

Modern passenger rolling stock is already equipped with on board computers that automatically advise home depots of any faults that arise, and also monitor in great detail how the trains are driven. The freight trains routinely convey 2,000 tonnes or more, in block load fully fitted trains, with powerful new locomotives.

The many freight marshalling yards on the Southern have gone, replaced by through services via the Channel Tunnel directly to their destinations.

The tracks are unceasingly monitored by teams of highly trained engineers. Network Rail has full control of the rails and liaises with many train operating companies. It is a new railway and it will be a good one.

But as I look back, I am thankful that I knew and worked the old railway, alongside men and women who were dedicated to their job, for whom, like me, the job became a way of life.

The old railway was very physically hands-on and relied very much on the input of human beings. Staff needed to be fit, energetic and committed, and keen to become experienced, to make the trains run efficiently and above all safely.

I suspect that even in this modern era with all the greatly sophisticated and complex equipment now in use or being brought into use, in the end, men and women will still have important roles to play. Their roles will be very different to those I grew up with, but they will be every bit as vital. I salute them.

One unexpected bonus that came a month after my retirement was a letter from the Human Resources office. As an encouragement to us to fill in all the forms, one of them was an entry to a raffle. I filled it in and forgot all about it.

The letter advised me that I had won the second prize, two tickets on Eurostar from Waterloo to Paris or Brussels. I chose to take my sister with me and go to Brussels.

A date was arranged but the day before we were due to travel there was a major fire on a freight train in the tunnel and it was closed. A new date was arranged, and we eventually made the trip just before Christmas.

It was a very enjoyable day, not entirely without incident, but all was well as we made our way back to the station for our return trip from Brussels.

There I was delighted to meet up with Jockey, my London Area Controller/Train Arranger at Waterloo and Croydon. I introduced my sister to him. We had a chat and arranged to meet for a drink once the train was under way. In due course we met up in the bar and swapped yarns about the railway while my sister listened patiently.

Jockey had brought with him a huge holdall that was crammed to the brim with a selection of beers that he had purchased in Germany and topped with Christmas presents. It weighed a ton!

After our drinks we returned to our own seats. It was now getting dark. I reached up and switched on the personal lights above us.

Instantly there was an announcement on the public address system. 'We regret to announce that, due to an electrical fault on the train, this service will terminate at Lille.'

My sister looked at me. 'What have you done?'

I said, 'All I did was switch the light on!'

I sat there working out where a replacement train would come from. I knew there were no spare trains at Lille, so a replacement would have to come either from Paris, Brussels or Coquelles.

As it happened, when we arrived at Lille they had held a train from Paris for us.

It was very crowded, but we managed to get on eventually. As we crossed the crowded platform, a broad Yorkshire voice rang out. 'Thank you Terry!' it said. I looked round and saw Jockey struggling with that enormous holdall.

'It was nothing to do with me,' I replied, 'I was just there when it happened!'

The End

The occasion of the Long Service Awards, Front left Clive,
rear left Brian A., front right Robin H. and centre right the author

My Retirement Presentation, my sister
and General Manager

Acknowledgements

There are a number of people to whom I am grateful and without whom this book would never have been written.

My sister, who has been a great support, and who attended one of the Emergency Services Presentations, and gave me the benefit of her honest opinion afterwards.

Peter Hancox, a retired professional Proof Reader, who kindly proof read all the text.

Kes Jones and Susan Knight, for their valuable advice on publishing the book, and for their encouragement.

My working colleagues, many of whom persuaded me and encouraged me to write the book.

The Publishers, Conrad Press, and particularly James Essinger, Margaret Dowley and Charlotte Mouncey, who gave valuable help and encouragement in producing the book.

And finally, the many professional dedicated railwaymen and railway women that I was privileged to work with, and from whom I learned so much. This book is a tribute to them.